PARTY LIKE A ROCKSTAR

PARTY
LIKE A
ROCKSTAR

THE CRAZY, COINCIDENTAL,
HARD–LUCK, & HARMONIOUS
LIFE OF A SONGWRITER

J.T. HARDING

TWELVE

NEW YORK BOSTON

Twelve
Hachette Book Group
1290 Avenue of the Americas, New York, NY 10104
twelvebooks.com
twitter.com/twelvebooks

First Edition: February 2022

Twelve is an imprint of Grand Central Publishing.
The Twelve name and logo are trademarks of Hachette Book Group, Inc.

The publisher is not responsible for websites (or their content)
that are not owned by the publisher.

The Hachette Speakers Bureau provides a wide range of authors for speaking
events. To find out more, go to www.hachettespeakersbureau.com or call (866)
376-6591.

Library of Congress Cataloging-in-Publication Data

Names: Harding, J. T., author.
Title: Party like a rockstar : the crazy, coincidental, hard-luck, and harmonious
life of a songwriter / J.T. Harding.
Other titles: Party like a rock star
Description: First edition. | New York : Twelve, 2022. | Summary: "In PARTY
LIKE A ROCKSTAR, J.T. Harding charts his life from a kid growing up in
Illinois to a chart-topping songwriter living in Nashville and working with
country music stars like Keith Urbahn and Kenny Chesney. As a kid playing rock
n' roll in his parents' garage, Harding's was a world in which every taste of new
music-from the Stones to the Beatles and everyone in between-was a revelation.
Inspired by his favorite artists, Harding abandons the classic "American Dream"
and runs away to Los Angeles, where he forms a band and becomes part of
the music scene there, all the while selling records to his favorite artists and
producers at Tower Records. A story of youth, rebellion, and determination,
PARTY LIKE A ROCKSTAR is a memoir for music lovers and an invaluable
how-to guide for anyone who wants to learn how to write a hit song. Fun and
heartfelt, Harding's memoir is the story of one man's unshakable love for rock
and roll, how it guided him through some of the greatest tragedies-and greatest
triumphs-of his wild and unvarnished life"—Provided by publisher.
Identifiers: LCCN 2021041283 | ISBN 9781538735404 (hardcover) |
ISBN 9781538735411 (ebook)
Subjects: LCSH: Harding, J. T., author. | Lyricists—
United States—Biography. | Composers—United States—Biography. |
Country musicians—Biography. | LCGFT: Autobiographies.
Classification: LCC ML423.H315 A3 2022 | DDC 782.42164092 [B]—dc23
LC record available at https://lccn.loc.gov/2021041283

ISBNs: 978-1-5387-3540-4 (hardcover), 978-1-5387-3541-1 (ebook)

Printed in the United States of America

LSC-C

Printing 1, 2021

*For my parents, Larry and Kendra Harding, and
my brother Lance. Anything special or
talented in me is because of you.*

Start by doing what's necessary; then do what's possible; and suddenly you are doing the impossible.
—Saint Francis of Assisi

Contents

CHAPTER 1

An American and an Australian Walk Into a Men's Room

The first country hit I ever had was a song Kenny Chesney released called "Somewhere With You."

As the song was climbing the chart, one day my friends started calling me, saying, "Dude, Keith Urban is talking about your Kenny Chesney song! He's telling his fans to buy it."

Keith had made an iTunes playlist of songs he recommended to his millions of fans. I had never met Keith Urban. He had no idea who wrote the song, but apparently he liked it. And with me being a huge Keith fan, you can imagine what a great feeling that was.

Keith's song " 'Til Summer Comes Around" was one of the reasons I wanted to write in Nashville. The imagery was like a three-minute movie and his melodies were simple yet infectious.

"Somewhere With You" went to number one on the *Billboard* chart and stayed there for three weeks. Even though he was already a superstar, it was Chesney's first song to sell a million copies. A few months later, I was given an award for the song at a black-tie event in Nashville. Washing my hands in the men's room, I looked up in the mirror and, at one of the urinals behind me, I saw Keith Urban taking a leak. So I waited for him.

As he stepped up to a sink and waved his hand under a faucet I said, "Hey, Mr. Urban. My name is J.T. I wrote 'Somewhere With You' and I wanted to thank you for telling your fans to buy it. You really helped us have a hit."

Keith's eyes widened and in his Australian accent that could melt butter he said, "Shit, mate, what a song! If I'd have heard that song first I would've put it on my next album."

"Whoa," I said in disbelief.

He continued washing his hands. "In fact, if I'd have heard that song before anyone else, I'd have put it on my next five albums."

I said, "That is so crazy—because I sent that song to your record company, to your publisher, and to Erika at the Blue-bird Cafe, who I think knows you?"

Keith laughed, saying as we walked to the door, "Do you have your phone on you? My wife loves that song." With the speed of Luke Skywalker arming his light saber when Darth Vader appeared, I handed Keith my phone. Surely I was about to meet Nicole Kidman right there by the hand dryer.

Keith punched his number into my phone, saying, "Next time you have a song that you love, don't do anything with it, just call me right away." We gave each other a bro hug and went back to our candlelit tables as the awards continued.

At seven o'clock the next morning, I texted him: *Hi Keith, it's the guy from the bathroom.*

I felt myself turn into the "slapping your own face" emoji. He never texted back.

Then one day, as Forrest Gump says, "out of the blue clear sky," Keith's name lit up my phone.

Keith and I got together and wrote a song called "Somewhere In My Car." It was a two-week number one in the USA and number one for several weeks in Canada.

By the time it was released it was my fourth number one hit. This book tells the stories behind those songs and hits I've continued to have. It takes you down the many paths I have traveled, from Toys "R" Us Big Wheels to rock star tour bus wheels around the world and back.

Along the way you will meet the characters that have made up the memoir of my life so far and see how an unbridled passion for music led me to become a hit songwriter.

This is a story about a kid from Michigan who loves '80s hard rock and dreams of being on the radio. With no music business connections whatsoever, he winds up in Nashville, Tennessee, writing giant country hits. If this was a movie, it would seem too good to be true, but it is true.

This is my story. It all began when I was brought into this world by a young couple. A man and a woman who loved me so much they decided to give me away.

CHAPTER 2

Born and Raised in South Detroit

Just like in the iconic Journey song "Don't Stop Believin'," I too was born and raised in South Detroit, and I like to think the universe did a mic drop when I appeared. More specifically, I was raised in Detroit, but I was born in Tennessee and lived there for my first years before we moved to Detroit's east side. There's no such thing as South Detroit. South Detroit is actually Canada.

I grew up thinking I was an orphan. However, I was born and adopted shortly thereafter. I would later find out that my biological father was a young DJ playing records on the overnight shift at a rock station. He'd met my biological mother over the request line—she and a few girlfriends attending a local college would call up and request songs while they were up late and dance around their dorm.

Since it was late at night and no one else was calling, my biological father began to recognize the voice of one girl who called regularly. She had a nice laugh and seemed fun. He would play songs she requested, dedicate them to her with some funny one-liners, and they eventually fell for each other over the air.

They started dating, and she became pregnant with me. Having an almost-cosmic Hollywood-style meet-cute like that, I'm surprised I didn't wind up a superstar on Elvis Presley's level. Either that or a college counselor handing out free condoms paid for by local radio stations.

My biological father, I later learned, had had big dreams of his own: A lifelong restlessness in him to be in entertainment. My biological mother thought they were going to get married, but he knew it was not to be.

"We have to give him up for adoption so he can be cared for properly," he said as calmly and as caringly as possible. My biological mother cried and worried what would happen to me. He told her, "He'll be fine. He'll be determined, like me. He'll figure it out."

So while Jon Terrell was in Tennessee, his heart and head were in New York City. My biological parents lived together that early 1970s summer before I was born, through football season, past Christmas and into the New Year, until one fateful night in March.

Hitting the back of his head repeatedly against a hospital wall, he closed his eyes in panic as he heard my biological mother screaming like a devil in church, "Look what you've done to me, look what you've done to me!" Nurses took me from her as I took my first breath. That's how it was done. No kisses or congratulations, no matching hospital bracelets with all our names on them.

That same night, Jon Terrell started driving his beat-up Volvo in the pouring rain straight to New York City. He had managed to land a nighttime radio job there so he could pursue an acting career by day.

One of his windshield wipers was broken. As the working wiper slapped against the window, he could barely see the road through the downpour coming not only from the rain but from the tears in his eyes.

As his headlights cut a path over the Tennessee state line into Kentucky, the car radio played "Bridge Over Troubled Water" by Simon & Garfunkel. Salt from his tears mixing with sips of truck stop coffee on the thirteen-hour drive, he repeated out loud the new name the radio station had given him: "It's midnight in the Big Apple. This is the Scorpion. Call me on the request line."

The sunrise was reflecting off the Empire State Building like a scoop of orange sherbet as he pulled into Manhattan. A few years later, on a Thanksgiving weekend he saw moms and dads out Christmas shopping. As they spun, smiling, through revolving doors at FAO Schwarz toy store, Jon Terrell felt overwhelmed with sadness wondering about me. He was certain God would curse him for giving up a child.

Drop-Kick Me, Jesus, Through the Goalpost of Life

An announcer yelling "Touchdown Lions!" blasted from the football game on a cardboard-box-sized wood-frame RCA TV in the den. Pumpkin pie with whipped cream was served while cranberry-sauce-stained dinner dishes clattered as they were being taken away. Grown men ate a few more pieces of turkey from a serving plate in the kitchen even though they were stuffed. Children sat at a blue plastic table in blue chairs that only reached their parents' knees. They sat quiet and obedient, then licked their lips, smiling as a piece of pie was placed in front of each child. One chair, however, was empty—mine.

"We all live in a yellow submarine, a yellow submarine, a yellow submarine..." Singing as loud as a trumpet, off-key but full of confidence, my three-year-old rock-star self was belting out my favorite song.

I stood on a grown-up chair waving my arms like an orchestra conductor I'd seen in a Bugs Bunny cartoon, until my parents, their parents and friends, and all the kids were singing along. A room away, the refrigerator was covered in bright colored Fisher-Price magnets shaped like letters from the alphabet. The plastic letters held up pictures of my brothers and me next to a piece of construction paper showing dripping green and yellow flowers in bloom made by my tiny hands and feet, which had been dipped in paint.

I sang even louder when my grandmother swatted at me like she was swatting a fly, telling me to get down, as I was sure to fall and hurt myself. I sang the song over and over until my dad picked me up from the chair and gave me a playful dinosaur roar that sent me running back to the other kids.

It was the first of many performances to come.

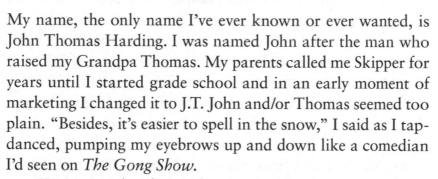

My name, the only name I've ever known or ever wanted, is John Thomas Harding. I was named John after the man who raised my Grandpa Thomas. My parents called me Skipper for years until I started grade school and in an early moment of marketing I changed it to J.T. John and/or Thomas seemed too plain. "Besides, it's easier to spell in the snow," I said as I tap-danced, pumping my eyebrows up and down like a comedian I'd seen on *The Gong Show*.

I'm not overly religious but I truly feel like I was taken by the hand of God and given to the greatest parents ever.

Their names are Larry and Kendra Harding, and I wouldn't trade them for anyone in the world. They never met my biological parents or had any knowledge of who they were. My mom used to complain that my dad, Larry, would carry me under his arm like a football. I don't remember that, but my dad seemed as tall as the Jolly Green Giant, so tall he literally had to duck through doorways to get into most rooms.

He caught a touchdown in the Rose Bowl for what I thought for years was the only college on the planet: Michigan State University. No other schools were allowed to be mentioned in our home. He met my mom at Michigan State. "Another damn stuffed animal" was what she angrily said when a dishwasher-sized box wrapped in a green bow arrived for her a few years into dating him. Inside the giant box was another, and she opened that to find another box. Five shrinking boxes later, she came to a minuscule velvet carton that contained an engagement ring.

He wasn't only a professional romantic, he played professional football with the Los Angeles Rams for a hot second until a knee injury changed those plans. Larry Harding lived and breathed sports.

As a child, at night I'd wake up in the dark and run to my parents' bedroom. Stepping on their bed's box spring like a ladder, I'd climb up on their mattress, then curl up in a ball, pressing my head against the back of my dad's warm T-shirt with a smile, and drift to sleep. I've never felt safer in the presence of a human being than I felt all my life with my dad.

My mom, Kendra, deserves to have her picture in every dictionary next to the word *beautiful*—a true living angel. She was caring and fun. My earliest memory of her is baking a cake and decorating it with red licorice for fire hoses and Oreos for fire truck tires. She brought me with her to deliver the cake to the firefighters at a new fire station near our house. Giving personalized gifts to my friends is one of my favorite things to do, and I got that from my mom. From the first second she held me in her arms, she told me there was no doubt in her heart I was hers, no matter how I got there.

There's no one else I'd ever want to be looking over me when I was home sick with a cold, going through a breakup, or especially when I went back-to-school clothes shopping. She would drive me to the farthest mall to find a Merry Go Round clothing store I had heard sold checkerboard tennis shoes or neon-colored shirts with zippers on the sleeves.

Once I got into music and wanted to dress the part, she

did her best to help. Before the days of Instagram, school was the place to show off my outfit, and I made a habit of walking to the pencil sharpener. For as long as I can remember, I always liked to stand out in a crowd. I tried to be normal once—it was the worst two minutes of my life.

"If the barber doesn't get it I'll take you to the beauty school to get your hair cut wild. They love to experiment," my mom said, pulling the electric cigarette lighter out from under the car radio and lighting a Virginia Slims, while my brothers and I bit into McDonald's salty chicken nuggets as we drove in her station wagon. From grade school all the way through high school and beyond, my parents always made me feel understood. Growing my hair long and bleaching it? No problem. Using so much hair spray sometimes you could taste it on the sloppy joes that had been bubbling on the stove? No problem—just shut the bathroom door next time.

Covering every inch of my bedroom walls with posters of rock stars (mostly men in makeup, and one of David Lee Roth in leather pants, without a shirt on, chained to a fence), sure— "It's your room," they'd say, "but use tape. Staples crack the walls."

As understanding as my parents were, every teenager pushes the envelope now and then. Sneaking out at one a.m. to try to meet Van Halen at a hotel in downtown Detroit was too far. I tightened a blanket around some pillows in my bed to look like I was in it, sleeping, and I think my never-worn penny loafer dress shoes I used as fake feet were sticking out of the blanket. My dad realized I wasn't in my bed and I got grounded for that. They never stayed mad for long. At least I wasn't chaining myself to a fence without a shirt on.

My brother Lee was adopted a few years before me. He seemed much older even though he was only a few years my senior. Lee was great at sports and with animals. Always in a baseball hat over his honey-blond hair, he could destroy any opponent's pride with his pitching and just as easily nurse an injured bird back to health. He had a hamster cage with a maze of yellow tubes that twisted like a dozen Slinkys set up in his room that he cleaned without being told.

My younger brother, Lance, was born nine months after me. My mom was told by doctors she couldn't get pregnant, but the moment I arrived she was unexpectedly expecting.

Lance is the spitting image of our dad. We shared a bedroom growing up, and to this day he's my best friend. He was huge too, even as a kid—Lance also carried me around like a football.

Music was always close at hand. While my brothers devoted themselves to athletics, wearing their baseball gloves like championship rings, my prized possession was a red Donny and Marie record player that folded up into a Cheerios box–sized suitcase with a white handle. I would carry it around, plug it in, and let it spin a 45 record of "Disco Duck," "Silly Love Songs" by Paul McCartney, and "You're a Mean One, Mr. Grinch," my go-to favorites. Saying "cheers" when my brothers and I clicked our pieces of pizza together at dinner, putting a Band-Aid on the back of my hand to pretend I was wearing a watch, and Thanksgiving table concerts at age three weren't my only early claims to fame...

After splashing around in a bath full of Mr. Bubble one Sunday before bedtime, my brothers and I somehow managed to escape from the house completely naked. We ran outside, streaking around the front yard doing bare-naked somersaults, gyrating and yelling, "Helicopter!" at mortified families in passing cars, then we climbed a neighbor's tree.

She was completely freaked out, enough to call the cops on a few children. Our bare-assed adventure caused such a furor the story made it into the local newspaper. So the first time I got press was for swinging upside down from a tree branch, naked.

Pyros "R" Us

The sounds of Mr. Coffee coffee gurgling into mugs, women gossiping, and Bob Barker yelling "Come on down!" from a yellow astronaut-helmet-shaped TV filled our kitchen as the screen door slapped shut behind me. Bouncing past my mom and her friends sitting at our kitchen table, I climbed up on the counter to reach the strawberry Nesquik I loved to mix into my milk.

My mom put her hands under my arms to help me get down, when suddenly she looked at me, shocked. Pressing her nose to my hair, she said, "Why do you smell like smoke?" I hadn't done anything wrong so I told her the truth. "Fisher barbecued his Big Wheel," I replied, then gulped down my sugary milk with a satisfied sigh.

Fisher was the neighborhood kid with greasy hair and a lopsided smile like a see-saw that no one was playing on. When we played army, most kids brought sticks or squirt guns. Fisher brought a box of his older sisters' tampons. He would pull the string, dip the cotton in RC Cola, and then throw it while yelling "Grenade!"

Fisher would wake up early on Christmas morning and open all of his family's presents while they were still asleep. Not just his presents—everyone's.

That morning, he'd poured his dad's lawn-mower gasoline all over his Big Wheel, then lit a Blue Tip match, the kind you could strike against any surface. He loved sparking them to life on the zipper of his cutoff jeans. (He had showed me that trick a dozen times, but usually blew the match out immediately.)

Today, after yelling "Don't touch that dial!" he purposely dropped the match on the gasoline-drenched Big Wheel, and we watched flames engulf it like Cookie Monster devouring a cookie. A black smoke tornado rose over it as the red, yellow, and blue plastic melted into a swirl of colors like Superman ice cream.

A cluster of young neighbors, barefoot, in shorts and striped shirts, stood around openmouthed like the cast of a hillbilly *A Christmas Story*. A Big Wheel was a big deal. It was our main mode of transportation at the time. "Y'all, a Big Wheel costs a thousand dollars, I seen one at Toys 'R' Us," a young girl said, between nibbles on a candy necklace that stained her neck pink. Fisher disappeared into a tree house as his mom was hosing it off, dressed in a bathrobe and slippers, her cheeks sucking in like a fish as she took a drag from a Kool cigarette, and I walked across their lawn back to my house.

As my mom pulled my smoky Popeye shirt over my head to throw it in the laundry basket, her friends around the table all laughed and echoed in their Southern accents, " 'He bar-be-cued his Big Wheel!' "

It's the first time I remember making a roomful of people laugh. It felt good, so I sang it over and over. "He bar-be-cued his Big Wheel he bar-be-cued his Big Wheel," smiling and waving my arms around like Grover from *Sesame Street*.

I liked the alliteration of that "B" sound even more. *Barbecue* and *Big Wheel*—it's something my ears still latch onto. Think of "Dancing in the Dark" by Bruce Springsteen, "Papa Don't Preach" by Madonna, and my own song "Smile"—"you make me smile like the sun."

I don't know what happened to Fisher. I haven't ever seen him on Facebook. Are people allowed to use Facebook in prison? In my fresh shirt and a strawberry mustache, I ran back outside as the *Price Is Right* theme drifted through the screen door.

Wide-Awake and Dreaming

We left our ranch-style house in Nashville, with its sweet smell of honeysuckle bushes in the yard, for a three-story brick house in Grosse Pointe, Michigan, with a seemingly funhouse-sized basement and skyscraper-tall Dutch elm trees in the yard with leaves that changed color in the fall as if Mother Nature had sprinkled Fruity Pebbles cereal on them. In winter, there was more snow outside than in the *Rudolph the Red-Rosed Reindeer* animated Christmas special we watched on TV. When the movers unloaded us in Michigan, the '70s were in full swing. *Star Wars* was dominating the movie theaters, and posters of Farrah Fawcett in her swimsuit smiled at virgin teenagers from bedroom walls. Reporters standing under spinning mirror balls described the disco music craze on the nightly news as the Bee Gees ah, ha, ha, ha-ed "Stayin' Alive," and John Lennon was still alive.

Like James Bond delicately deactivating a bomb, my new best friend, Marty Westervelt, slowly slid his library card behind the channel dial on a digital alarm clock–sized black box sitting on top of his TV set. Most TVs had channels 2 to 13; you clicked through them, turning the clunky dial by hand, and some channels were nothing but electric snow, but his father had ON TV, the first-ever cable box that showed dirty movies on Saturday nights. My friends and I had lots of weekend sleepovers. Marty's birthday sleepover had been specifically planned to be on a Saturday night so we could hack into ON TV.

After his parents had fallen asleep, six other kids and I excitedly sat like kittens about to pounce, staring at the blurry green-and-blue scrambled images on the TV that flashed to a full picture once every few minutes for a second. "I saw a nipple!" somebody screamed. "Shut up!" Marty scolded in a whisper. "Don't wake up my parents."

It was no use—the cable box was too tough to hack—but we had other things of great importance to discuss as we dug into a tinfoiled exploded Jiffy Pop pan. Mind-boggling questions such as: How can the Professor on *Gilligan's Island* make a radio out of two coconuts but he can't fix a hole in the boat? Why is the kid talking to the wise old owl in the Tootsie Pop commercial not wearing any clothes? We traded survival tips for one of life's most treacherous dangers certainly awaiting us all someday: falling into quicksand.

The latest news we'd heard from the older kids in town was shared between sips from Faygo soda cans wrapped in tinfoil to keep them cold, things like how if you ate too many Pop Rocks they'd get stuck in your throat and kill you, or if you wanted to French-kiss a girl you had to give her green M&M's because they make you horny.

Another friend at the sleepover, nicknamed Beaker due to his fire-red hair and twitching, manic demeanor, like the scientist's assistant on *The Muppet Show*, said excitedly, "Every cent of my allowance would be spent on green M&M's for Princess Leia if she visited Earth." "Dude, she died. *Star Wars* is from a long long time ago, duh!" came Marty's retort.

I don't know how these urban legends got started or how they managed to spread seemingly across the entire universe. Who needs the internet when you have older sisters and brothers you can eavesdrop on?

It Takes a Village to Raise the Roof

It was at a birthday sleepover for Jake Saad, when the late-night TV lit up with yellow sparkly words appearing in cursive like someone writing them with Cheez Whiz. They spelled out *The Best of the 70s*. I was pulling cherry Twizzlers apart and handing strands to my friends, while trumpets blasted a triumphant melody over a disco drumbeat and a line of men all from different walks of life paraded onto the screen. A leather-jacketed motorcycle man, a Native American, a construction worker, and a sailor in all white marched in place behind a grinning, singing police officer.

It was a song I had heard on the radio, but I didn't realize you could spell the title with your arms by moving them in triangles and half circles like an airport runway flagger.

Jumping up out of my Boba Fett sleeping bag, I began talking like a used-car salesman trying to sell my friends on an idea. "Guys, let's do this for the school talent show! Everyone knows this song. I can borrow a leather jacket from your mom, Jake. I could be the motorcycle man." Pointing and assigning roles like a casting director, I was possessed by the thought of performing. "Someone must have a cowboy hat and cap guns in a toy chest—they could be the cowboy. We could get a tool belt and a hammer from my dad's workshop for the construction worker."

Two cups of Hulk-green Kool-Aid and a pack of Twizzlers later, "The Star-Spangled Banner" began playing over an American flag waving in the wind on the channel, letting us know TV stations would be shut down for the night. My friends dozed off as I flipped my pillow to the cool side, imagining our show in my head.

I convinced my friends, and every day after school for a week we rehearsed, and it was an epiphany. I didn't mind going over the routine, trying to get it perfect. In fact, I loved it. I hated yard work, I despised washing the family station wagon, I gagged changing the litter box, and I secretly pressed a thermometer to a lightbulb, then showed my mom my "fever" to get out of doing the dishes after dinner. But rehearsing, making up moves, and lip-synching to a 45 record, spinning round and round like a clothes dryer, was more exciting than finding a dusty *Playboy* magazine in someone's garage. Almost.

The hundreds of children that made up Defer Elementary School all sat cross-legged in fidgety rows on the gym floor facing the stage. A sixth-grade boy, who blinked constantly and was the school's official film projector operator, volunteered to start our record before pulling the rope and parting the purple velvet curtains in short jumps like my dad fluffing his newspaper to straighten it while reading. A teacher with black curly hair wearing a mustard-colored dress adjusted her drink coaster–sized reading glasses and cleared her throat. From side stage she announced on a silver handheld mic connected to a PA system, "Don't forget, students, Popsicles with the Principal is next Thursday. Tell your parents to attend. Now please welcome The Village People of Defer!"

The teacher held the microphone up to the tiny record player speaker as my second-grade friends and I came out marching with army-like precision, turning left to point at one another at the start of every verse, then back to the marching position for the next line, dancing in time to the excited high-pitched screams of our fellow students. Before New Kids on the Block were "hangin' tough," *NSYNC sang "Bye Bye Bye," or Backstreet Boys "wanted it that way," the Village People of Defer got an entire school raising their arms above their heads spelling out YMCA. I only broke rank to point at my brother Lance singing along in the gym full of kids.

We won the talent show and I craved the stage after that. Every time I opened the refrigerator and the light inside shone on my face, I sang and danced for a full minute until my dad said, "J.T., you're letting all the cold air out, the milk's going to go bad!" I honestly thought I was in trouble when my mom, carrying an overflowing laundry basket, sighed, "If only I had Johnny Carson's number I'd call him and tell him about you."

Grosse Pointe was a great community to grow up in. We left a key to our house at the neighbors' in case we got locked out, and they left one of theirs at ours. We all trusted each other and looked out for one another.

Our street was close enough for us to walk to and from

school and safe enough to play outside for hours after. We ate dinner as a family every night. You could have blindfolded me and I could have made it to my house from the corner following the smell of spaghetti, chicken pot pies, or my personal favorite dinner—pancakes—coming from our kitchen.

After dinner we had to ask to be excused and had to clean our plates. I became an expert at moving my cooked carrots or green beans around like a master chess player to make it look like I had eaten some.

Grosse Pointe is one of Detroit's most exclusive suburbs and has a reputation that everyone there is rich and snobby— on Lake Shore Road, for example, there are a lot of big Beverly Hills–style houses on the waterfront, some of which are owned by the Henry Ford family, and it's home to one of the country's nicest yacht clubs, but plenty of us had our own hardships.

Everyone's parents worked hard, including mine. That's where I get my work ethic. It's the Michigan way. When people ask me where I'm from, I say Detroit without hesitation. Detroit is the city that put the world on wheels, the home of Motown Records, which inspired the Beatles and every generation since with its music, and the streets have potholes big enough to eat cereal out of. What's not to like?

Sparty Like a Rockstar

Vinyl records by Captain & Tennille, Tom T. Hall, and the Carpenters were stacked on top of each other like large black tortillas, each one making a *slap* sound as it dropped onto the turntable, the record player's tonearm moving over like a robot to drop the needle onto the record, where a *pop* was heard before the music began. My parents liked music but the only instrument they played was the stereo when their friends were over for beer and bridge card games. My mom's smile appears in my mind anytime I hear the perfectly sweet Carpenters melody "Why do birds suddenly appear, every time you are near?"

My dad's favorite song was the "Michigan State University Fight Song." He would blast it every Saturday morning in the fall as he and all the other parents would go up to Lansing to cheer on State football, my dad wearing a black-and-white-striped referee shirt and blowing a whistle although it was only tailgating he was an official of.

My parents always invited us kids along. They were so good about encouraging us in our ways. "Let your mitt hit the dirt if it has to stop the grounder," Dad would say to Lee. Punching his mitt at the ready, then adjusting the visor of his hat to hide his eyes from the sun, Lee could stop every ball my dad sent spinning his way across the grass in the backyard.

"Measure twice, cut once," Dad instructed Lance as a zipping sound emitted from a black-and-yellow measuring tape in our basement workshop. Lance loved building stuff in Dad's workshop with its wall full of screwdrivers, hammers, and enough scrap wood to rebuild Noah's Ark.

Throwing a Nerf ball to each other with dramatic catches, Lance and Lee jumped in the family van, excited for the Michigan State games. Football wasn't my thing and my parents didn't force it on me.

"Love you, Mom," I yelled as she placed a five-dollar bill for my babysitter by the microwave before leaving for the game in her white pants and green turtleneck. Avoiding the eyes of a missing child staring at me from the back of a milk carton, I filled a bowl to the rim with Cap'n Crunch's Crunch Berries and milk, then gingerly lifted it off the kitchen table and walked to the TV room. My Saturday morning ritual of cartoon watching had begun.

"Conjunction Junction, what's your function?" came singing out of the TV between episodes of *Scooby-Doo* and

Hong Kong Phooey. Eating around all the pink Crunch Berries, saving them for my last spoonfuls, I sang along to *Schoolhouse Rock* not knowing what the words meant, just loving the melody. The sound of girls' laughter and stomping caught my attention.

Boom-boom clap. Boom-boom clap. Feathered hair, painted-on Calvin Klein jeans, and movie star smiles greeted me in the kitchen. As if I wasn't already enamored enough with my babysitters, the gorgeous Keelan sisters who lived up the block, now there was the sound of a wild marching band in my kitchen. *Boom-boom clap, boom-boom clap.* The windows vibrated as they smacked their hands, stomped, and sang along to "We will, we will rock you!"

The babysitters had the radio turned up to ten playing a group called Queen. When I ran from the TV room to join in, they cheered me on as I used a silver egg whisk for a microphone, lip-synching and stomping around to a song I'd never heard but immediately could sing.

The power of music. If it's a good song, it's amazing how through the decades it can find new audiences. "We Will Rock You" is just as powerful now as it was then. I guarantee you someday on Mars "We Will Rock You" will be playing. Unlike milk, good music has no expiration date.

We moved to Michigan because my dad landed a job at a talk radio station, selling advertising. WRIF was the big local rock station. It was connected to my dad's station, and thanks to my babysitters I became an avid listener. One day my dad took me to work with him for fun. That morning, I catapulted out of bed, dressed up in my Kmart gold-button suit coat usually reserved for Sunday church, and standing next to him on a chair by the sink so I could see myself in the steamed-up mirror, I put shaving cream on my face and used a Popsicle stick to "shave."

A security guard looked up from his detective magazine

and waved my dad's midnight-blue van through the station gates. I leaned forward to stare up at the WRIF sign glowing cinnamon Red Hots red and marvel at the giant radio tower that was sending music as if by magic into our radios.

WRIF, or "The Riff," as it was called, gave away colorful bumper stickers with famous bands' names on them. You could order them for free by mail or get them from the Riff van if you saw it outside a concert or at the annual Detroit Auto Show.

The stickers were hard to come by and were coveted by everyone who had or wanted them. High school kids had AC/DC or the Who stickers on their notebooks, and it was my goal in life (at the time) to have a few of my own. Sitting in my dad's office, I poked the air with my finger like a woodpecker pointing toward WRIF, whispering, "I want to go next door."

Covering the receiver of the phone during a sales call, my dad said, "Okay, pal, tell them Coach Larry sent you." The WRIF sign got bigger and bigger as I walked across the parking lot, approaching the glass doors of the mighty rock station.

"It's 63 degrees in the D. I'll be at Harpos Saturday giving out tickets to the Autorama auto show. Come on down, say hi, and let your freak flag fly." A DJ with a brown mustache as thick as a Milky Way candy bar sat in a booth plastered with posters of rock stars and women in bikinis. The man's lips were pressed against a blue fuzzy microphone as he spoke. I was captivated. A secretary with canary-yellow hair and wearing a white leather jacket informed everyone, "Coach Harding's son is here to learn about radio," as she chewed her gum and smiled me past her desk.

Gold and silver records in frames on the walls above my head caught my eye like an usher's flashlight in a dark movie theater. "See something you like?" a short man in a suit coat over an "I'm a Pepper" T-shirt asked, noticing me grinning like Charlie entering Willy Wonka's factory. Jerking his chin up to point at a Bob Seger disc, he added, "Those are gold and platinum records. Rock stars get those when they sell a shit ton of records."

Walking backward away from me, the fast-talking man continued: "You know how they sell a shit ton of records? Riff plays the records." Facing me and pointing his fingers in my direction like a pair of cowboy pistols, he kicked the men's room door behind him open and slipped inside.

Glossy WRIF stickers that read AEROSMITH and PAT BENATAR passed from the secretary's hand into mine, but my mind was elsewhere, lost in thought over those gold records.

"Lunchtime, pal!" my dad called to me from in front of the radio station cafeteria across the parking lot. Stickers in hand and gold record dreams in my head, I ran to him.

Welcome to the Jungle Gym

A plum-colored rubber ball the size of a globe left the hands of a fifth-grade boy and furiously rolled toward a pizza box being used as home plate. Another boy standing at the ready over the pizza box kicked the ball as hard as he could before taking off in the direction of a dusty baseball cap that marked first base on the baseball field.

On the playground twenty yards to the right, girls chased after each other yelling "Tag, no tag-backs" in a game of Who's Got Cooties.

Running from the slide to the swings to the monkey bars and back again was a swarm of a few hundred grade schoolers in bright-colored windbreakers, sneakers, and Detroit team jerseys, blurring like an exploding gumball machine. Our forty-five minutes of daily freedom had begun. It was recess at Defer Elementary School.

Sitting on the swings passing a Rubik's Cube back and

forth, my friends wanted every detail about my radio station visit. "WRIF wants me to be a DJ on weekends. Call me on the request line, I'll get you on the air." Of course that wasn't true, but it made for a good playground story.

From the parking lot that was surely off-limits to students, the toughest kid in school started walking toward us with a strut you could keep time to. He acted like a sixth-grade Fonzie from *Happy Days*. His oil-black hair was slicked back, his wallet rolled up in his white T-shirt sleeve like a pack of cigarettes, and he had one hand behind his back. Rumor had it his older brothers were really rough on him, so in turn he picked on younger kids. Schoolyard trickle-down economics. With each step he took toward us, my mouth started to dry and my stomach tickled, a little more nervous. My friends raised their eyebrows when he pushed my chest with a closed fist.

"You the kid talking to all the girls about music?" he asked, not smiling. "Yeah—I guess," I replied, trying to play it cool. I looked down to the ground, looked up to his eyes staring at me, then back down again. Was he going to pick a fight? Where's my big little brother, Lance, when you need him?

Slowly pulling from behind his back a record that opened up into two big wide squares like a *Playboy* centerfold, the tough kid asked, "Ever heard this?" I'd never seen a record like this before. Right before my eyes were four otherworldly beings with guitars, black hairdos as big as cotton candy, and sparkly boots. They wore Kabuki-style makeup that covered their entire faces and clothing like I'd never seen.

The beings were standing in between giant fireballs that were as high as palm trees. One of them was in a silver foam space suit, one looked like a cat with whiskers holding drumsticks over his head. With puckered cherry-red lips, a sparkly garter belt on his thigh, and a perfect black star drawn on around his right eye, the singer was pointing at the camera like a hairy-chested, muscular Marilyn Monroe.

The last one on the cover was sticking its lizard-like tongue out longer than any tongue should ever humanly stick out. The tongue creature had knee-high boots with teeth and eyes like an alligator.

Were these men or women? Were they superheroes? Were they proof that aliens had landed? Behind them was a giant lit-up sign the size of a movie screen. Two *S*'s in the sign were shaped like lightning bolts. The sign spelled one giant glorious glowing word: KISS.

"I'm a member of the KISS Army. You're recruited. This is *KISS Alive II*. Keep the album until you know it by heart, then pass it on to someone else," schoolyard Fonzie said to me. Once I'd taken the record from him, he nodded, satisfied. Then looking around at my friends with a scowl, he produced a switchblade knife. Beaker jumped like he'd been poked with a pin when it sprang open, but instead of a blade it revealed a comb. After a quick styling of his hair, young Fonzie huffed, then strutted back across the playground, sliding the switchblade comb into the back pocket of his Jordache jeans.

KISS and Makeup

When I slowly placed the needle on the record, it crackled like bacon cooking until the sound of a crowd hissing to life collided with the band blasting into a song called "Detroit Rock City." The guitars chugged like a locomotive at full power. The drums popped fast like a machine gun as the "Starchild," Paul Stanley, screamed above the music: "You gotta lose your mind in Detroit Rock City!" I did lose my mind, but I found my calling. That day I started air-guitaring and using a black Sharpie to draw a star around my right eye. I've never stopped.

It was unimaginable that these people, KISS, knew of Michigan. Better yet my hometown.

The record had been played so many times that it started skipping due to the scratches on the vinyl. Somehow I figured out that if I put pennies on the tonearm of the record player it would hold the needle down and stop the record from skipping.

Lance, wearing a Garfield T-shirt that said NEVER TRUST A SMILING CAT, sat and listened to me talk nonstop about how KISS were never seen without makeup. They could have walked past us at the mall undetected; they could be coaches at our baseball games for all we knew. As "Detroit Rock City" played for the hundredth time, Lee sat in the den with his nose practically touching the TV screen as he watched M*A*S*H, the volume turned up full blast in protest against my music.

After air-guitaring and lip-synching to the record for months, my mind was in overdrive wondering who they were, where they were from, what they looked like without the makeup. On late-night TV shows there'd be a short frantic clip of KISS and I would be glued to the screen.

Every few months a magazine like *Circus* or *Creem* would come out declaring "KISS Without Makeup for the First Time Ever!" I'd spend my hard-earned allowance on anything KISS. The mystery of who they were caused many sleepless nights. Despite the bragging of the magazines, it was always more pictures of them covering their faces with a scarf, and a bodyguard throwing a punch at the camera. There wasn't any internet then, so all I had was my imagination.

Whether they were on the cover of *People* or their iconic band logo was respelled to read KRAP in *Mad* magazine, I had to have it.

For Halloween, Lee and Lance, in matching Detroit Lions football helmets and jerseys, waited impatiently as my mom studied my KISS *Dynasty* album cover like Norman Rockwell, then turned to me, arching her neck back as she delicately applied black makeup in the shape of bat wings on my face. Gene Simmons—the fire-breathing, blood-spitting member of KISS—was my trick-or-treating costume of choice for a decade. My mom sewed black bat wings onto my black turtleneck sleeves and used Lee's model paint to paint white alligator teeth and red eyes on my snowmobile boots to complete my costume.

Mixing water with red food coloring from my mom's spinning spice rack on a kitchen shelf gave the desired blood effect but ruined many of my shirts.

My dad overheard me saying something about spitting out gasoline to breathe fire, and he looked at me with such fury in his eyes I never mentioned it again.

Every now and then school supplied one of the great joys of youth: a substitute teacher. "Ms. Anna, for real, our teacher said I could hang this up." A Gene Simmons poster I kept in my desk next to a soon-to-be-confiscated Pip Squirt pen and rock-hard stale Swedish Fish was covering up my face as I held it up. "If she was here she would tell you," I pleaded. *Surely a boy wouldn't just keep a poster like this in his desk*, the substitute mused. The truth was, I actually did.

Pushing silver tacks into the poster's top corners, I stared proudly at the rock star demon sticking his six-inch tongue out for all to see, hung up in between a purple octopus pointing his eight arms at the letter O and a top-hat-waving Abraham Lincoln driving a yellow school bus.

"Sad eyes, turn the other way" sang out in sorrow over the speakers at the roller rink where my parents dropped my brothers and me off one Saturday a month. I rolled off the rink, skipping the "couples' skate kiss" to feel the rush of another KISS. Blinking lightning bolts and the song "Shout It Out Loud" came to life as quarters I stole from the rusty Planters Peanuts can above our washing machine were fed into the KISS pinball machine. My roller skates put me at the perfect height to reach the bumpers.

KISS for some reason weren't on the radio much, but I would scan it all the time for them regardless.

"Clean the House Sunday" was the bane of my existence at the Harding residence, but there was no escaping it. Soft fuzzy headphones and my Walkman radio were my saving grace. *Casey Kasem's Weekly Top 40* was on every Sunday.

I rolled a vacuum from room to room cleaning, my ears bathed in the sound of "Start Me Up" by the Rolling Stones, "Keep On Loving You" by REO Speedwagon, "Bette Davis Eyes" by Kim Carnes. Because of her raspy voice I thought Kim Carnes was the same person who sang another one of my favorites, "Da Ya Think I'm Sexy?" by Rod Stewart.

Pop songs about yearning and lost love were my favorites, songs that somehow made me feel sad and happy at the same time. I wonder, Do I like pop songs because I'm lonely sometimes, or am I lonely sometimes because I love pop songs?

A KISS Army membership card was taped to my bedroom wall. They were my undisputed first love, but other bands and songs were whispering in my ear, getting stuck in my head and seducing me at every turn of the radio dial.

All those otherworldly guitar riffs, drumbeats, and voices that would sing, squeal, and haunt me in the best way have been running through my head all these years like a dozen Keebler Elves running in and out of their tree on a cookie commercial. Maybe the songs were all mixing with each other and coming back out recycled into brand-new melodies whenever my fingers strum a guitar and my voice makes up songs now.

Cicadas buzzed like a barber's hair clipper in the oak tree above our house on a warm summer evening. The band Journey were constantly played on the radio thanks to their infectious song "Don't Stop Believin'." Their new album was due and I read the song titles in a magazine ad.

Clutching a hockey stick for a guitar on the front porch of our house, my cheeks puffed up like the chipmunks Chip and

Dale scarfing acorns as I made a distorted guitar sound with my voice vibrating my teeth and lips, I sang a new Journey song as I imagined it might go.

Long before albums were leaked to the public digitally, if a DJ or a babysitter's boyfriend informed me about a new album coming out, all I could do was wait for it to be released. The anticipation of new music by a band I loved made me Christmas-morning excited no matter what time of year it was.

Balancing a giant piece of plywood on a stack of bricks at the end of our driveway, my brother Lee and his friend Rich Waller were making a ramp to jump Lee's Mongoose bicycle over. As I belted out my lyrics, Lee and Rich put their index fingers in their ears and booed me while I bowed exaggeratedly with pride.

Feeding the fire burning in me to hear new music that was unavailable, I made up songs inspired by the titles I had seen. Kicking my legs back and forth to get higher on the swings at Defer School, I did the same for an unreleased Van Halen album that was coming out. That was the first step toward songwriting. I made up lyrics to songs that I'd never heard.

The *Smokey and the Bandit* movies made me want to get a black Trans Am. Lighting an entire pack of Black Cat firecrackers made my heart race with mischief. Gobbling blinking ghosts, playing Pac-Man at the arcade was a two-minute thrill, but music—music was in a league of its own.

Music gave me goose bumps. Music made me dream. Music made me strut instead of walk. Music was always there for me—happy, sad, or in between.

Music transformed my front porch into a stage. Passing cars became imaginary fans I pointed at. A sunset through the leaves of a tree became a dozen perfect spotlights. Fireflies were cameras flashing, taking my picture in a stadium, a robin's nest high in a tree became the people in the "cheap seats" that I gave a shout-out to. It was a portal to another world.

Today when I hear songs from my youth like "(I Just) Died in Your Arms" by Cutting Crew or "Jump" by Van Halen, it's like a time machine flying me back to my bedroom on Berkshire. Whether it's fifteen years or fifteen days ago, listening to music has a magic that turns memories into movies, but when I was growing up, music was a time machine zooming me into the future like Marty McFly's DeLorean.

Standing behind the outstretched arms of a crossing guard on a corner after school, I saw a pimple-faced teenager with a peach-fuzz mustache kissing a girl at a red light in his car. I wanted that to be me leaning past the steering wheel, tasting her Bubble Yum tongue.

My babysitter would blow-dry her hair at my house. Talking loudly while waving our white Conair back and forth, she would excitedly talk about a backyard keg party she was going to when my parents got home. I ached to go to that party. Listening to songs gave me a secret look into the world I wanted to be in. I wanted to be a teenager. I wanted to run the streets all night, go to dances, make out on a couch like older kids did as Eddie Murphy talked like Gumby on *Saturday Night Live*.

Flipping through the pages of *16* magazine, with pictures of rock stars riding in limousines, flying to Japan, and being mobbed at the airport by their fans, only intensified my yearning to grow up.

Like a bored Little League outfielder waiting for a fly ball to come my way, I knew there was life beyond my bedroom but I was too young to live it. Music got me there, if only in my head. Songs were supernatural. Luke Skywalker had the Force, J.T. Harding had rock 'n' roll.

The sound of paper slipping through the mail slot on the side of our house made me run to it from my room. Digging through a *Better Homes & Gardens* magazine, a *TV Guide* showing the kids from *Diff'rent Strokes*, and throwing a white envelope featuring an old man named Ed McMahon saying my family had ten million dollars waiting for them, I saw a box addressed to me. "Yes!" I cheered before I carefully opened the box with scissors from the kitchen.

Weeks before, I had taped a single penny to an order form in the Sunday paper and mailed it to the Columbia House tape club. The prize was ten cassettes of my choice. I was in my room immediately with the stack of cassettes that I laid out on the floor like precious gold bricks. After dinner, lighting a Virginia Slims cigarette, my mom curiously looked over the box. "J.T., you have to buy a new cassette every month in this club and you don't have the money for that. Pack the tapes up, we're returning them," she explained. "Mom, let's return the ones that come and keep these. I sent the penny and everything," I pleaded. "J.T., it's stealing," Mom said, blowing smoke upward. Where was my mom when Napster was invented?

The cassettes were taped up and handed back to the mailman in his sideways mail cap. I'm thankful now that my parents raised me not to steal, but it was pillow-punching frustrating at the time. Records and cassettes were expensive. I waited eternities for birthdays and Christmas to arrive to get new ones. If someone had told me that in the future I would be able to play all the music I liked instantly out of a handheld telephone, I would've told them they had watched *The Jetsons* one too many times.

...Catching OZZZZZy's

Silver words printed on two gold rectangular tickets stared up at me from between my fingers: WRIF PRESENTS OZZY OSBOURNE WITH SPECIAL GUEST MÖTLEY CRÜE.

My dad had gone over to WRIF and traded his MSU football tickets for concert tickets.

Being the hero that he was, Dad encouraged me and my love for music. "J.T., when you grow up you can do whatever you want to do, just do it your best."

Two boring school weeks later we were headed to the show. Because the radio station tickets came directly from Ozzy's record company, we had amazing seats only a few rows from the stage. Walking down to the main floor into the skunk-smelling smoke and a sea of people with long hair and jean jackets, we heard a guy yell at my dad: "Hey, look, Grandpa is bringing his grandkid to the concert!" My dad smiled as he gave the heckler a thumbs-up. "Typical spastic—his dad probably went to U of M," he told me.

The lights went black and the crowd roared to life like Blue Angels jet engines I'd once heard fly over Detroit. The hair stood up on my arms poking through my bubble gum "Jail-O" and "Minute Lice" temporary tattoos. Standing on my chair on my tiptoes to see above the heads of the rockers standing up in front of us, I balanced by putting my hand on my dad's shoulder.

Mötley Crüe took the stage. The backdrop was a city in ruins under an ash-gray sky. The band looked like future criminals and bounty hunters from a Star Wars movie.

Vince Neil spat out lyrics while pumping his leather-gloved fist into the air. His bleach-blond hair seemed to glow like E.T.'s finger. At one point during the first song, bass player Nikki Sixx must've had something wrong with his bass guitar, which was painted to look like a blood splatter.

Frustrated, Sixx clenched his teeth as he took it off by the shoulder strap and slammed it against the stage. His bass didn't break, it balanced on the edge of the stage like a teeter-totter.

A mob of fans reached up and grabbed the expensive bass. At that exact moment Mötley Crüe roadies ran out onstage for it, and there was a screaming tug-of-war between the crowd and the roadies, who were gripping the neck of the bass guitar and pulling.

Security guards along the front row moved to aid the roadies in the tug-of-war, inspiring another long-haired shirtless fan from the audience to jump unnoticed up onto the stage. The fan grabbed Vince Neil's cordless microphone, then dove headfirst back into the crowd with it.

A guitar tech ran out from side stage and dove into the main-floor mob, trying to rescue the stolen microphone. It was total chaos. I didn't blink; I wasn't going to miss a moment of this spectacle. "Shout at the Devil" roared through the speakers, with Tommy Lee pounding his drums like a monkey on Red Bull the whole time. He was hitting the cymbals so hard, pieces of wood shot off from his drumsticks, which he magically spun like tiny cheerleader batons every few beats.

People lit bottle rockets from the back of the arena that whistled over all of our ducking heads like missiles. It wasn't part of the show. These concertgoers were lighting bottle rockets indoors.

Between songs, Neil brought cursing to an Olympic level—he could have made Andrew Dice Clay blush. Pretty girls leaned over the barricade to touch him. The things he shouted at them made me stare straight ahead, not looking at my dad, pretending I didn't understand a word.

The red-and-white flashing stage lights, electric guitars so loud that my body vibrated, transported me into a kind of trance I never wanted to break.

After Mötley Crüe, the most notorious rock star on the planet at that time came out: Ozzy Osbourne. Ozzy's music was causing what was called Satanic Panic among adults opposed to his loud music and devil persona, while fans lovingly called him the Prince of Darkness.

He'd recently bitten the head off a bat that may or may

not have been alive at a concert in Des Moines, Iowa, so you can see where he may have gotten the nickname. Morning radio shows talked about the bat incident constantly, adding fuel to Ozzy's fire. Every parent was disgusted as every kid discussed it.

When Ozzy took the stage, it was Superbowl touchdown–style pandemonium.

Guitars squealed as Ozzy grabbed his microphone with both hands, gnashed his teeth, and shook his copper-colored shoulder-length spiked hair like he was being electrocuted by the local PTA.

"Do you think I'm crazy? Do you think I'm really crazy?" his voice boomed through the two-story PA speakers hanging above his band. We all cheered like a heavy metal congregation. Ozzy paused, then gripped the top of his head and pulled his giant hairdo off.

It was a wig. He was bald underneath. Some sort of confused, testosterone-fueled euphoria came over the crowd. Their Heavy Metal God had committed the ultimate sin: He'd cut his hair.

Fifteen songs later, confetti poured from the ceiling over the crowd as sparks shot up over the stage from cannons behind the drum set as if it were New Year's Eve in Times Square. The flying sparks warmed my face like a stove burner on full.

Confetti settled on my cheeks like snowflakes. Catching some in my hands, I filled the pockets of my Levi's with it, proof that I had been to a concert to show my friends on the playground.

The house lights came on, and I could see the main floor of the arena was a cluttered mess of collapsed folding chairs, bras, crunched cigarette packs, empty beer cups, even a shoe.

Ghosts of explosions appeared in my eyes every time I blinked, like after a camera flashes at a birthday party. Two hours of wall-to-wall amplifiers turned up to 11 caused a high-pitched ringing in my ears.

The loudest experience of my life had come to a cymbal-smashing end. Next to me, Dad sat in his chair, a popcorn bucket between his knees and pink confetti in his salt-and-pepper hair. He was sound asleep.

"Dad, it's over. Hey, Dad. Dad, it's over." I poked his shoulder and rubbed his strong arm through his dark-blue suit jacket. Inhaling loudly through his nose, he opened his eyes wide and said, "What a bunch of wild Indians." A normal pace for his long legs was twice as fast as mine, so as we walked back to our van, I had to skip to keep up with him. As soon as we got to the van I tossed my preppy Grosse Pointe polo shirt in the back seat like a losing lottery ticket, then clicked the seat belt over my new Mötley Crüe concert T-shirt. We'd bought shirts for Lee and Lance as well.

Turning on the talk radio station he worked for as we pulled out of the parking garage, my dad smiled. Holding out the "s" sound like a snake hissing, he said, "Wait 'til my sales team hears the ol' man went to see the Prince of Darknesssss."

Dreams of Mouth-to-Mouth Recitation

Mickey Mouse beach towels around our necks, our Walkmans blasting tunes through our headphones, my friends and I would pedal our BMX bikes through the tree-lined streets of Grosse Pointe, past all the three-story houses and the bank sign flashing the summer temperature, to the local park pool.

Popping wheelies, jumping the curbs, and then jamming on the brakes to leave black skid marks, we tattooed the streets with our tires. An ace of spades playing card clamped with a clothespin in the spokes of my bike made it buzz like a motorcycle engine as I pedaled. Grosse Pointe summers as a kid were total freedom. No one told us what to do; we were as wild and free as Max from the book *Where the Wild Things Are*...until the streetlights came on.

One day a gorgeous lifeguard started talking to us at the entrance of the park as we locked our bikes to the bike rack. My seven-year-old heart was beating like a hummingbird's. She was seventeen and the first teenager I ever saw smoking a cigarette. Imagine every beautiful girl from every John Hughes '80s movie rolled into one teenage dream. That was her.

Dressed in a one-piece bathing suit as red as Jake Ryan's Porsche in *Sixteen Candles*, mirrored sunglasses, and a sugar-white seashell ankle bracelet that seemed to glow like a Halloween light stick against her perfect tan skin, it was like she was a magnet and my eyes were metal. The pool had a "Sixteen and Under Out" rule for fifteen minutes every hour so senior citizens could swim without fear of our cannonball jumps drowning their beauty salon hairdos. We would slip silently into the pool hoping to get caught by her as a conversation starter, but never had we run into her outside the pool.

Spinning the hunters-orange thread of her lifeguard whistle on her index finger, she patiently listened to my friends and me excitedly talk over each other about how Han Solo was the only one who could understand what Chewbacca was saying in *Star Wars*.

I caught a glimpse of her braces as I watched her chew on her sunburnt lip. She pointed at my spokes and made fun of my "motorcycle" sound maker before heading back to the lifeguard shack. All we could do as she walked away, her flip-flops popping with every step, was wonder aloud if you could feel a girl's braces when you kissed her.

If only Lee wasn't baiting fishhooks a football field away out on the park pier. I could have hooked the lifeguard with my favorite thing to do at the pool: stand on his shoulders as he held his breath and squatted down underwater. Once balanced, I would lightly tap his head when I was ready. Feeling the tap, Lee would stand up as fast as he could, his strong body flying me out of the water like Iron Man blasting off out of the ocean.

Without my big brother there, my flying trick couldn't catch the attention of the lifeguard, but I had a better plan. That day was the end of my "motorcycle" but the beginning of my career.

Jake Saad, one of my friends at the park with me, had a guitar at home. After swimming until our toes were too scratched from the pool's bottom to walk barefoot anymore, we rode back to his house. Hands off the handlebars, my outstretched arms balancing as my bike rolled along, I yelled, "Let's write a song for the lifeguard! She'll want to make out with me forever."

Dropping our Schwinns in a tangled metal heap at the steps of Jake's back porch, we rushed up the stairs to his room. Jake sat on his bed and held his electric guitar. He knew all of two guitar chords, but endless nights staring at record covers and the lyric sheets that came with them had taught me a few things.

Songs all had a title, and they all had words. The words needed to rhyme, that much I knew.

I took a pen and a blank piece of paper out of Jake's Trapper Keeper folder with a silver sports car on it. Tapping the pen like a drumstick, I began singing and writing lyrics as he stared at his hands and strummed clumsily.

Later, Jake's mom set down a can of Tab soda to hold up the lined yellow paper with my lyrics on it. With macaroni and cheese boiling on the stove under the paper, Jake's mom read the lyrics aloud to my mom over their kitchen phone: "When your lips are stunned you can't have any fun."

Jake's mom was concerned. My mom laughed.

The very first song I ever wrote, like almost every song

I would ever write, was inspired by a girl. A lifeguard with braces. The song was called "Lockjaw."

Charcoal from backyard grills perfumed the air. Dads mowed lawns around abandoned Slip 'N Slides and Coppertone bottles where kids had played as the summer sun began to set. The "Lockjaw" lyrics folded up in my pocket, I pedaled from Jake's house under the butterscotch clouds across the baseball diamonds to get home in time for dinner. As I rode by on the grass, I saw my older brother, Lee, the only kid in Grosse Pointe who would never age, hitting fly balls to his friends on the field.

CHAPTER 3

Kids Alive 2

The crowd was screaming in anticipation, the stage pitch black. Standing on the drum riser ready to rock, I curled my toes in my tennis shoes as butterflies ballet-danced in my stomach. The multicolored bandannas around my ankles were tied tight so I wouldn't trip.

In one giant motion the first guitar chord struck, the drums boomed to life. Jumping off the drum riser doing a Bruce Lee kick as the lights came on, I was thunder and lightning in a rock 'n' roll storm.

Spinning my arm like a windmill over my guitar, I brought the audience jumping to their feet. Singing, swaying, sweating, I did a double take, teasing three beautiful high school girls that looked like the real-life Charlie's Angels reaching over the barricade in the front row, trying to touch me. I was posing, pouting, and pointing, the packed arena in the palm of my fingerless Mötley Crüe–style leather glove, backstage pass stuck to my pants for the entire audience to see.

The audience sang every word I was singing right back at me. I was a natural. During the guitar solo I fist-punched the air to every down beat of the drums with kung fu precision.

When the song ended, the lights went black perfectly on cue. The crowd's cheering rose like a wave as I yelled "THANK YOU!" Seven years old and playing a sold-out show in Detroit's

Cobo Arena—I was already a legend. Covered in sweat, my head back in triumph, and one arm held up like Rocky, I looked off to the side of the stage where my roadie stood.

Walking offstage, I smiled at him and said, "Sweet! Okay, let's do it again. Double nice with the light but this time flicker it on and off as fast as you can like a strobe during the guitar solo—I'm pretty sure it'll give me a cool robotic look. I'll jump off a chair instead of the couch this time, the couch cushions are too soft to stand on, I freakin' wobble. Whoever heard of a wobbling rock star? No one! Okay, I'm starting the song over—get ready!"

The crowd and music were coming from *KISS Alive II* on the family stereo, the stage was the living room of our house. My guitar was a hockey stick that I held with a crusty golf glove with the fingers off. The sweat on my face was water from a Kmart spray bottle, the backstage pass a HELLO MY NAME IS sticker from a PTA meeting my mom had attended.

The Charlie's Angels of my imagination were my real-life babysitters, the Keelan sisters. My roadie, my groupie wrangler, and my lighting man was my younger brother, Lance, his cheek the size of a golf ball as he held a half pack of Big League Chew bubble gum in his mouth.

Lance didn't always stay for my entire performance. As I sang the ballad "Beth, I hear you calling," the basketball net over the garage was calling to him. I didn't mind. I needed intimacy to really charm the audience. There's nothing more personal than shining a spotlight on your most private heartbreak in front of twenty thousand people. As Lance dribbled and threw himself an alley-oop on the driveway, the streetlights flickered on through the front window.

Only forty-five minutes left before the Little Caesars pizzas my mom ordered were delivered and their tomato sauce scent filtered through our house as my dad walked in from work and hollered, "Wash your hands, rock star, it's dinnertime."

CHAPTER 4

The Six Million Dollar Man

A white parachute cut perfectly through the wind, swinging slowly from side to side like a pendulum in a grandfather clock. Three other parachutes dotted the blue sky behind the first and floated toward the earth. An announcer ten thousand feet below was yelling into a microphone on a stage standing before a sold-out stadium.

"Look to the sky! Van Halen is parachuting to the stage! Look to the sky!" The audience threw their heads back and cheered, waving cups and T-shirts above their heads as their rock 'n' roll heroes made the greatest concert entrance they'd ever seen.

I didn't get to see it. It happened in 1978. A high school kid who lived across the street taped it off the radio and lent me the cassette. It made me love the energetic wolf-howling singing and mind-blowing guitar sounds of the band even more.

The parachute I was looking at was my hand hanging out the car window, cupping the blowing wind. From the back seat of my dad's van, I told Mom and Lance about the Van Halen concert as we drove home from a Tigers baseball game one perfect summer night in Detroit. Lee had stayed back at home to play baseball with his friends.

Broken windows in abandoned buildings, dilapidated houses without roofs, burned-out streetlights, and cars without tires made Detroit look and feel like a war zone. Dogs roamed freely as men sat in lawn chairs on corners sipping from bottles concealed in brown paper bags under the fading sun.

As my dad looked both ways before rolling through a nonworking stoplight, I noticed a McDonald's restaurant that was boarded up. Children in the empty parking lot jumped on a rust-stained mattress, pretending it was a trampoline. Looking back, I think even as a child I knew how lucky I was.

After a twenty-minute drive through Detroit, the scene change was drastic. Crossing into Grosse Pointe from Detroit felt like Dorothy going from black-and-white Kansas to Technicolor Oz.

One street separated the two cities. On one side it was all deserted gas stations with broken pumps, empty beauty salons with cracked graffitied windows, on the other were beautiful brick homes, manicured lawns, and teenagers driving brand-new sports cars on streets as clean as a new pharmacy.

"Time for bed, guys," my dad said as Lance and I jumped out of the van and I trotted into the house, headed to my room to listen to music.

Petting our cat, Pickles, I turned on WRIF radio and sat on my bed, flipping through a copy of *Dynamite* magazine with Mork from *Mork & Mindy* on the cover standing next to the silly deli owner from the show.

Over the sound of "m-m-m-my Sharona" playing in the background, I suddenly heard my dad's voice echoing up the laundry chute. A lot of Michigan homes have these chutes—we could drop clothes from the second floor and they would all land in a basket in the basement.

"Kendra, Kendra, help!" he yelled like the house was on fire. The blood froze in my veins. I'd never heard my dad yell like that. I remember it better than I remember last night. I ran down the stairs to the first floor, my socks sliding on the steps. Following my dad's voice, I ran through the kitchen to the basement, calling out to him in fear and confusion.

Zigzagging through our basement past the washer and dryer and through my dad's tool shop, I saw my dad in the small room where we kept cans of soup and old suitcases, holding my brother Lee up by his waist. He was still in his baseball uniform and cleats. Lee's feet were dangling at my dad's knees. A stepladder lay on its side next to him. Around my brother's neck was a yellow rope.

In a panic, my mom appeared with a large kitchen knife. Using all his might, my dad held my brother up with one arm and then cut the rope with his other arm as he and my brother tumbled to the cement floor.

"Wake up, it's your father. Lee, I need you to wake up, it's your father," my dad commanded as he lightly patted the cheeks on my brother's face, which was turning gray like ash.

Running into the laundry room, I grabbed the phone off the wall receiver to call for help, but the sticker with the hand-written emergency and doctors' numbers had been rubbed off after years of regular phone use. Instinctively I dialed 911. My mother grabbed the phone from me in the confusion and hung it up but couldn't get a dial tone to make another call.

Lance stood in shock as my dad said over and over, "Lee, wake up." Grabbing Lance's shirt, I insisted we go outside to the tree.

My father had instructed us all that—heaven forbid—if there was ever a fire or any sort of emergency, we should all meet at the giant Dutch elm tree that stood on our front lawn. Lance and I ran out to the tree in the dark. We could hear sirens as a police car and an ambulance sped up to our house faster than any vehicle had ever been driven in our neighborhood.

Neighbors in robes and nightgowns appeared on their lawns as red sirens cut through the dark everywhere around us, like something out of a movie. But this wasn't a movie or a bad dream. Lee was wheeled out on a stretcher and put into the ambulance, and my mother and father climbed in after him. Our next-door neighbors walked Lance and me over to their house, asking what had happened.

In their kitchen, we were kindly offered Kool-Aid and cookies. At some point my mother and father returned from the hospital, coming to the neighbors' house where they told us that Lee had died. "They're lying, the doctors are lying!" I screamed out loud as my dad wrapped me in his arms trying to calm me down.

My parents, Lance, and I walked back to our house arm in arm. Later that night we somehow managed to fall asleep together on Mom and Dad's bed above the covers, wrapped around each other like a shield guarding us from the outside world.

A few days later, friends and family, kids of all ages, and Lee's entire Little League team in their uniforms crowded into a church for the funeral service. The only funeral I had ever attended before was one Lee presided over. When our goldfish, Yoda, died, Lee flushed it down the toilet, whistling "Taps" as it swirled to its resting place.

My dad stood and from the front of the congregation spoke to everyone who had gathered.

"I've been driving myself crazy trying to figure out why Lee passed away. I finally figured it out. It's a lesson to let all you other kids know not to fool around, not to take the fast track in life. Lee's favorite show was *The Six Million Dollar Man*. While we named him Lawrence after me, he asked us to start calling him Lee after Lee Majors, the guy who plays the Six Million Dollar Man. Lee thought he was invincible. He wasn't." My dad teared up. I had never seen him cry. Exhaling slowly, he continued his plea: "To all of the young people here, I beg you: Stay young. We need all of you. We need everything you will offer the world as you grow up."

In the front row I buried my eyes into my mom's shoulder and bawled for the first time since Lee had died.

Standing tall, my dad continued: "As bad as this is, I'm still the luckiest man on earth. I can't imagine going home alone to an empty house after this. I'm going home to the best wife ever, Kendra. I have two other boys—Lance, who's great at math and great at sports, and J.T., who's seven going on twenty-nine." The entire church laughed, bringing a much-needed release to all the tears. "J.T. is going to be a great salesman or a rock star someday. You are all welcome to stop by our house today. Thank you for coming."

My brother was buried in his Little League uniform. My parents placed words from a flower wreath that read OUR NUMBER ONE CHAMP gently on his chest before the coffin was closed.

Kids played tag, laughed, and ate Fudgsicles on our front lawn as dozens of grown-ups drank beer, ate noodle salad off paper plates, and told stories in seemingly every corner of our house on Berkshire. The reception was quite a gathering, like nothing I had ever experienced.

An hour into the party, a girl in tight white tennis shorts, with brown fluffy bangs and a Marcia Brady smile, arrived on a black moped with the word *Spree* written in purple cursive on the side. She went to school with Lee and took out her sadness on me. With a touch of cinnamon-clove cigarettes on her tongue, she kissed me in the bushes next to our house as the wake went on around us.

Even as Kim was putting the *"fun"* in *funeral*, I noticed in our driveway both my parents had one arm around Rich Waller, Lee's best friend. Rich's head was lowered, the rim of his baseball cap pointed to the ground. He was the only kid not smiling, running around, or reminiscing. My parents were doing their best to comfort him. They gave him Lee's bike.

When he finally climbed onto the bike, the setting sun cast a long shadow from his tires. Rich rode off alone.

I was too young to process what happened. I remember being sad, of course, but death at that age is unfathomable.

My mom later took Lance and me to Toys "R" Us to buy us an Atari, trying her best to help us deal with what had happened to Lee.

My friends rallied around me. The rest of the summer was spent riding our bikes to the pool, roasting marshmallows over a bonfire at our cottage making s'mores, listening to records, and dreaming of being famous. My mother dove into suicide awareness charities and traveled around Michigan talking to parents and teenagers for years afterward. I know she made a difference and saved lives. It took me quite a while to talk about my brother's passing—maybe I haven't ever accepted it. To this day, no one can explain it. It's a mystery what led my brother into the basement. But somehow, life became normal again.

Little did I know everything was about to change. It was the 1980s, and a man was about to land on the moon.

CHAPTER 5

Houston, We Have a Problem Child

Four, three, two, one—we have liftoff." Giant tangerine flames billowed upward to the sky. White smoke thrust into the air, high as a skyscraper. A rocket ship with the letters *USA* on it lifted off the ground as if in slow motion, heading for outer space.

An astronaut in the iconic white space suit bounced off the ladder onto the lunar surface, where he planted the American flag.

A cold chill tickled my arm like a spider running from my elbow to my shoulder.

The flag was not red, white, and blue. It was electric pink, fluorescent green, bright yellow, and even leopard print. There were no stars and stripes on this flag. On the flag was a giant letter *M* with the letters *TV* spray-painted across it.

If the big bang created the universe, MTV was the big bang that created J.T. Harding. My life would never be the same. As if someone had sprinkled acid on my Oreos, I felt the world around me change shape.

What had been only in my imagination was now alive right in front of me, and I couldn't believe my eyes. The music that I lived and breathed was now mixed with images that my young mind could barely process.

Madonna singing "Like a Virgin" as she rolled around in

a wedding dress. Michael Jackson dancing as he lit up the sidewalk to "Billie Jean." Duran Duran chasing a half-naked girl through a jungle, singing "Hungry Like the Wolf."

My idols Van Halen lighting a gong on fire over the black-and-white prison-striped drums, as David Lee Roth, shirtless and muscular, shaking his blond mane like a rock 'n' roll Tarzan, did the splits in midair like Bruce Lee with a jet pack on his back as Eddie Van Halen's fingers did acrobatic tricks on his guitar.

MTV started in 1981 but it took a few years to get to Grosse Pointe. Their catchphrase "I Want My MTV" was actually created by the channel so people would call up their local cable provider and pester them to make MTV part of their cable service.

The week sixth grade started, a pink envelope addressed to me sat on our kitchen table. It was from a girl named Melissa, who I had met at my grandparents' lakeside cottage in Northern Michigan and had a major crush on.

Over Labor Day weekend Melissa had pulled me into the cottage bathroom, closed the door, and flicked the light in a bear-paw-shaped switch plate to off. In the pitch black, her fingers found my shoulders as I awaited her saltwater taffy kiss. Her soft hands slowly turned me toward the mirror and she began to whisper "Bloody Mary" over and over.

As my eyes reconciled with the dark, a witch missing teeth and with knives in her hands took shape in the mirror. I screamed and ran back out into the safety of our cottage's shag-carpeted living room. As infectious as her laugh was, I never followed her into a dark room again, but her letter had my full attention.

Cursive writing under a heart-shaped Hallmark sticker of Snoopy puckering his lips read: "J.T. I miss you and your silly songs. Have you heard about the music TV channel?"

On Christmas Eve our house was filled with friends and

family. My dad's coworker had a son in high school. Grabbing a Pizza Hut glass with E.T. crossing the moon in the basket of a bicycle on it, he went out to our back porch, where the alcohol was kept because it was so cold out, splashed some vodka into his glass, then downed it. The cold air turned his breath to smoke as he went on and on about the music movie clips on cable TV.

Was it true or a rumor like the kid who ate too many Pop Rocks?

On Christmas break, sitting in front of the TV pulling Oreo cookies apart and licking the frosting from the center, I stared at the screen in happy bewilderment.

The rumors were true.

No matter what else was happening in the world, my new mantra was "I Want My MTV."

Every day after school I ran straight to the den, dropping my schoolbooks like a wet umbrella, to study MTV. Friday and Saturday nights I watched MTV until my eyelids were as heavy as concrete blocks. Before breakfast and after, music videos were all I cared about. The days of Lance and me arguing about whose turn it was to play Pac-Man on the Atari were over forever.

If I wasn't home, the VCR was set to record to make sure I didn't miss any David Lee Roth interviews.

Every now and then my dad, a *Sports Illustrated* magazine tucked under his arm, commanded "Go play outside" as he clicked the TV off. Sitting in the drive with a Mr. Sketch grape-scented marker, I would draw the MTV logo on my tennis shoes.

My parents thought I had a problem but I persisted. "You guys think about it, you never have to hire the Keelan sisters again. I don't need a babysitter anymore—as long as MTV is on I'm not going anywhere."

Crawling inside the TV wasn't an option, but someway, somehow, I had to be a part of this magical world. The group a-ha in their iconic animated video for the song "Take On Me" showed the singer trying to break out of his black-and-white world. That's what I wanted to do.

How on earth do you get on MTV? Gripping and flipping my dynamite stick–sized nunchucks around my shoulders in the basement night after night trying to figure it out, I thought it through backward. You have to have a video, which means you have to have a hit song, which means you have to have a band.

Music historians always like to point out that "Video Killed the Radio Star" was the first video ever played on MTV. For me, video killed playing pretend out on the front porch with a hockey stick for a guitar. I was going to start a band.

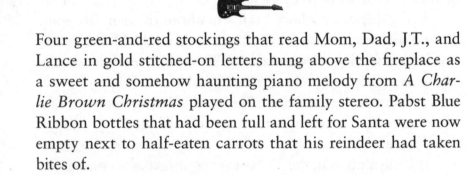

Four green-and-red stockings that read Mom, Dad, J.T., and Lance in gold stitched-on letters hung above the fireplace as a sweet and somehow haunting piano melody from *A Charlie Brown Christmas* played on the family stereo. Pabst Blue Ribbon bottles that had been full and left for Santa were now empty next to half-eaten carrots that his reindeer had taken bites of.

A dozen wrapped presents sparkled and waited to be opened under the real Christmas tree, which smelled like pine cones, but my eyes were glued to the string of white lights, blinking like a marquee, that were reflecting off a silver drum set that Santa brought me.

Smashing it like Animal from *The Muppet Show*, I played the drums in the basement until the paint practically came off the walls, and I broke the two pairs of drumsticks that came with it faster than you could say "more cowbell." I asked for new ones. "Money doesn't grow on trees," my dad replied, and neither do drumsticks, apparently, so I drummed with some old Lincoln Logs I found in a forgotten toy chest.

Since Lee's death, Rich Waller and I had become inseparable. We bonded over music. I had lost a brother but gained another. He had the magic touch on the drums, and girls swooned over him because they thought he looked like Judd Nelson in *The Breakfast Club*, so he took over that instrument. He would play drums and I would shout along in our basement with no other instruments. "Every Breath You Take" by the Police was one of our faves. It's a miracle my parents didn't throw the drum set out with the constant racket we were making.[1] Once, when visiting us from Florida, my grandpa had had enough and yelled down the basement stairs, "Jungle music!" Rich's eyes met mine like two secret lovers and without a word we blasted into "I blessed the rains down in Africaaaaa."

Spray It, Don't Say It

Dropping a lit cigarette into a can of Vernors, a long-haired guy with John Lennon glasses exhaled smoke, then waved me into a back room at the local music store, Fiddlers. The phone-booth-sized room contained two chairs and a Dukes of Hazzard TV tray covered in guitar picks. "Cool mom you have getting you guitar lessons for your birthday," he said, handing me a guitar and picking one up for himself.

She was cool. For my birthday that year my mom called

---

1 Songwriters: The songs we liked were so simple and catchy we could sing them with only a drumbeat. To this day, when writing a song, if I get confused by a melody I say, "Put the guitar down, let's sing it just by clapping along. If that works it's simple enough for 80,000 people to sing along."

the store and got me lessons. My biological father, Jon Terrell, now living in Los Angeles, got a call from his long-lost girlfriend reminding him that I was out there somewhere and it was my birthday and I was probably alone.

In reality I was so electrified about my first guitar lesson I could hardly sleep, but after a few Saturdays in a cramped room with the guitar teacher and Bo and Luke Duke grinning up at me, I grew frustrated. Trying to figure out where my hand should go on guitar frets guided by chord charts felt like math homework. I wanted to play music, not work at music. For the moment, guitar was out.

I did not have the discipline to learn guitar back then. I did, however, know how to be the lead singer. I was a natural. I could pose and point to the imaginary audience like no one else in town.

A tiny bell above the door at Village Records and Tapes rang as I pushed the door open. Usually I was asking the owner if I could have the KISS promotional poster advertising their new album when he took it out of the front window, but today I asked if he knew any good guitarists.

He informed me of a few kids in town who played, and I held an audition in my basement. One of the guitarists was a high schooler in a buttoned-up shirt who played jazzy, complicated notes. Adjusting sheet music on a black metal stand in front of him between songs, he played gently, as if he was serenading a librarian. Another guy came in wearing shorts, breaking a cardinal rule for me: Unless you dress in a full schoolboy outfit like AC/DC, you cannot rock in shorts.

The other guitarist auditioning, John, was a baby-faced blond kid with a mischievous smile. Wearing stonewashed jeans and a sugar-white Jordache jacket, he turned his amp up to window-shaking volume, then lifted his Stratocaster guitar to his face and played "The Star-Spangled Banner" ... with his teeth. Throwing the guitar on the ground, John then played the chunky power-chord-driven song that played at the top of every hour on MTV—with his feet.

John sent the jazzman and the shorts guy packing. Every weekend after that we jammed for hours in my basement. We played any song we could think of for a few months, but it still didn't feel like what I was seeing on MTV or what I had seen at that concert.

"Here's what we are gonna do. We're gonna get some orange extension cords from my dad's workroom and we are gonna play out in the back driveway," I confidently told my new as-yet-unnamed band.

Our driveway had a little cement square part expanding out into the grass. To me it looked like the part of the stage that Van Halen had so they could be closer to the audience.

We had the drums and one knee-high amplifier for the guitar. We plugged my microphone into that same amp. With the sun as my spotlight, we launched into a song as my dad watered the lawn.

I want you to want me, I neeeeeed you to need me…

Pointing over the grass imagining a crowd, I sang the Cheap Trick classic with all my heart. Our song in all its noisy glory, my voice shouting more than singing, drifted over the fences into the backyards of other houses, but my neighbors knew me. No one should've been surprised we were playing a concert outside. A roaring engine on the other side of the house caught my ears.

A woman who lived a street over had pulled her rusty station wagon full speed up our driveway and started shrieking at us. "Are you out of your bastard-picking minds? What is the matter with you people? How can I think with all this racket? You should all be arrested!" Her unkempt hair looked like a tumbleweed. An eyeglass chain hung between her ears and the stem of her glasses, which were steamed up and crooked over her scrunched-up nose as she tried to catch her breath and assault us with more insults.

Our song stopped on a dime. She had sped her car up to us, the bumper practically kissing the drums, and screeched to a halt, sending our cat, Pickles, darting up a tree. Turning to my dad, I felt heat rise up from the collar of the MY PARENTS WENT TO HAWAII AND ALL I GOT WAS THIS LOUSY T-SHIRT shirt, I was so afraid we were in trouble.

Dragging the green hose, my dad approached her car like Bill Belichick staring down a referee after a questionable call. "Lady, number one, get off my property. And number two, you should be honored to hear my son sing." On the word *sing* he put his huge meaty thumb over the end of the hose and sprayed water at her through the open car window she was scowling out of.

Screaming like a vampire doused with holy water, she threw the car into reverse, her face and hair soaking wet as she swerved backward down our driveway, her bumper banging the curb as she left. If there's not a street somewhere in America named after my dad, there should be.

Donut Stop Believin'

That afternoon I interrupted Lance outsmarting his pals with his math skills, huddled around a game of Monopoly. As a woman water-skied to the theme from *Jaws 3* on TV, I spoke: "Lance, we're putting on a concert in the backyard Friday night. Do not pass go, do not collect two hundred dollars, go tell everyone you know." Lance immediately ran next door and told Beaker and his two younger carrot-topped brothers. Inspired by explosions of smoke in music videos, two packs of Black Cat firecrackers hidden in my T-shirt drawer surely could bring us the same big-time effects.

Putting a milk-carton-sized bottle of Johnson's baby powder on the kitchen counter, we hatched our plan. "We're going to put baby powder in Dixie Cups, put firecrackers in the baby powder, and Lance is going to light them. INSTANT SMOKE BOMBS!" I cackled like a mad scientist.

The next Friday evening, as the sky above our back-yard turned from blue to red, my dad flipped sizzling Ball Park franks on the grill before placing them one by one into Wonder Bread buns held out by a dozen kids looking like the Peanuts gang come to life. Marty Westervelt arrived on his Huffy bike dressed in his Sunday best, telling everyone he was our manager, and I loved it. The melting sun would be the only fire that night—my mom had confiscated the fire-crackers.

Ten minutes before showtime my brother squeezed out of a bedroom window onto the flat roof looking over the patio where we would play. The drums were being set up below as his hands took from mine three multicolored Dixie Cups filled with baby powder. "Sprinkle it down over us when I point to the sky making the devil horns with my fingers. It'll at least look like a smoke machine."

On the brick wall behind the drums was a king-sized bedsheet held in place by duct tape to the side of our house. Spray-painted on the sheet and surrounded by a yellow light-ning bolt inspired by the logo of Jolt Cola was our band name: JET BLACK.

"This is called 'Rock of Ages' by Def Leppard," I yelled, doing my best Bruce Lee–style karate kick as Rich hit the cowbell with flawless precision. John played the guitar behind his head as the Radio Shack microphone, taped to a broom-stick for a mic stand, sent my voice booming through the neighborhood.

In honor of David Lee Roth, colorful bandannas wrapped my legs, making them look like a pack of Fruit Stripe gum. From his perch above us, Lance did as he was told. My trusted roadie and bodyguard of a brother emptied the cups of baby powder from the roof. The powder fell into my hair in big white clumps like snowballs that didn't melt.

Wiping ketchup and mustard from their lips, the kids watching all clapped dutifully. Jet Black turned into The Powdered Donuts, but it was a fun show.

CHAPTER 6

The Art of War Memorial Dances

A white sliver of the moon shone over Lake Saint Clair like a thumbnail. On the water's edge teenagers danced inside a mansion once owned by a Michigan governor. The mansion was now a community center called the Grosse Pointe War Memorial.

The War Memorial hosted middle school dances every few months in the massive ballroom with hardwood floors. Hundreds of students from several schools around Grosse Pointe would attend.

The dances were a petri dish of teenage fun—wild jumping and thrashing about to loud pop songs such as "Kids in America" by Kim Wilde and Joan Jett's "I Love Rock 'n' Roll" that a DJ spun on a record player through a PA system.[2]

Nervous slow dances under a spinning mirror ball to "Total Eclipse of the Heart" by Bonnie Tyler led to the awkward bumping of braces. The bathroom stalls hid sips of room-temperature beer smuggled in by brave students in the sleeves of jean jackets.

One weekend, instead of a dance they had a High School

---

2 "Kids in America" chants the title with a new melody at the end of the song. I try to put a new melody at the end of my songs for the audience to sing along to. I did it with "Smile" and Keith Urban's "Somewhere in My Car."

Battle of the Bands. Disappointed there wasn't any dancing, my friends scattered like seagulls a dog was chasing to flirt with girls. Not me.

Squeezing through high schoolers, making my way to the front of the stage, I stood as close to the action as possible. A high school band called Ronnie's Ray Gun was slogging through a Led Zeppelin song.

Dirty bare feet poking out from under his bell-bottom jeans, the singer's eyes would roll up in the back of his head like a Baby Alive doll going to sleep when he sang. Swinging back his mane of buttery-blond hair, he guzzled orange Faygo soda between verses.

Hippie rock wasn't my scene, but this guy seemed to be in a trance. "Think there's booze inside that pop bottle?" I yelled excitedly to another kid, who shrugged.

When one band finished, another band would take ten minutes to set up. In the interim, anyone who looked like a parent was subjected to twenty questions from me about how to get Jet Black in the next battle.

Eventually a mom doing a *Detroit News* crossword puzzle in the coat-check booth pointed me to the man in charge. Picking up cups near a trash can, he told me the next Battle of the Bands was in September.

He pointed his business card at me, pinched between two of his fingers like a cigarette. "You have to be in high school and you have to be good. That's it really. Auditions are in August."

Thanking him with all the politeness my parents had taught me, I carried the man's card in my hand like an engagement ring the rest of the night, worried it might fall out of my pocket. My first music business connection was not going to end up on the sticky floor with trampled blue-and-red Pepsi cups. Making it into the Battle of the Bands was my new obsession.

Rich knew a bass guitar player named Bob from South High

School. Bob's checkerboard shirt, brown hair as long as Jesus', and fringed knee-high moccasin boots only added to his coolness. Bob was the missing piece our band needed to fill in our sound.

The swimming pools and bike rides were left outside that summer. We practiced every single day. Yard work, schoolwork—any type of work—I'm allergic to. But jamming, rehearsing, and practicing with the band was not work. Maybe that's why it's called "playing" music.

It felt like a dream, but we were wide-awake. The only time we left the basement was to walk a mile to Village Records and Tapes to get a 45 record of a song we wanted to learn. Rich and I knowingly looked at each other stepping over Lee's name where my brother had written it with his finger in the wet cement a few years prior.

A cigarette behind his ear, Bob the bass player was jumping up, slapping stop signs as we walked. John and Rich walked arm in arm, their legs in unison crisscrossing to the left, then to the right, singing "Hey, Hey, We're the Monkees" like we had seen on the *Monkees* TV show. Bob loudly disapproved. "The Beatles are a real band, Monkees are a fake band, created by a TV executive." "But any three-year-old can sing their songs so they became hits," I added, tapping my finger on my head.

Awkward silence followed us. Marty, who lived up the street from me, pulled up to us on his ten-speed bike with two other kids I didn't know. Marty and I had sleepovers practically every weekend since we met in second grade, but we hadn't hung out all summer.

"Hey, man. We're going to audition for the Battle of the Bands," I said, trying to bring the two groups together.

Marty and his friends looked at Bob with his long hair, smiling like a jack-o'-lantern with an unlit Marlboro between his teeth, and pedaled away. It was autumn, the leaves were starting to change, along with my friendships.

Back in my basement we played a new 45 record and listened hard, as if learning the song could save Earth from an oncoming meteor. As the small black plastic circle spun round and round, the band collectively figured out the musical notes of a song by plucking away at our instruments. Scribbling the words down on paper as quickly as I could decipher them, I would then lay the lyrics on the floor and peek down at them as we worked on the song as a unit.

Audition day finally came. The man from the War Memorial who had given me his card showed up in a suit and tie, chewing on a golf tee. My mom, beaming, sat him and his secretary in folding chairs, confusedly facing the closed garage door in our driveway.

"They're here, they're here!" I excitedly whispered to my band, putting them all in place, posing like rock soldiers ready for battle. I nodded at my brother, Lance, and he slowly opened the garage door, like a metal curtain rising in front of us. Our band was revealed to the grown-ups as we blasted into a song.

We skipped the baby powder trick. We didn't need it. We were oozing confidence. We were unstoppable. The secretary plugged her ears and scrunched her face like she was smelling bad cheese as we played, so I knew we were really rocking. We were a shoo-in for the battle, no questions asked.

We never received a follow-up phone call. For days after the audition, every time the phone rang I would jump like a bomb went off, grabbing the phone off the wall, and wheeze "HardingresidenceJTspeaking" every time.

It was always the same thing—"It's cloudy, is there baseball practice today?"—a coach on the other end of the line looking for my dad, who was the president of Little League. I was an MTV junkie trapped in an episode of *Sports Center*.

Reading the disappointment on my face, my mom hugged me and said, "J.T., if it's meant to be it'll happen."

It was the first of my many musical rejections. For a week

I lay awake in bed at night staring at the silent Van Halen posters on my wall for guidance, wondering what we could have done differently. I skipped dinner, and my mom would put applesauce or Hostess CupCakes by my bed, hoping I'd finally eat, before tousling my hair as she walked out of my room. But the universe had my back—we soon found out a band *not* from Grosse Pointe had auditioned, so they were disqualified...and we were offered their spot!

"What's the name of your band?" the man in charge asked me over the phone. Rich Waller, our drummer and my new best friend, was sitting at our kitchen table, eating city chicken with my family.[3]

"What's the band name now?" I whispered, one hand over the receiver. Rich replied in a low-pitched haunted-house movie-trailer voice, his lip curled like Elvis's: "Dirty Tricks."

"Dirty Tricks," I repeated into the phone, before adding, "and please spell *Tricks* with two *x*'s." Taking after KISS and the lightning *S*'s in their name, I knew bands should have an eye-catching logo, cool enough that fans want to draw it on their school notebooks and simple enough that they are able to do so.

"Dirty Trixx with two *x*'s it is...Okay, great," the guy responded slowly, like taking a hot dog order at Coney Island. "By the way, you guys are in high school, right?" the guy asked.

"Umm...pretty much. The bass player and the drummer are in high school." Using the only math I ever paid attention to, I faked confidence, continuing, "That's half the band. When you do a fraction you always round up." The guy from the War Memorial said okay.[4] Without hanging up, I spun the

---

3 **City chicken** consists of meat scraps to fashion a makeshift drumstick on a wooden stick. It was a working-class food item started in the Depression. Despite the name, city chicken never contains chicken.

4 My dad told that story for years, he loved it so much.

phone's curled cord like a lasso full speed and then caught the phone above my head like I'd seen the singer of the Who do with a microphone on *Entertainment Tonight*. "We're in!" I yelled. The dinner table cheered, each holding their city chicken up like four Statues of Liberty.

Rich really taught me how to write songs. When we would hear local Detroit bands on the radio during the WRIF *Homegrown Show*, the songs didn't have the same effect on us as songs by famous bands did. What was missing? How could we avoid that humdrum local sound?

We used our favorite artists as teachers. Listening to Bryan Adams, Rich would tell me, "Listen how the drums drop out in the last chorus and then come back in. That's called dynamics." I realized it takes the listener on a roller-coaster ride without them really knowing it. There was a part in every Bryan Adams song that felt like the roof of the car was coming off as you sped on open highway in the sun. As if the song itself was changing gears. "That's called the bridge," Rich said.

Van Halen songs have the same kind of dynamics. In their chart-topping song "Jump," after the frantically paced keyboard solo the drums and the bass drop out. Suddenly the listener is in an elevator free fall. The catchy keyboard riff is all we hear. After a few measures a drumroll leads the bass and vocals crashing back in. It's a simple but effective songwriting trick.

All my songs pretty much do that before the last chorus. In "Sangria," which I wrote for Blake Shelton, the trick happens at the end of each chorus under the lyrics "Your lips taste like sangria." The singing and the sexy lyric are suddenly alone grabbing the listener's attention as if a cool wind is blowing through the curtains of a beachside hotel.

So many of my songs use that trick at the end of a guitar solo, my co-writers and I thought, *Why not try it in different parts of our songs?* Might as well mix things up and have fun. Take the listener on a roller-coaster ride when they least expect it.

At age eleven I didn't have the life experience to put into any songs of merit, but every time I sit down to write a song today, my mind goes right back to Rich Waller teaching me these invaluable songwriting tools.

CHAPTER 7

Teenage Dream

Bathroom-mirror-sized posters were hung up in the halls of all the local schools. Six band names on the posters and Dirty Trixx was one of them. I loitered around the high school one day after everyone but an unshaven janitor had gone home and quickly taped our posters inside stall doors in all the girls' bathrooms. When any girl sat down on the toilet, she was looking at our band's logo.

Other bands told anyone who would listen that we took the place of a disqualified band. We were too young to be any good. People wrote "SUCKS" in marker under our name on some of the posters.

But come on. Have you met me? MTV was in my blood at this point. While other kids were dissecting owl pellets in the woods for science class, I was dissecting songs on the radio, making sure we played them perfectly. We rehearsed like a small army training for war. Looking back, I can't really remember what I had expected, but I was ready.

Three bands played on the hardwood floor in the ballroom, eye level with anyone watching but obscuring the view of most of the crowd. The other three bands, including ours, had the good fortune to play downstairs in the auditorium. The auditorium had movie theater seats and a stage with lights. I had seen a picture of David Bowie peeking through the curtain of one of his sold-out shows before it started. I always wondered what that must feel like. Before we played I did the same just for fun. Peeking out, I unexpectedly lost my breath as if an asthma inhaler had been squeezed in my lips. The auditorium was wall-to-wall packed with teenage girls.

Every seat was taken—even the stairs leading up to the lobby had girls elbow to elbow sitting on them. A silver jam box cassette radio sat ready with the theme from *Rocky* cued up. To this day, before every show I make sure there's intro music, something fun to get the crowd pumped up, like for a prizefighter walking into the ring. These days my favorites to play before one of my songwriter shows are "Jump" by Van Halen and "Cherry Pie" by Warrant. Holding my microphone up to the jam box so it would be heard through the PA, I pressed play as the auditorium lights went down.

Dirty Trixx was the only band with drums up on a shoulder-high drum riser. Lance and my dad built it in the workroom with ramps going up each side that I could run up and down. We left nothing to chance—this was a real concert.

The ruby-colored velvet curtain opened as John's guitar screamed to life like a World War II plane dive-bombing a boat. In perfect time Bob and Rich launched into their parts, a barrage of bass and drums.

I ran onstage in red pants, a white sleeveless shirt, and a purple bandanna, the Grosse Pointe War Memorial morphing into Madison Square Garden as I yelled into the microphone, "Alllllllriiiiiiiiite—" Screaming girls greeted us as if we were the Beatles.

Dirty Trixx played eight hit songs of the era, the entire audience singing along the whole time.

At one point, I smashed an electric guitar we'd spray-painted to look like tiger stripes—an homage to KISS. (It was a beat-up guitar we found at a garage sale, and breaking it was a planned part of the show.) My palms were full of splinters and

the fillings in my teeth rattled when I unsuccessfully tried breaking it at home in the driveway. It was too solid to break for real
in one swing. Smashing it over and over until it broke in two,
I glued it lightly back together in my dad's workroom a week
before the show. It was the only way to pull it off. During Def
Leppard's "Foolin'," as John tore through a solo, I quickly disappeared offstage, then reappeared with the pre-broken guitar.
The audience foamed at the mouth when the sacrifice began.

Swinging it like a convict breaking rocks, I shattered it
in one blow on the hardwood stage. A pile of teenagers began
fighting for it when I hurled the body of the guitar into the
audience like a slab of raw meat.

A madman began elbowing people and pushing other kids
down. He was fighting for the smashed guitar like a shipwreck
survivor grabbing the only flotsam in the ocean. It was my
brother Lance. "Lance, let someone else have it!" I shouted at
him, off the mic, in between lyrics.

Todd Wire, a friend of Rich and my late brother, Lee, was
doing lights for the show, watching us as he clicked faders up
and down, flashing colored spotlights in time with the music.
Lights always go black at the end of a song at a real concert.
Todd left them bright between songs.

During Bob's bass intro to U2's "New Year's Day" Todd
yelled, "You're killing it, buddy, they love you!" as I appeared
at his side of the stage. I yelled at him over the music to go
pitch black at the end of every song.

Todd's hands were on the lighting buttons and my hand
was dragging my microphone. In the excitement, as he leaned
in to listen to my instruction our foreheads hit together and
an indigo-blue spark zapped us both between our heads like
the lightning that brought Frankenstein's monster to life. I saw
stars and was light-headed for a second. Rubbing my forehead,
dazed, I yelled "Fuckin' rock 'n' roll!" then led the charge
through the next twenty-five magical minutes of stardom.

John threw guitar picks into the crowd like he was skipping rocks on a lake. Rich bowed, tossing his splintered drumsticks to a high school kid yelling to him and miming a drummer playing with his hands.

Bob, as always cool as a fan, smiled with an unlit Marlboro between his teeth.

Eight hundred Grosse Pointe teenagers all chanting "Dirty Trixx...Dirty Trixx" washed over me in one glorious wave. As the curtain closed slowly in on me from the left and right, I stood like Freddie Mercury with one hand above my head. Rich ran up, shaking me like a Magic 8 Ball that wasn't giving him the prediction he wanted as he yelled, "We're gonna win! We're gonna win!"

Mary Ellen Royce was my first.

Standing alone under the metal stairwell that led up to the band dressing rooms, she made a hook with her index finger, motioning me to come to her. I looked behind me, wondering if she was talking to someone else. She wasn't.

It was dark except for the taillight-red letters that spelled EXIT above the door next to her. Stepping closer, she whispered "Hi" as she tugged on my T-shirt without letting go. Mary Ellen smelled like vanilla ice cream with honey.

She was the kind of girl mirrors stared at when she walked by. The only interaction we'd had prior to this was when she passed me in the bustling halls at school, embracing her schoolbooks against her chest as she walked. The confidence that possessed me onstage had yet to spill over into my social life. Kids were still chanting "Dirty Trixx" inside the building, echoing out through the empty backstage around Mary and me.

What happened next was something I'd only seen pictures of in a magazine or in a flash on late-night cable TV. I'd fantasized about it and practiced it with my right hand alone, always in private. Mary Ellen was my first autograph.

Handing me a multicolor Bic pen and a poster, "Can you sign this?" she said. It was the poster with our band name on it.

Clicking the color green, I signed "Mary Ellen, Good luck with me! J.T. Harding," the *A* in my last name replaced by a star like I had practiced on countless scraps of paper and backs of school homework.

After I handed the poster back to her, Mary Ellen pushed her dark hair behind one ear and stared at me. Kissing her didn't cross my mind—I had signed my first autograph and I couldn't wait to tell the band.

I caught up with my bandmates, and we walked into the lobby of the War Memorial. Dozens of teenagers engulfed us like people crowding onto a New York City subway.

Voices from every direction cheered and yelled—"J.T., that was awesome!" "Duuuurty fuckin' Trixx"—as Lance held the remains of the smashed guitar over his head like Hulk Hogan with his championship belt.

In the throng of teenagers someone squeezed my butt cheek, causing me to jump.

Looking over my shoulder, I was greeted by the biting-her-lip smile of an Izod shirt–wearing girl chewing mint-smelling gum. She handed me her phone number before she broke off half of the gum in her mouth and put it in my mouth. It was the 1980s version of an Instagram DM.

Kids voted with their ticket stubs. Each band had a box on a table with their name on it. At the end of the night, the Dirty Trixx box was comically overflowing with ticket stubs like a frat house trash can longing to be emptied. Even my friend Marty was patting me on the back, once again saying he was our manager, and it felt great.

Whistles blew and marching drums boomed over the

South High School football game the very next day. Waving their hands, smiling strangers greeted me from the crowded bleachers.

People pointed, then looked wide-eyed at whoever was sitting next to them to proclaim, "That's the Dirty Trixx singer."

Meanwhile, a hobbling football player with a varsity jacket over his shoulders and his hands gripping crutches barked, "Move it, faggot boy, there's no stage here." I was unfazed—I was only in the eighth grade, but I knew singing would be my career.

The sun was bright as a sprinkle of sailboats dotted the lake outside floor-to-ceiling windows in the War Memorial office later that afternoon.

"I don't know how you guys did it. You're the hands-down winner of the Grosse Pointe Battle of the Bands. First place gets first prize." Leaning over his desk, Suit-and-Tie Guy handed me a thousand-dollar check pinched between his two fingers. "Hell of a job," he said, shaking my hand.

Seeing me excitedly waving the check like an undeveloped Polaroid picture in the empty War Memorial parking lot, my dad smiled and said, "Way to go, pal. Make sure I get to drive the limo when you're famous." The band and I split the money and traded stories about being recognized around Grosse Pointe.

What's Black and White and Read All Over Town?

The phone in our house was ringing off the hook from girls calling me. Talking on the phone with one of my parents in the room was awkward. I'd set the receiver down, run upstairs to another phone, then yell "Hang the phone up, please" down to where my parents sat. A South High junior who I had met and who reminded me of Molly Ringwald called me Jit instead of J.T. when she phoned. I liked her and she asked me to go to homecoming. I was excited but I thought for sure I would have to spend my Battle of the Bands winnings on a nice suit coat and a corsage, but once again my parents were able to ease my worry: "You are not going to homecoming. Don't be in such a hurry to grow up." The mom had spoken. No homecoming for me.

Because we won the Battle of the Bands, we were asked to play a dance at the War Memorial a few months later, so we prepared just as much for that. I had spied purple pants with zippers on each leg that I wanted to wear at our next show, and Rich wanted to spray-paint the drums. Money didn't grow on trees—we returned empty bottles and cans to get money to buy what we needed.

A cashier at the local submarine sandwich shop counted out three garbage bags full of cans I'd collected as my dad grabbed a bag of pork rinds and Lance bit into a thick, greasy slice of Detroit-style pizza.

Coins rattled in the cash register drawer when it popped open as I awaited my booty.

Looking down at my feet, I saw stacks of the Grosse Pointe newspaper, and shockingly there I was, staring back at myself. Dirty Trixx were on the front page of the local paper!

The *Grosse Pointe News* headline said MEET THE CHAMPS. In all the excitement of winning the "battle," we'd forgotten the guy who showed up out of the blue at one of our rehearsals with three Nikons around his neck to take our picture.

It wasn't *Rolling Stone* magazine, but it was to me! Thousands of households in my hometown had my face on the cover of their paper. Girls would cut it out and put it on their walls, I'd add it to my growing Dirty Trixx scrapbook, football players would line their parakeet cages with it. I was walking on air.

The Mothers Club had a food sponsorship to pay for a dance and they asked us to play. Posters would be printed up with no other band names on them but ours.

I peeled the Gene Simmons pictures off my bedroom wall to make way for the poster with only our band's name on it.

One Monday morning, passing two student council members putting up the American flag in front of the school, I strutted through the doors knowing the new posters had been delivered and hung up in all the halls.

Kids tossed their math books, spinning in the air like pizza dough, and sang Def Leppard in Italian accents when I walked to my locker. I was confused.

The posters meant to read DIRTY TRIXX and FREE PIZZA were somehow printed up to say DIRTY TRIXX PIZZA AT THE WAR MEMORIAL. All that was missing was my smiling face as pepperoni on the picture of the pizza. *Class clown* took on a whole new meaning. The poster wasn't hung on my wall but I saved it and still have it.

The school year faded into summer. We chased girls, rode roller coasters at Cedar Point in Ohio, and stood outside a downtown hotel for hours to meet Van Halen. I still have the guitar picks Eddie Van Halen himself handed to me as he ran past us to a limousine. Mowing the lawn and cleaning the house once a week funded my Donkey Kong, music, and movie habit.

Man in the Mirror

The smell of rotten vegetables rose from garbage cans in an alley behind the Esquire movie theater on a boring oven-hot humid summer night. The theater's exit door opened with a jolt, and a hand waved me in like Thing from *The Addams Family*. The hand belonged to Rich. My eyes adjusting to the dark, I found a seat to bask in the purple glow of our newly crowned king. His name was Prince and the movie was the R-rated *Purple Rain*.

Rich used his older brother's driver's license to get a ticket, then snuck me in. We spent the whole weekend watching the movie over and over.

Prince's rock guitars mixed with dance beats blew my mind. It was something new to my musical palette. Watching him pout, pucker, and sweat as he sang, then simulate an orgasm, spraying a stream of water from his guitar as he gyrated two stories high on the silver screen, was overwhelming.

Prince didn't just sing a song. He took a bite out of it. Sometimes he swallowed it while licking his lips, other times he spat it back out while spinning in Paisley suits and high-heel boots. David Lee Roth and Madonna seduced you when they sang into the camera's eye. Prince made you feel like you were watching him watching himself getting off in a mirror.

Drunk on Junior Mints, fountain Cokes, and the Minneapolis sound, we would walk back to my house and try to learn the songs from *Purple Rain* in my basement. Soon the purple haze of August turned to orange plastic jack-o'-lanterns and yellow bags of candy corn, the Halloween aisles at Kmart letting us know another summer was coming to an end.

Since we were too young to play at bars, that was it for gigs for the foreseeable future. The next Battle of the Bands was a year away.

Sitting on my bed, his back against the wall, Rich strummed a guitar as I sang. Channeling our restless rock star dreams, we started writing our own songs.

The best bands had lyrics about the wild lives they led, so I imitated them, using details from my own life. "With my red pants I'm looking so fine," I sang.

Rich's face turned red as he fell off the bed laughing. I laughed as well with a shrug. Looking back now, I realize I didn't have nearly enough life experience to write great lyrics or the wisdom that makes for good lyrics.

After a few attempts at original compositions, we figured out how to play "Do They Know It's Christmas?," a charity song featuring tons of our favorite rock stars.

We recorded it on a cassette and mailed it to local radio stations. It didn't matter that it wasn't ever played—the sheer possibility of it being played kept our fire burning as MTV kept throwing gasoline on it.

One Saturday the following summer, I sat cross-legged, less than a foot from the television for twelve hours straight watching Live Aid on MTV. The girls sunbathing at the park pool had no hold on my heart that day. The carnival tent melody drifting from the Good Humor ice cream truck passing with Bomb Pops, and my dad's drill-sergeant commands to "mow the grass," were both drowned out by the magic of Madonna and Duran Duran in Philadelphia, U2 and Queen in London, as the broadcast ping-ponged back and forth over the ocean into our den. Watching Phil Collins play "In the Air Tonight" alone on a piano was mind-bending. To hear a song that inspired a generation to air drum, one of the greatest drum fills of all time, stripped down to only a microphone and his hands tickling the ivories, I didn't even know that was possible.

A person on someone's shoulders waved a lone white flag above the sea of people in Wembley Stadium like a shipwreck survivor. In black block letters the flag read U2 as the band U2 filled the stadium with siren-wailing guitar sounds and a military drumbeat. Their singer, Bono, took the stage and had the audience in the palm of his hand like Julius Caesar conquering Rome. Bono sang two songs before desperately pointing at a girl in the audience.

When the yellow-shirt-wearing security guards wouldn't help him, Bono leaped from the stage, then pulled the girl from the audience over the barricade, embracing her in a long slow dance. I moved closer to the TV, staring at the screen as if I was Moses staring at the burning bush.

At our next rehearsal I had Lance put on a blonde wig and pretended I was singing to a girl like Bono at Live Aid. It didn't have the same effect. In the wig Lance looked like E.T. when Elliott took the alien trick-or-treating. We had to find another place to play a real show.

Years later I read that U2 were furious at Bono after Live Aid, because his dance prevented them from playing their newest song. Bono says he even considered quitting U2. Funny how such a tense moment for a rock band from Ireland was such a transforming moment for me in the sunlit TV room at 1151 Berkshire.[5]

Fast Times at Grosse Pointe High

A history teacher pointed at a map of Egypt as students yawned and doodled on paper at their desks. Tucked inside my history book, the headline PRINCE'S WOMEN stared up at me from the cover of a new issue of *Rolling Stone* magazine.

Prince didn't do interviews. There was no social media. The internet didn't exist. To know what was on his mind you had his music—that's it. The mystery was everything and honestly I miss those days. It's kind of like when KISS showed their real faces on MTV finally. All I could think was "Yikes, no wonder they wore makeup." This *Rolling Stone* was the Holy Grail of music, with glossy pictures to match. His band members were breaking the mysterious silence and I had to

---

5 I also read a lot of the bands were doing tons of drugs backstage. If only they had spent that money on the people starving in Africa.

read it immediately. Egypt for the class, deciphering the hieroglyphics of Prince's life was all I cared about.

It's been thirty years—you could ask me right now any question from that interview and I would get every answer right. History, math, and science, however, not so much.

South High School, with its five-story-high redbrick clock tower and golf-course-perfect lawn, looked like a college campus and it felt like one too. Cars belonging to those kids old enough to drive screeched out of the parking lot, racing to Burger King and back at lunchtime.

Senior girls who looked like Elle Macpherson and smelled like Love's Baby Soft walked the halls; notes were passed in class with a student's address whose parents were in Acapulco for a week and was having a party. High school brought a whole new dimension to my social life, and the classroom desks taught me how to fall asleep in any sitting position.

"You sure that's a dude?" a *Back to the Future* Biff look-alike would ask me condescendingly, seeing pictures of Poison's Bret Michaels wallpapering my locker. "It's a dude, but with a boob job he could win the Ms. Michigan pageant, don't ya think?" I said quizzically. There was a sense of freedom that didn't exist in middle school, and best of all, the South High Talent Show was holding auditions. But luck wasn't on my side.

"You're grounded. You can't play with the band until your grades are up," my dad said sternly.

My parents and I were sitting at the kitchen table. Cradling a coffee cup, having long given up her Virginia Slims, my mom stared disappointedly at my lackluster report card.

"Report cards come out like every hundred years! I'm not going to wait that long," I huffed.

"J.T., the band is done unt—"

Slapping my knees, I interrupted him. "I'll study more, I get it, but I can't just stop being in a band."

"Colleges are looking at grades earlier than ever, J.T.," my mom added.

"I said I'll study! Is everyone deaf around here?" I yelled.

Dad immediately put me in my place.

"Son, I've got news for you: Until the next report card comes, *there is no band*. Now apologize to your mother."

Lance, standing nearby in his basketball shorts and jersey, lightly crunched on a Cheeto.

"Sorry." Stomping down the stairs to the basement, I yelled back, "Sorry for loving music!"

The drums and amps in our basement sat silent around me like supportive friends. Stewing for an hour, I decided to do what any teenager who respected his parents more than anything in the world would do.

"We have to practice at your house from now on. Don't tell anybody—just have your sister drive you over to get the equipment this Saturday."

"What happened?" John asked through the phone.

"Bad grades," I sighed.

"That sucks."

The basement light clicked off. "I'm down here," I called out. The light clicked back on. "Go to bed," my dad said as I gingerly put the phone back on the receiver.

Wardrobe Malfunction

John's house overlooked the lake. Buzzing off the sugar of watermelon Slurpees, we rehearsed in secret for a month of Saturdays in his basement. When the time came, we auditioned for South's student council and were welcomed with open arms into the talent show.

After nervously bouncing my knees under the table and staring at the digital clock on the stove all through dinner, I finally excused myself. "Going to the library," I called out to my parents as I rolled up three shirts into a backpack before heading out. Streetlights glowed over empty streets as I pedaled in my checkerboard Vans like I was being chased by Jason from the *Friday the 13th* movie. When I arrived at the school parking lot, it was already full of cars.

Two high school football players emceed the show with jokes that didn't land. The act before us consisted of a group of girls lip-synching to the Jackson 5. Another act juggled and a guy played a very sad song alone on an acoustic guitar. Our equipment had been set up beforehand and was ready to go. Watching from the wings and knowing my band was a well-oiled machine gave me the confidence of a winning politician.

"You may have seen these guys before," the emcees said. "Let's give it up for Dirty Trixx!"

Running out at full speed, I slid on my knees into the U2 song "I Will Follow." Dirty Trixx were as tight as ever. The stage lights on my face were sunlamp hot, and so bright I could only see the outlines of people's heads in the crowd bopping up and down in the school auditorium.

Strumming a guitar that wasn't even plugged into an amp (it was all for show), I belted out "Somebody" by Bryan Adams, pointing at silhouettes of girls when I hit the lyric "Somebody like you!"

Prince's colorful wardrobe inspired me to change outfits two times during my brief twenty-minute show. With my back to the crowd I hooked my fingers in my belt loops and swung my hips, like C-3PO doing a striptease, as I danced and disappeared to the side of the stage for a moment. People whooped as I reappeared in a South High Blue Devils football shirt for the next song.

During the second outfit change, there was a tall, alluring girl standing above my backpack smiling like I was a Popsicle and it was the hottest day of the summer. Her pretty face and dishwater-blonde curls were familiar to me. She was the president of the student council. We'd never spoken. She was a senior and I was only a freshman.

Rifling through my backpack, pumped with the adrenaline of performing, I smiled to her, saying "What's up?" Crouching down next to me, she said: "You guys are so great."

Pulling the South T-shirt off over my head, I hurriedly put on a bright polo shirt that was meant for my final song. Somehow my arms got stuck.

The band kicked into the song onstage, while I twisted around in the shirt in a panic. "I can't get my shirt on!" The girl pulled my shirt down like it was a window shade. When her fingers brushed against my stomach, it jumped with excitement.

Grosse Pointe is very preppy, and at that time upturned collars on short-sleeve polo shirts were a country club trend that had gone mainstream. "I have to pop the collar!" I yelled. She popped the collar for me as a confused look came over her face.

I darted back out onstage gripping the microphone, with lyrics coming out of me instinctively before I realized my shirt was on backward. The collar was popped up over my mouth and nose, muffling me as I sang. The whole audience burst out laughing.

"Not bad for a freshman, eh?...Not bad at all," the two football players emceeing the show said to the audience after we were done, their shirts now on backward. The place was howling.

Calling all the acts out onto the stage at once, the emcees read our name aloud as the winners. The entire student body were on their feet, cheering.

Standing in front of a glass case overflowing with shiny sports trophies, students who had passed me like a ghost just a day before shook my hand and high-fived me. What was it,

I wondered, about being onstage that makes people see you differently?

"As the winners, you're going to get to skip school for a couple of days and perform around Michigan at other schools. It's part of the student exchange program," the girl from the student council told me, beaming.

Arms held over his head in triumph, Rich crowed, "Holy shit! It'll be like we're on tour!"

"Totally," the girl said, then added: "Someone's mom or dad has to go with you though."

The next day, the South High newspaper had a perfect shot of me, on my knees singing, for all to see. I'd never dreamed of being prom king, and after that I didn't need to. I did need to face my parents though.

Van Halen posters stared at me over my mom's shoulder. Her arms were folded. My dad sat on my bed next to me. Tears welled up in my eyes and streamed into my mouth the second I started to speak.

"I've been rehearsing at John's—we won the talent show tonight. We were really *really* great. I'm sorry my grades are bad, I'll do better, but I'm not going to college. I'm going to be in a band and I'm going to make it. I know you're worried, but you don't have to be—I know what to do."

My dad rubbed his fingers against his forehead.

"You need something to fall back on. You need a plan B," my mom said sternly.

"I know, Mom, I'll study." Headlights from a passing car floated by outside as we sat quietly. Using the forearm of my sleeve to dry my wet, bloodshot eyes, I continued. "There's something else. Other schools around Michigan want us to play for them, like in their gymnasiums. No one else's parents are cool enough to chaperone us. It has to be you or dad."

"Study every night seven to nine," my mom said. "Okay," I sniffled.

Dad grinned. "I finally get to drive the limo. That's cooler than hell."

Bowling Them Over

We played at two other high schools a few hours from Grosse Pointe with Dad chaperoning us. Both shows were in gymnasiums swarming with students. It wasn't the Houston Astrodome but it was to me. Fan mail arrived at our house for me after those shows, and I still have the letters. Dirty Trixx also played a few bars around Detroit who had called to book us despite our being teenagers. My favorite was a place called the Falcon Rock Fortress.

I heard about the Falcon Rock Fortress when the loud booming voice of a monster-truck rally announcer spilled out of WRIF: "The Falcon Rock Fortress—beer specials and killer bands all Saturday night."

Then in the paper I was mystified by a drawing of a big winged bird with guitars in its claws flying over a castle called the Falcon Rock Fortress. What an amazing spectacle of all things rock 'n' roll this place must be. They called the house and I jumped at the chance to play there.

Once all of our music equipment was jammed into my mom's station wagon like a winning game of Tetris, we set off to play the club. Since it was a twenty-one-and-over show, my mom had to chaperone us. I was drumming on my knees with excitement when we pulled off the highway and approached the Fortress.

Imagine my surprise when I saw a flashing sign— FALCON LANES—with a few letters burned out. It was a rundown bowling alley.

Floors sticky with old beer and full ashtrays greeted us as we unpacked the drums and plugged in our amps. The stage was tiny, so we put the drummer onstage by himself and played on the floor. There were colored lights over the stage. Band logos, profanity, and WRIF stickers covered the walls backstage, which was one room, with a couch that looked like it had chicken pox due to all the cigarette burns on it, and a leaky toilet without a seat.

All of these factors made the bowling alley Madison Square Garden–big to us.

A local band called Wizard was playing with us. They were much older and condescending. "Kiddie rock," they kept yelling as they sipped whiskey and fluffed their long, receding-hairline Afros during our nine p.m. set.

Someone from Wizard spent a few hours drawing a life-size wizard with long robes, long hair, and a skeleton head in Lord of the Rings–level detail on the wall. The wizard was holding a giant crystal ball in his palm with lightning shooting out of it. They were saying to all the other bands in Detroit, "DON'T MESS WITH US." Wizard took the stage after we packed up our equipment for the ride back home.

Standing on the ripped-up backstage couch with a black Magic Marker, I reached up and drew three black circles in a triangle onto the wizard's crystal ball, turning it into a bowling ball. After yelling "Wizard sucks!" at the top of our lungs like the crowd on *Wheel of Fortune*, my band and I frantically ran like the Three Stooges to my mom waiting in her station wagon and laughed all the way back to Grosse Pointe.

CHAPTER 8

Talking to Girls About Duran Duran

A bed of roses exploded like confetti as a groundskeeper named Carl swung at them with a rake like a golf club. He then slurred to himself about the spectacular shot.

"This guy's a legend," Rich said to me, laughing and sipping a beer he'd snuck from our refrigerator. The groundskeeper was Bill Murray, it was one a.m., and we were watching a Blockbuster rental of *Caddyshack* in our basement, lounging on the big couch.

The clocklike sound of a ten-speed bike chain clicking caught my attention. "Oh shit, they're here!" I whispered. Rich and I ran up the cement steps that led from a door in our basement outside to the driveway.

Bianca Euginio and her best friend, Christy, were there in the dark holding up their bikes. Bianca, wearing a multicolored Benetton sweater and a dozen thin rubber bracelets in homage to Madonna, smiled as she chewed gum. She and I had talked on the phone and passed notes in school for a few weeks. Christy looked bored. They'd each told their parents they were sleeping at each other's houses to sneak out.

We all tiptoed back into the basement. "I'd play you a song I wrote, but I don't want to wake my parents," I said, trying to be cool as the flickering TV provided the only light.

"When is your band playing again?" Bianca asked.

"Well, we need to make a demo and get it to some record companies. We have to write our own songs. That's the only way to make it, so we're just focusing on that," I whispered.

"I like the lyrics you wrote in the last note you gave me," she said. I didn't have the guts to tell her it was actually a Duran Duran song I had copied.

"How do you write songs?" Christy asked in a snobbish tone.

"It's easy," I explained, stretching my fingers in a circle holding an imaginary record. "We play the Disney Haunted Mansion record backward and wait for Satan to tell us what to do."

Rich spit his beer out laughing, then added without joking, "J.T. is getting mobbed for autographs—at schools he's not even a student at. Trust me, he'll get discovered."

"I'm so sure, and like, why do you have a picture of Lance Harding in his football uniform?" Christy asked, pointing at a picture on the wall of Lance in his South High Blue Devils blue-and-gold jersey.

"He's my brother. It's weird—he looks like my dad, but I look like the milkman," I said.

"I'm so sure," Christy said, annoyed.

"He's joking. J.T.'s adopted," Bianca explained, giggling and throwing a couch pillow at Christy.

An hour later Rich and Christy had fallen asleep. Bianca and I took our shirts off under a blanket, and her body was comforter-straight-from-the-dryer warm against mine. Her fingers gently traced my shoulder and arms as I lightly touched her stomach with the back of my hand.

We would have had the teenage night of our lives if I'd stopped talking. I think I was nervous. I had commentary for every MTV video that glowed from the TV. Bianca finally grabbed my cheek and we kissed until the sun crept around the corners of the lawn.

Before shaking Christy's shoulder to wake her up to go, Bianca pulled my shirt on over her head. It was a sleeveless Journey concert shirt. (I had noticed that Sting had cut the sleeves and collar off his shirt in the Police video "Don't Stand So Close to Me," so I'd done the same to my Journey shirt.) Bianca, still barefoot, waved at me with her tennis shoe from the top of the stairs as they climbed on their bikes and rolled down the drive.

A moment later, the girls let out a bloodcurdling scream. In his socks, knocking over empty beer cans, Rich darted up the stairs behind me and we both ran out to the front yard, only to find Dad raking leaves as the girls pedaled away at Lance Armstrong speed.

"Oh, hey, Dad, you're up early," I said.

"Hey, guys," he replied, "I yelled 'good morning, ladies' to your girlfriends, scared the living shit outta them."

Pulling off her FRANKIE SAY RELAX shirt, Bianca would sunbathe in her bra on the gravestones behind an old church and complain to me how boring Grosse Pointe was. When we could see our breath because of the cold weather, we would haunt the mall, drinking Orange Julius smoothies and pretending we were a celebrity couple. We hung out after school and played "seven minutes in heaven" under a pool table at parent-approved basement parties where stolen wine coolers sat open, but mostly full, and cans of Coca-Cola were sipped dry.

Spinning the black-and-white numbered dial on my school locker a few weeks later, I saw a short, muscular guy with a pierced nose in a Journey shirt with the collar and sleeves cut off. My heart sank. Thinking back to Bianca casually mentioning him, I knew that was my shirt and she must have given it to him. Did she stay the night at his house? I didn't let my mind wander any further. I just tried to breathe and remember my locker comb.

My suspicions were confirmed that weekend when I saw

them passing a pack of cigarettes back and forth, walking out of *Ferris Bueller's Day Off*, as my band and I waited in line for the next screening. Rich grimaced and John said, "If she smokes, she pokes" as he sipped his blue ICEE. As much as my songwriter mind loved that rhyme, my heart felt like a Zamboni had run me over like it did to the goalie on the TV show *Cheers*.

I'd fallen for Bianca harder than the Karate Kid after getting his leg swept by Cobra Kai. I wanted to talk to her constantly on the phone. I imagined us living happily ever after. When we hung out, the sun seemed brighter, jet trails becoming X's and O's in the sky. I even called my favorite DJ, the Electrifying Mojo, to dedicate a song to her on the radio. I spent days making a mix tape of songs for her as a birthday gift.

Almost everyone has their first teenage breakup, but this one leveled me for months. Looking back on it now, I wonder if it had triggered delayed mourning for my brother Lee and I just didn't realize it.

A single pack of M&M's with the edges of the wrapper frayed sat on my desks as I went from class to class at school for a week. My heartbreak made my stomach so sick it took me that long to finish the pack. I went to school late and left early so I wouldn't see Bianca walking the halls, but then I would ride my bike past her house at night to see if that guy was there. She stuck to my clothes like smoke.

Snow crunched under my shoes as I took long walks after school listening to music, trying to forget her. Holding a jam box over my head in her yard playing our song crossed my mind, but I'm pretty sure that only works in the movies. I stayed in my room a lot.

I didn't need to tell anyone how I felt because George Michael knew. Hair metal was wrapped in sex and good times and I still rocked out to it, but I needed a new station to dial my heart into. George's songs "Father Figure" and "One More Try" told me he understood. Don Henley's "The Boys of Summer" was everything I wanted to say but didn't know how to. The songs were not only Band-Aids for loneliness, they inspired me to write.

One night in our living room on Berkshire Road listening to George Michael songs on the stereo, I wrote down the sections of the song "Wake Me Up Before You Go-Go" in a Garbage Pail Kids spiral notebook so I could capture that feeling in one of my own songs. Wham! songs were on more girls' lips than cherry-vanilla ChapStick every summer. The melody was stuck in my head like a bill I couldn't pay. I wanted to write songs, and I knew this was a real hit. After recording it on a cassette, I paused the tape to write down the sections of the song. I scribbled, "Catchy part comes three times, new lyrics happen when the drums drop out in the middle of the song." While I didn't know the musical terms or musical notes, I learned how to arrange songs listening to "Wake Me Up Before You Go-Go" and deciphering it like the Ovaltine code in *A Christmas Story.*

I couldn't read music—I still can't—but unlocking the songs in my own way I would memorize these directions to myself.

Plunking the chipped keys on the upright piano my parents had found at a garage sale, I had the sections and a simple melody for an original song, but words as cool as the ones on the radio eluded me like a puzzle without edges to give me a start.

After pressing play and the red record button on a boom box at the same time, I quickly sat down at the piano and taped my song "I Can Hear You Cry," which impressed Rich. "This sounds like a movie theme," he said, and coming from him I took it as high praise. He also complimented my lyric— "I walk these city streets but all I feel is the rain." Very melodramatic, I know, but I was trying my best.

Licking a dozen American flag stamps and pushing them down on a package with my thumb, I dropped the package with my cassette inside it into the post office mailbox, opening the lever to make sure it had fallen into the box. The address on the package was Burbank, California, an address on the back of so many of my albums, and I got a letter back immediately. A rejection letter, but seeing the Warner Bros. Records logo on the letterhead made me feel like a treasure map was in my hands. I just had to keep digging.

Paper Boy

The first hot day of the year, I was in a convertible full of senior girls who were spraying Sun In on their hair, blasting "Walk Like an Egyptian" and whistling the hook of the song as we sped out of the South High parking lot. In the music section of the *Detroit News* I read that my favorite DJ, Casey Kasem, was furious that a disc jockey in LA had said on air, "Walk like an Egyptian, smell like an Arab" after playing the Bangles hit.

The girls had asked me to model for their photography class final as my hair was now long and my colorful style made me model worthy, apparently. Imitating the posters on my wall, I posed for them on an empty jungle gym by the lake. As they clicked their Nikons, checked their shutter speed, and clicked some more, the attention made me realize I had wasted enough time thinking about Bianca.

The record company rejecting my tape didn't bother me, but a rejection of another sort was waiting for me. Bob Button, South High's cool journalism teacher, asked me to stay after class on the last day of school.

"J.T., I see you signed up to write for the school paper next year, but you need at least a B average in journalism to be in that class, and you got a C minus," he said, taking banana-yellow highlighter pens from his drawer and placing them in an open briefcase. "I'm sorry," he added

I sat there shifting my weight at a desk in his empty classroom, not quite sure what to do. The sound of squealing students having a shaving cream fight on the lawn trickled through the window.

Closing his briefcase, Mr. Button broke the uncomfortable silence between us. "But I do think you would bring great energy to the school paper, a unique perspective. If you can assure me you'll do the work, I'll bend the rules this time. I'd love to have you."

"Yes, sir!" I said, shaking his hand, and my sophomore year I did do the work. I wrote articles about concerts, movies, even books. Trying to really stand out among the volleyball articles and interviews with the Prom committee, I cold-called the *Detroit Free Press* and interviewed their music critic, Gary Graff, who regularly talked to real rock stars.

Walking through the school lunchroom like a private detective, I would seek out girls in Tretorn shoes and fluorescent Swatch watches. Clicking the red record button on a small tape recorder, I would hold it up and ask them about new songs they liked. Then I would wander out to the students smoking cigarettes in jean jackets with Pink Floyd patches sewn on them and ask them the same question. I knew the song disagreements would give an entertaining yin-and-yang effect to my article.

Writing for the paper taught me how to look for the details in every story I wrote about, which turned out to be a lifelong skill and has helped me write better lyrics over the years.

A delivery truck dropped stacks of the paper at school every Wednesday. Flipping to my article, seeing it in black-and-white, and watching students reading my words at their desks was a thrill. Mr. Button, rubbing his beard sitting behind his desk, always gave me a thumbs-up after reading my articles.

In a teenage dream come true I was picked to go to South's rival high school, Grosse Pointe North, for a day, sit in their classrooms, wander their halls, and write an article about it.

I don't remember what I wrote about them, but thanks to me being in the band and by now sporting my hair long and spiked half a can of Aqua Net high, North High School put me on the cover of their paper in the What's Hot column of their Hot or Not list.

I know life is not a popularity contest, but I proudly admit it felt good to know that if angry jocks pushed me inside some girl's locker, most likely my picture would be hanging in it.

One Sunday after begrudgingly spraying our bathroom mirrors with Windex and vacuuming out the family cars, I went to the local Guitar Center to kill some time before seeing a movie with Lance. I sat happily strumming a bright pink lightning-shaped guitar. Behind the glass counter I noticed the cool rocker who once taught me a few chords in third grade. He was still wearing those John Lennon glasses, but now his hair was short and a Guitar Center name tag was pinned to his buttoned-up long-sleeve shirt. A flyer for his old band hung in a frame by the cash register like a consolation prize for trying.

Seeing him click the trigger of a label gun as he priced guitar strings brought up fears in me of growing old and playing other people's songs in half-empty bars at a Holiday Inn. Dressing in purple pants and checkerboard shoes, streaking my chocolate-brown hair blond like Kajagoogoo, winning the talent show, another Battle of the Bands, I did it all, but it wasn't enough. It wasn't the big time. Being in a popular high school band was certainly a blessing but there was something else out there—I knew it in my blood and bones.

Blessed with great parents, a great community, and close friends, I should've been happy. But like a kid with the flu who can't get comfortable no matter what position they lie in, I couldn't get comfortable with life. I had rock 'n' roll pneumonia. Music was whispering in my ear, "Come closer, any way you can."

I was California dreaming every long Michigan day.

CHAPTER 9

The Grosse Pointe of No Return

K endra, Los Angeles is no place for a seventeen-year-old boy. What's he going to do, run around the streets of Hollyweird all day? Not on my watch."

With the phone receiver up to my ear and my right hand over the mouthpiece to conceal my breathing, I listened to my mom talk to a friend of hers who lived in Los Angeles.

Earlier that spring, that friend told my mom I could stay with her and her husband in California when school let out in June. Whether it was for a week or for the summer I don't recall. All I knew was school would be out soon, and mowing lawns and swimming at the park pool was not going to get me closer to a record deal.

Scanning the credits on the back of my CDs, I had seen they all said the same thing: Sunset Boulevard, Los Angeles, California. Every single record company was in Los Angeles.

Some CDs listed record companies in New York City, but low on money, living without air-conditioning, sounded much easier than living without a heater. If you're going to be a starving artist, do it in the sun. Moving to Los Angeles had become the plan, but the plan was now toppling like a game of Jenga.

Gently clicking the button on the phone, I stood in the kitchen in silence. Pencil lines and birthdates on the kitchen wall where my parents measured how much my brothers and

I had grown every year caught my eye. Lee's never moved. Lance and I were both taller than him now. The prickling heat of anger rose from my stomach straight up into my head. Los Angeles was on my mind and it was a bell I couldn't un-ring.

My parents patiently listened to me rant about the injustice of it all after dinner.

"What's the big deal? I could stay on their couch for a week. What a bunch of old farts. All I have to do is get out to Los Angeles. I'll just walk into a record company's office— once they meet me I'll get a record deal right away. I have a tape of me singing Bryan Adams songs and a song I've written myself." My parents sat quiet. "Hello, McFly! I have the *Grosse Pointe News* with me on the cover. How many kids like me could there be? No one thinks about music like I do," I said, exasperated.

Scraping Hamburger Helper off a plate into the sink, Mom replied, "Maybe another time."

My heart raced with frustration and determination. To me there was no "some other time." I recently read that teenagers' brains have a piece that makes them feel invincible during puberty, and that's why they are so daring. If that's true, then that part of my brain was popping like movie theater popcorn overflowing from the tub.

Fish flies cracked like Rice Krispies under the tires as I cruised Lake Shore Road blasting "Purple Rain" and imagining myself singing the songs. My Velcro wallet with the Rolling Stones red tongue logo now had a driver's license in it, freeing me up to spend weekend nights driving around Grosse Pointe in a white station wagon with an oil leak and only one working speaker.

I also had a new love interest, Grace, an outgoing girl with orange-blond hair the color of a Florida sunset who wore Obsession perfume and blue jean overalls with one top buckle undone over R.E.M. shirts. We shared a fascination for New York City and each other's bodies.

Grace got straight A's and lived in a Grosse Pointe house with a circular driveway that backed up to a golf course and was the star of the debate team. All the more puzzling was when I heard from friends she was spotted swiftly riding her bike away from her house with her Converse tennis shoes untied and a black eye. The rumor mill said her dad found out she was getting an A-minus in a class. I never asked her about it.

Slipping my brown leather wannabe Bono boots off and leaving them on the SPOILED GRANDCHILDREN LIVE HERE doormat by the kitchen door, Grace snuck me into her baby-sitting job one Saturday night after the kids she was looking after were asleep. I loved raiding the strangers' fridge before we made out. Grace closed her SAT prep book full of green sticky notes, grabbed the remote, and, pointing the red laser to the Zenith TV, lowered the sound of Bon Jovi purring "I'll Be There for You" on MTV.

With her elbow on her knee, her chin resting on the back of her hand, she smiled as I excitedly whispered about how a songwriter named Desmond Child wrote not only my favorite KISS song but also co-wrote great stuff on the new Bon Jovi album.

Grace and I shared a shadow for the last few months of the school year, but the California sun was calling.

"I'm leaving and I'm not coming back. I'm going to Los Angeles," I told her one night as we leaned up against my dusty station wagon, the words "almost as dirty as your mom" finger-scribbled into the dust on the passenger-side door by a fellow smart-ass.

Her arms tightened around me like I was a soldier going off to war. "You're gonna make it, I know it," she sighed. I pulled my shirt to my nose, smelling her cinnamon-like perfume as I drove away the last time we hung out.

I was determined: Los Angeles was going to feel the bottom of my checkerboard Vans if I had to hitchhike, hop a Greyhound, or skateboard there. Advertisements for cheap flights on Southwest Airlines were always on TV. Thanks to the money from the Battle of the Bands sitting in my bank account, I soon had a one-way ticket in my hands. My bag was already packed: red pants, a couple of T-shirts with Japanese characters on them like the ones rock stars wore on MTV, a toothbrush, and a hair dryer—only the essentials.

The sun wasn't up when I shook Lance awake to tell him I was off. We gripped hands like two championship arm wrestlers. No tearful goodbye, just two brothers there for each other no matter what. I left a note for my parents on the wooden chopping block in our kitchen: *I love you. I'll call when I get to California. Don't worry. J.T.* Standing by the towering Dutch elm tree on our lawn, I took a long look at the house that built me and I was off. I was seventeen years old.

If you're reading this and thinking, "That sounds nuts," you're right. It was. Maybe I was afraid they would have said no. (Of course they would have said no—I had great parents.)

Once I got to LA, I took a taxicab into the city, crawling bumper to bumper through traffic on a freeway with no less than twelve lanes. Passing the occasional palm tree poking up between apartments and highway billboards for *Home Alone 2* and Whitney Houston in *The Bodyguard*, I directed the cab-driver to the only place I knew besides Disneyland: the Sunset Strip.

My parents had taken my brother and me there on vacation the year before. On that trip, my dad behind the wheel of our rental car, I leaned out the open window in the back seat as we passed the famous Tower Records. It was the biggest record store I'd ever seen. Tower was covered in hand-painted murals as tall as elephants advertising all the latest albums.

At the time, a sign above the Tower parking lot read

GUNS N' ROSES AUTOGRAPH SIGNING TUESDAY. I clicked away on my disposable camera as Dad passed the Roxy and the Whisky a Go Go, where Van Halen and Mötley Crüe had gotten their start. Sunset Boulevard was what I knew, so that's where I went.

The cabbie let me out in front of a crumbling hotel a block away from Tower Records. Loading a nearby pay phone with quarters, I called home. My mom answered on the first ring, fuming. "I'm on my way out there to bring you home."

"Mom, I'm perfectly okay. I'm at a hotel. I'm not on drugs. I didn't steal money from your purse for the trip and I promise to brush my teeth." Cars zoomed behind me like waves crashing on a beach. "Mom?" No answer. She had hung up.

Lance told me later that after she'd hung up, my dad told her she needed to let me do my thing.

"So they saw the note right away?" I guiltily asked.

"No," Lance informed me. "Mom yelled 'Larry, the hair dryer's gone!' They didn't need to see the note."

I hadn't taken my mom's feelings into account. I was too young to process that after losing Lee, the thought of me leaving must have been scary for her. It's a lame excuse but it's the truth. Years later, it dawned on me and I felt really bad about the way I left.

Somewhere Over the Rainbow Bar & Grill

That night the Hollywood sidewalks in front of the clubs were littered with colorful flyers and dreamers. Dudes with huge Dolly Parton hairdos and leather jackets trying to become the next Guns N' Roses or Poison handed out flyers and yelled like state fair carnies advertising the clubs their bands were playing shows at.

Teenagers from all over Southern California stood around

flirting, sipping alcohol from concealed bottles they kept stashed in their purses and cowboy boots, and crowded into the all-ages clubs to hear live music. Then they spilled back onto Sunset to shoot tequila, eat pizza, and mingle with real rock stars who hung out at the Rainbow Bar & Grill next door to the Roxy.

The cab and hotel devoured what little money I had. Undaunted, I set out to meet future rock stars like myself.

A hairy-armed bouncer outside the Whisky a Go Go stamped my hand and I walked in. It was like walking into the alien cantina in *Star Wars*. Everywhere there were zebra-striped clothes, pale white arms graffitied in colorful tattoos, pierced noses with chains connected to earrings, a mass of rock 'n' roll people like I'd only seen on TV.

"Are you in a band?" two girls in short leopard-print skirts and teased hair asked me over the music. "Not yet, I just moved here from Detroit," I yelled, proudly pointing my right index finger at the open palm of my left hand.

"Is there hair on your palm?" They laughed, leaning into each other.

I laughed too. "No, that's just what we do in Michigan! Michigan looks like a mitten." The bright lights hitting the crowd from the stage hid the embarrassment coloring my face.

Writing a phone number on a Big Red gum wrapper, one of the girls said, "We just moved here from Orange County. We need a roommate if you can pay your share." Two days later I was out of the hotel. After walking a mile to their place, I threw my bag down, and I walked right back out and found a job. Passing Hollywood High School and a Scientology building, I then marveled at the Sunset Sound recording studio, their building logo written in a seventies-style Brady Bunch font, where Tom Petty and Prince had recorded their biggest albums. I wandered into a restaurant that was hiring.

On the job application I was thrown by the line asking for my Social Security number. I wrote in numbers from a song— 867-53-0999. I started the next day.

"Hey man, can I get a beer?" It was ten in the morning. Wiping down tables at the restaurant, my Michigan eyes were in disbelief: Jeff Spicoli from *Fast Times at Ridgemont High* was asking me for a beer. Sitting on the patio in the morning sun, Sean Penn was lighting a cigarette off another already between his lips. Yes, I was starstruck. And yes, I got him an ice-cold beer for breakfast.

Hooray for Hollyweird

That July and August in LA was like summer camp. But instead of singing Bible songs around a campfire and making friendship bracelets out of fishing lures, I was dancing up a storm at the Cathouse nightclub playing a Where's Waldo version of Spot the Rock Star. A fake ID that made bouncers roll their eyes during my high school spring break worked like a charm in Hollywood.

One minute I was stomping my boots, whipping my hair back and forth to Joan Jett's "I Hate Myself for Loving You" in a swaying crowd of tattooed vampires that looked like they hadn't seen the sunlight in years. The next I was a wallflower eavesdropping on Axl Rose in a black leather jacket with white leather skeleton bones sewn onto it, talking to Lars Ulrich of Metallica in his faded jeans and high-top sneakers as big as water skis. I nursed a flat Dr Pepper next to Lars, who winced as he sipped a strong drink, with a lime floating up in it, like the Wicked Witch of the West's smile.

There was also a lot of Californication. The hair metal scene had just about shaken the hair spray can dry, but West Coast girls and "someday I'll be a rock star" guys still fell madly in bed with each other. I was most intrigued by a talkative girl with a platinum pixie-bob haircut and skin that was paper-sack tan.

With her fingers in my belt loops to pull me close to her, and Poison's "Nothin' but a Good Time" pumping through the club, we danced up a sweat, then spilled out of the club to lay down in the back of her peanut-butter-brown 1975 Dodge van, which looked like a real-life Hot Wheel.

She grew up by Disneyland—as a kid her curfew was when the fireworks went off over Cinderella's castle. Nose to nose under a blanket, using her jean jacket for a pillow, I quizzed her like I was a detective before she waved and blew me a kiss, pulling away on her late-night drive back to Orange County. I couldn't fathom skipping homework to go surfing or bumping into movie stars at the mall as if it was the most normal upbringing. She also played songs for me on an acoustic guitar, something I myself didn't do yet, as I relied on a band, but she inspired me to sing and play.

Back-to-school sale signs with smiling googly-eyed pencils on them next to cutouts of Bart Simpson carrying a stack of colorful books began popping up in store windows around Hollywood. In Grosse Pointe my friends were asking each other to homecoming and applying to colleges. I was moving forward in another way.

"If I were you, I'd get nails and a hammer. Hammer the nails facing out into the hall so the sharp ends stick out the door. Every junkie, hooker, and homeless freak will at some point jiggle this doorknob hoping there's stuff in it they can steal."

I was standing in a dimly lit hallway that was strewn with candy wrappers and cigarette butts and smelled of urine, getting advice from the landlord of a four-story building with a defeated elevator. Bands referred to the building as "the Billiards" because it stood over a Hollywood pool hall, on the most unglamorous corner in Los Angeles. It was on the verge of being condemned, but in the meantime the long-forgotten offices with smashed windows were rented to bands to rehearse in.

"There's a sink at the end of the hall." He motioned with his elbow, unlocking my room.

"Cool, and the bathroom?" I questioned.

Rearranging the crumpled green faces of Lincoln and Hamilton I'd handed him for the first month's rent, "There's a sink at the end of the hall," he replied, before adding, "You like Jane's Addiction? The lyric 'She walks up on Saint Andrews... pulls her dinner from her pocket' was written about the corner of Saint Andrews right outside." He grinned, his teeth decaying and bronze like an Oscar award.

"I love stuff like that!" I said. "Is there a sub shop or something out there?"

"No. 'Pulls her dinner from her pocket.' He's singin' about heroin," the landlord yelled as he walked down the stairs, his belly laugh turning to a coughing fit as it echoed up the stairwell.

You can take the boy out of Michigan, but you can't take Michigan out of the boy. I was as green as the Grosse Pointe golf course grass when it came to drugs. It's a miracle I didn't experiment with getting high, but my veins already had ambition running through them, mixed with a good upbringing and a straight-up fear of drugs.

Record companies were handing out deals like Halloween candy to bands, and I wanted to be next. I was great at putting bands together. I printed up pink flyers—SINGER LOOKING FOR BAND—with my apartment phone number on them. Walking the elbow-to-elbow packed sidewalks of Sunset Strip on weekends, I would hand the flyers out, and soon enough other Hollywood hopefuls were calling me and we were ready to rock.

Wiping tables, ripping movie tickets, serving frozen yogurt—I always had a job, but paying rent and paying for a rehearsal space while working minimum wage proved difficult. In Michigan, you rehearse in band members' basements, but I didn't know anyone with a house in LA. Besides, California had earthquakes, not basements. I decided to leave the apartment I was living in and move into the rehearsal room. *A book will be written about this someday*, I told myself as I hauled my suitcase and guitar onto the bus headed to the cracked-concrete corner stop at the Billiards.

"Slash, play us a song!" a man with a wandering eye who had peed himself yelled at me on the bus as I tried to find the Hollywood sign through the thick smog clouding the skyline as we rolled along.

My lack of funds kept me creative in my quest for fame.

I didn't have a TV, so with my feet dangling from the fire escape at the Billiards, I watched pretty girls walk with guys as big as King Kong out of the gym on the corner and made up songs about where they met. I didn't need to work out, since I was skinny as ever. McDonald's had a scratch-off game of some sort going on, no purchase necessary. Everyone wanted to win a million dollars, but I soon figured out that French fries and orange juice seemed to appear next to the word WIN-NER on most of the tickets I scratched with a quarter. I survived on free French fries and orange juice for a long while.

On the landlord's advice I hammered nails into my door from the inside, the sharp points of them sticking out of the door into the hall to ward off thieves, then my new band and I hammered out songs, all originals, after work. The gigs we landed were at uninhabited clubs, and we played before the sun even set as bartenders restocked the beer cooler, but I felt like I was moving in the right direction. At night, to pass time away from the firetrap drug den I was living in, I walked Hollywood Boulevard. I'd see a movie at Mann's Chinese Theatre and put my hand into the cement where Harrison Ford and C-3P0 had made handprints when I was a kid.

Standing for hours at a newsstand on Hollywood Boulevard, I'd read the latest *Rolling Stone* so I didn't have to buy it. Walking back to the Billiards passing a faded mural of Charlie Chaplin and Bruce Lee, I'd give them both a thumbs-up while asking myself the questions I'd read in the magazine as if I was the one being interviewed.

Still learning the landscape of my new surroundings, I knew I was getting closer to my place when the Universal Studios gift shops morphed into twenty-five-cent peep show stores, and families of tourists were replaced by a woman in a wheelchair, pulling herself forward with her leg, and girls in napkin-sized shorts and half-shirts fixing their heavy red lipstick in the side mirror of a Toyota with a pile of parking tickets thick as a phone book under the wiper.

"Hey, cutie, looking for a date?" the girls would ask me. For months I thought everyone in Hollywood wanted to be in a relationship. Somehow I figured out that *date* was a code word for prostitution.

I don't recall feeling lonely or scared in Los Angeles, just lost at sea. I'd gone from being the popular high school rock star to feeling like I was in the Witness Protection Program. I was a nobody, washing my hair in the same sink I went to the bathroom in. A thrift store guitar was the driftwood that I clung to, and a pay phone on the corner was my lifeline to the world.

Record companies didn't show up at our gigs or return my calls when I inquired about setting up a meeting.

A pulsing gold-and-silver blanket of lights that made up Los Angeles stretched for miles in front of my eyes. The cacophony of heavy metal music blasting from the other rehearsal rooms made it hard to write songs, so at night I would walk up the graffiti-kissed stairwell to the fire escape, pushing open the broken exit door leading to the roof, and serenade the city.

Police helicopters scoping the area would shine a chalk-white spotlight on the rooftop. I'd rock out and thrash on my guitar like I was in the spotlight of a sold-out arena. I would move around the roof to stay under the glow of the police light as long as possible.

"I saw Billy Idol on his Harley motorcycle cruising around, no helmet on, just his blond hair perfectly spiked," I wrote on postcards, showing the stack-of-records-shaped Capitol Records building, that I sent home to all my friends.

Rich had moved from Michigan to South Carolina to live with his sister, not sure if he wanted to pursue music. John joined a heavy metal band as my influences leaned more pop. But they both loved hearing about my brushes with famous people. Grace mailed me yellow-and-orange leaves to remind me of Michigan fall weather, the envelope sprayed with a dash of Obsession perfume to remind me of her.

A season-less year had passed. The bathroom-hand-dryer–warm Santa Ana winds blew through Hollywood, letting me know it was another October, and falling asleep on the stiff carpet was starting to get difficult. It was like that scene in the movie *Big* when Tom Hanks is watching TV and hears gunshots and sirens. He turns off the TV and can still hear the chaos. That was the Billiards to a T. I slept with one eye open, as there were always bottles breaking in the halls, and most nights a rogue cockroach ran across my arm after I covered myself with newspapers for a blanket and squeezed in between the drums and amps just to fit myself onto the floor of the shoebox-sized windowless room.

A confident and sassy girl from Texas had come to see my band a few times. We had a connection, and after watching us perform, then lug our equipment up four flights of stairs after a gig, she was shocked to see my suitcase full of clothes, the milk crate shelves, and my Teenage Mutant Ninja Turtles toothbrush in an empty McDonald's cup. In her Southern drawl that could cut glass she said, "Good Lord, come stay at my place." She was my savior. Having a TV, a shower, and a kitchen felt like I was living at the Ritz-Carlton after all that time living in the rehearsal room.

Kitchen dancing to our newest favorite songs—"Damn I Wish I Was Your Lover," "Achy Breaky Heart"—Ms. Texas and I had a great time until my bandmates moved in and took over like Thing One and Thing Two from *The Cat in the Hat*. The place became a rock 'n' roll frat house and was destroyed in the process.

Phone numbers were written on walls in marker, beer cans and ramen noodle wrappers littered the kitchen floor next to the overflowing never-emptied trash can. A revolving door of girls came in and out at all hours. One bandmate got his heart broken by a stripper and started smashing the apartment drywall with a cheerleading baton she used in her act. No stranger to heartbreak, I cheered him up by putting on his American-flag-striped motorcycle helmet and ramming my head into the wall, leaving a circular hole.

Immature and not something I'd do now, but we were a band of brothers for a short time. Texas Girl left me a "John Deere" letter that said "These boys are all hat and no cattle" and disappeared back to Dallas.

Loving the echo sound my voice had in the apartment's empty parking garage, I sat with my back against the concrete wall, singing and writing more and more songs, trying to get what I heard in my head out of my guitar and onto a demo tape.

In Between Stars

After quickly tiring of bussing tables, I got my next job at a clothing store on Melrose Avenue where all the hip shopping was.

The clothes on the Marilyn Monroe mannequins in the window display were not allowed to be sold. I remember one such shirt was turquoise with white ruffles around the cuffs and neck. Imagine something Austin Powers would wear but for real.

I was folding jeans behind the counter at the store one day, when the little bell above the door rang, letting us know someone had walked in. Looking up from the jeans, I felt a chill go up my spine like an ice cube was rubbed on it. Pointing toward the mannequins in the window, the man who'd walked in said in a soft, commanding voice, "I want that shirt." He looked right at me. The eyeliner around his brown eyes made them as big as Bambi's. It was Prince.

But the shirt wasn't for sale. The boss wouldn't allow it to be sold. So I told Prince without hesitation, "No problem."

Prince stood talking quietly with the beautiful girl he was with. I was pulling the mannequin down when my boss came in, his big belly bouncing and his voice hissing, "We don't take clothes out of the window."

Carefully unbuttoning the frilly shirt, I replied like a calm parent giving a stubborn child an ultimatum: "You can fire me, you can arrest me, you can do whatever you want, but I'm giving the man who wrote 'Another Lonely Christmas' anything he wants in this store."

My boss arched an eyebrow, then backed down. I'd never talked back to him in the six months I'd worked there. Twisting the earring in his right ear, he whispered, "Okay, take it easy, sheesh. But don't give it away for free. He's rich, y'know."

I stared out the bus window from Melrose to my apartment, taillights jamming Hollywood Boulevard like red ants marching into the night as I thought: *Prince has his own record label. If I had a demo tape of my own songs, it would have gone in the bag with his new turquoise shirt.*

Hometown newspaper clippings and singing other people's songs on a CD was not a quick way to fame and fortune. The few record company offices I had contacted didn't reply or, worse, told me to move back home. I knew I had to get a move on with my own music.

Later that same week, a long-haired redheaded dude who looked like Carrot Top the comedian, in jeans with a chain hanging from his wallet, came into the store. His faded T-shirt said PAISLEY PARK. Paisley Park was the famous studio that Prince owned.

"Cool shirt," I told him. "You from Minneapolis?"

"Prince's guitar tech," he replied, not looking at me. "We're filming a video tonight downtown at City Hall."

That night, instead of going to my apartment, I took the bus all the way to Downtown LA. Watching Prince film the video on the steps of City Hall was like being the first kid in Grosse Pointe to cut open a Stretch Armstrong doll and see what was inside. I was witnessing something that no one else I knew ever had.

There was no one there but his band, the camera crew, and myself standing a limousine's length away from Prince.

The guitar tech glared daggers at me when he noticed me so close to the star. I could see *Don't get me fired, kid* flashing across his face.

Around close to two a.m. the video shoot wrapped. Passing homeless people's feet sticking out of cardboard boxes like bodies in an open grave, I walked back to my bus stop. The limousine's headlights cut through the dark as it pulled around the corner of the empty street. *Prince must be in there*, I thought as my stomach dropped.

"Prince is the best! *Purple Rain* changed my life! I gave you that shirt on Melrose," I yelled to the car with my hands up in the air.

The limousine stopped and the rear window slowly rolled down. It was a hot night and the air-conditioning from the limo spilled onto the sidewalk at my feet like cool, invisible water. One marble-sized white light turned on inside, illuminating Prince's face. He smiled, then without a word he clicked the white light off and the limo rolled on. I truly felt he was saying, "Rock on with your bad self."

Walking around the house when I was growing up, my dad would snap and sing, "It never rains in Southern California." It was always sunny in Los Angeles, but it practically *rained* celebrities. Not long after seeing Prince, I was walking the aisles at a grocery store called Rock & Roll Ralphs on Sunset Boulevard. I stopped in my tracks like the librarian who saw a ghost in *Ghostbusters* when I saw Jon Bon Jovi buying a bottle of wine.

Too excited not to, I introduced myself and asked him for advice on making it in the music business. He said, "It's easy to get if you never take a day off." I took the advice to heart, then stretched my paycheck and bought a cheap loaf of bread the length of a guitar, a giant tub of no-name mayonnaise, and a dozen cans of on-sale tuna.

At the apartment I'd fill a brand-new garbage bag with the tuna and mayonnaise, shake it up, and keep the whole thing in the otherwise empty apartment fridge. As the *Cheers* theme played from our TV late at night, I would grab two pieces of bread and use them to scoop out some tuna fish from the bag when I was hungry.

I Met a Man from a Record Company and All I Got Was This Lousy T-shirt

Bumping into famous people and dressing like a rock star was fun, but I wasn't meeting anyone in the record business who could help me. Irish bars blasting U2 and serving green beer for St. Patrick's Day turned to Bobby "Boris" Pickett singing "Monster Mash" through low-rider radios on Hollywood Boulevard as kids trick-or-treated. Another year had passed, and I knew something had to give. Every single person I met wanted to be famous and was trying to get discovered. Myself included. It was as if God had picked up America like a bath mat and shaken it real hard, and all the secure people hung on and everyone else landed in LA. I had to be smart and do something to get ahead.

The warehouse-sized Tower Records store was my favorite escape: wandering the long racks of CDs, reading rock magazines, and listening to headphones that allowed you to sample new releases. On Friday nights, while other people would go to a nightclub, I went to Tower.

Standing in the new-release section one night, I finally put two and two together. Record companies must send their employees here to make sure their CDs are on display and being played in the store. If I got a job here, I'd meet those people and they could play my music for the big shots that actually signed bands.

It sounds naive now, but something like that actually did happen. I filled out a job application on the spot and was soon hired. I loved talking to people about music.

"To anyone who thinks they're gonna get famous working here, you're not." The general manager of Tower was giving new employees a "pep talk" in the break room. Many like me had big dreams and big hair to match. The general manager was wearing a Grateful Dead shirt over his huge belly. He looked like he ate Jerry Garcia.

"What about Axl Rose?" I offered, raising my hand.

"He worked at the video store," the manager snapped.[6]

Negative people didn't faze me. I believed in myself as much as the manager's belt believed it could keep his Levi's from snapping. I was now working at my favorite place to hang out and I kept my eyes and ears open for anyone that worked for a record label while I was helping customers.

Countless people would come in and say, "I don't know the band name but they sing a song that goes like this: 'Ohhhh, I'm a loser, baby...'"

Confidently I'd reply, "Oh yeah, that's Celine Dion." When they arched their eyebrows like the *M* in a McDonald's sign, I'd laugh. "Just kidding—it's a guy called Beck." Being the fan I am, I truly loved connecting people with the music they were searching for.

All kinds of interesting people came through my store. One lady came in furious with a stack of ruined CDs, demanding a refund for faulty products. She had put them in her dishwasher to clean them.

While I still couldn't seem to get ahead, this was Hollywood—the place where dreams come true.

One day, a college girl pushed the glass doors of Tower open with her foot and she laid a stack of mint-green flyers inside the door by the stacked plastic shopping baskets: *Would you like to be on a game show? CALL VH1.*

Punching the numbers into the pay phone on my lunch break, I called the number on the flyer.

"The show is called *Rock & Roll Jeopardy!* We tape it in Santa Monica. You can be on the show as long as you're not

---

6 Rivers Cuomo, who is the singer of Weezer, also worked at Tower Sunset before me. Successful Musicians, 3; Dream Crushing Manager, 0. Game on!

an actor. We've had a lot of repeat contestants," a man said through the receiver.

"Hell yeah, I'll be there." Not only was I going to be on TV, I could probably win some money.

On set, blue TV screens glowed in a movie-screen-sized square just like real *Jeopardy!*, but the questions were all about music in some way. The band Green Day stared at me from the TVs and the question was: Who is this band? Simple question, but you couldn't push the buzzer too quickly or you'd be locked out of the question. Before pushing the handheld answer button with your thumb, you had to wait for a string of lights off camera to light up like the beginning of a NASCAR race. Once I figured that out, I absolutely killed it and destroyed the other contestants. All of the work I'd put into my music education over the years was finally paying off. I even had to correct the show producers when the host said, "From the Van Halen album *Jump*." I interrupted: "The album was actually called *1984*," I said as I looked at the studio audience, my hand on my chin like the thinking emoji, making them LOL.

The episode aired soon after it was filmed. "Dude, you've hit the big time! I yelled 'I know him' to the whole room when you came on!" my friend Todd from Michigan told me over the phone, laughing, and it felt good.

A first-place check for two thousand dollars arrived in my mailbox from VH1, along with a care package from my mom. Over her anger, but not her worry, she had placed Oreos, Cherry Pop-Tarts, and cigarette-pack-sized boxes of Tide detergent under a letter reminding me that I owed some of that winning money to the government when taxes were due. I used most of the money to book a small studio and record three of my newest songs.

A stack of demo tapes bounced around in my backpack as I walked past the crowded sidewalk cafés on Sunset Boulevard to work every day. Studying the credits of popular CDs,

I learned who produced the records and who the songwriters were. Flipping through *Billboard* magazine during lulls at the cash register, I'd memorize the names and faces of record executives who stood next to rock stars in pictures above the articles.

To use an analogy, a record producer is to a record what a movie director is to a movie. A record producer picks the musicians, helps pick the songs, helps the artist form their sound. Think of George Martin, who produced the Beatles; Quincy Jones, who produced Michael Jackson; and Buddy Cannon, who has produced every Kenny Chesney album.

Names of A&R people were also in all the CDs. These are the people who discover bands. A&R stands for "Always Wrong." Kidding—it stands for "Artists and Repertoire." They also help pick the songs for albums and find songs for artists who need a hit. Barry Manilow is an incredible writer, but a lot of people might not know he did not write his iconic song "I Write the Songs." His A&R person found it and presented it to him.

Most artists write their own songs these days, but in Nashville, artists still record songs they have not written. For example, Tim McGraw is a huge superstar with hatfuls of number one songs—but he didn't write a single one of them. Professional songwriters did. That's one reason why Nashville is called Music City.

"That'll be thirty-two dollars. Cash or credit?" I asked a young guy with a beard wearing a Polo shirt and a Boston Red Sox baseball cap.

"Credit," he said, handing me his American Express card. The name on the card was Brian Koppelman. My heart started beating like a locomotive. I wondered if he could hear it.

After I swiped his card, I began putting his purchases in a plastic Tower Records bag and said casually, "You produced Tracy Chapman, yeah? Her song 'Fast Car' is a masterpiece worthy of the Grammy. Her whole record is one great song after the other."

"Wow, thanks, man. You must love your job!"

"I do. Working here is part of my 'get rich slow scheme,' " I said. He laughed as I handed him his purchase, then added, "You do A&R at EMI Records, right? I have a demo, is it cool if I give it to you?"

Walking into my apartment later that night, I saw the red light on my answering machine was blinking. Throwing my backpack on the floor, I dove for the machine. Brian Koppelman must have already called. He must have loved the songs. "Holy shit..." I muttered as my finger shakingly pressed play.

"How many Dr Peppers you drinking out there trying to get a girl to cuddle with you? *Jeeeeeesus Chriiiist!*" It was my brother, Lance, calling from a kegger in full swing at his frat at Michigan State. Thanks to his good grades in math and his prowess on the football field, he was now a Michigan State Spartan. Three messages in a row, the last one just him saying to his buddies, "I'm not slurring, I'm talking in cursive."

Crumbling onto the unmade sheets of my futon, all I could do was wonder if Brian was listening to my songs. The song list on my demo was printed on yellow paper. I'd chosen it because of a Discovery Channel show I'd watched about New York City explaining that taxicabs are yellow because it's the most eye-catching color to the human eye. If my CD was going to be lost on a messy desk, I wanted it to be seen.

Koppelman didn't call but an EMI Records intern dropped off some Wilson Phillips and Debbie Gibson shirts for me to wear to promote their new CDs. Despite the disappointment, I kept working the cash register, writing songs, and passing out my demo to anyone and everyone I thought could get me on the radio.

One record exec came in a day after he'd accepted a copy of my demo. He was anxiously pacing the aisles, looking for me like a mother whose child has wandered off, asking all my Tower coworkers if they knew where I was. I was eating dollar rice with soy sauce, the only thing I could afford from the hip restaurant Chin Chin, when a fellow employee told me a guy with headphones on was asking for me.

My plastic fork broke in the rice when I heard the news, and I sprinted out to find him. This was it—someone was finally going to offer me a record deal. "J.T., I'm so glad you're here. Can you watch my dog while I shop? She's a poodle and terrified of her own shadow," the exec said, handing me a leash attached to a shivering ball of fur.

So many celebrities came into Tower and they all left with my demo. George Michael happily accepted one after I asked for his autograph; Matt Groening, the creator of *The Simpsons*; even Sylvester Stallone got one. Chewing a toothpick, he looked down at the song titles through coal-black sunglasses as he left with the tape.

"Eye of the Tiger" was unknown before he put it in *Rocky III*. Stallone had wanted "Another One Bites the Dust" by Queen to be the theme song, but Queen wouldn't let him use it, thus paving the way for "Eye of the Tiger" to become an all-time classic. Who knows, I thought—maybe Sly was making a new movie that needed one of my songs.

Moonwalking on Sunset Boulevard

Singing along to the sugar pop melody of Mariah Carey's "Dreamlover" playing over the store sound system, I picked up the black plastic phone that was ringing at the information booth, which stood in the middle of the record store like a military command center. "Tower Sunset, J.T. speaking, how may I help you?" I answered. A very soft voice on the other end said, "Hi, is the manager there? This is Michael Jackson." Without missing a beat I answered back, imitating a teenage girl in an equally high-pitched voice: "Oh, hi, Michael, this is your sister Janet. Remember when I was Penny on *Good Times*? I'm much older now. Call me Miss Jackson if you're nasty." The caller on the other end lightly giggled before adding, "I'd like to come shopping after midnight, when you're closed, like last time, thank you so much." I hung up the phone, reminded of all the epic prank calls I made growing up, and began alphabetizing discarded CDs, getting ready to end my shift.

"Future rock star J.T. Harding sweeping the floor at Tower. Enjoy it while you can, people, I'm destined for greatness," I said loudly to my fellow employees as I swooshed the high school janitor–style broom around the feet of the security guard flipping the front door OPEN sign around to read CLOSED.

It was midnight, and I may have been a future rock star, but a real rock star was pulling into the parking lot. "Michael Jackson's here," the jaded manager of the store said to me, exasperated. "Stay if you want, but I'm out, there's a cold beer calling my name."

Tower was as empty as a church on Monday, but excitement raced through the few employees like me who decided to stay. Cupping my hands around my eyes to see through the store window, I saw a two-door Toyota Corolla in the parking lot kill its headlights. The driver opened his door and leaned his seat forward. Wearing jeans, a ruby colored sweater, a light blue surgical mask over his face, and his famous black loafers, the King of Pop, Michael Jackson, climbed out from the back seat...as his ankle got caught in the seat belt.[7] Balancing

---

7 Since the COVID pandemic, masks are normal, but at the time I had only seen surgeons on TV wearing them. To see Michael in one was perplexing, to say the least.

on one leg, Michael jerked his other leg back and forth like a fisherman reeling in a big catch, trying to free his famous foot.

The biggest superstar in history, only two handicap parking spots away from me, and his foot is caught in a seat belt. I remember it better than I remember yesterday.

With curious almond eyes blinking above his mask, Michael very politely said hello to us as he sauntered in. Too starstruck to talk to him, my fellow employees pretended they were busy shuffling CDs around and sweeping the already spotless floor. Not me. After about ten minutes I approached: "Anything I can help you find, Mr. Jackson?" In the same soft voice from the phone call, he said, "Led Zeppelin."

"No problem." I spun around as excited as Ace Ventura, eager to help, and walked to the L section in the CD racks, not knowing if he was behind me or not.

"Anything in particular?" I said out loud, surveying the iconic Led Zeppelin catalogue. An inch from my ear he whispered, " 'Black Dog.' " Flipping through the plastic CDs, I found "Black Dog" and handed it to him. He then asked me if I knew what the top-selling albums were. I told him I did not but maybe I could get a *Billboard* magazine he could look through. Michael nodded yes. I grabbed a *Billboard* magazine, folded it over to the Hot 100 Albums page, and handed it to him. Michael shopped looking at the magazine, crossing off his finds one by one with a black felt tip pen as he dropped them into a red plastic shopping basket.

Although it was now past one in the morning, Michael didn't appear to be in any hurry, and it was clear that the last thing on his mind was how much anything was going to cost. He spent a good half hour leisurely looking at *Simpsons* comics, and I remember him wincing at one point when he noticed a magazine with a picture of a stuntman on fire on it, no doubt reminding him of the accident he had when his hair had caught fire.

As his driver grabbed the half-dozen yellow Tower bags overflowing with goodies and put them in the Toyota, Michael signed autographs for all the employees. We were all giggly like schoolkids. Before he left, I approached him very calmly and said, "I have something I wanted to give you. It's a dream come true to give it to you." "What is it?" he said, his cheeks rising up, indicating a smile under the surgical mask. As proudly as a kid showing his parents a report card full of straight As, I held up my demo tape. "I know you have a record company. These are my songs." I beamed. Michael's mask changed shape as his smile turned upside down. "I'm so sorry. I can't take it from you. Too many people try to sue me. They say I steal their song ideas." Putting his hand on my shoulder, he added, "Just keep believing in yourself, you can do anything if you believe in yourself."

As the Toyota pulled out, my mouth was dry. I felt confused and rejected. Why would I ever accuse him of stealing my songs? That's ridiculous. How ironic that years later, when I walk out of the Bluebird Cafe after shows of my own, people always try to give me their music, but due to my publishing deal I'm not allowed to accept it. Like LA in the '90s, Nashville has its own fair share of lawsuits to this day. Human nature, I guess.

It wasn't only Tower Records I was covering. A spunky girl with short braided hair caught my attention playing cool acoustic songs at an open mic night.

One night while at her house, I discovered her roommate worked at FedEx. She lent me his company jacket.

Just as Obi-Wan Kenobi infiltrated the Death Star, record companies that would never have let me in, otherwise, let me pass the security desk unquestioned. My demo tape was hand-delivered into every A&R mailbox in Hollywood.

Is that illegal? I don't know and I don't care. Well-behaved women seldom make history, and neither do well-behaved aspiring songwriters.

Calling in favors to musicians I'd met, I put together a new band. I'd spend the few dollars I had left over after paying my rent and eating rice to book an hourly rehearsal space. Running to the bus stop every night after work, I'd practice for hours. On my days off I'd call record companies, write new songs, then try them out in between comedians' sets at any open mic night I could find. I was working harder than a drunk person trying to whisper a secret, but the demo wasn't getting any traction and it began to weigh on me.

Visiting Grosse Pointe once a year, I was greeted like Neil Armstrong returning from the moon. Girls were attracted to my adventurous spirit and continued to sneak into our basement through the outside stairwell; old bandmates foamed at the mouth for stories of my brushes with real rock stars like Bret Michaels and Mötley Crüe at nightclubs I had been to. Neighbors asked me with stars in their eyes what being on TV was like, but I felt like a wannabe. The attention was like eating a Big Mac. It filled me up for a moment but ultimately left me feeling empty.

Lance had made the Michigan State University football team, and I went to visit him and cheer him on. His Transformer-tall muscle-bound teammates were shocked, thinking he had brought a girl into the locker room the first time they saw me with my key lime pie–green pants and past-my-shoulders long hair, walking around as they showered after practice. Lance was following his dream too, and I was proud of him. My mom was still worried.

"It's been a few years. You're on a treadmill—maybe you need to try something else," my mom said, moments before she and Dad dropped me off at the Detroit airport for my flight back to LA.

She meant well, but her words frustrated me. Hugging me under the departures sign, she added, "We love you, whether you're famous or not." As I shook my dad's enormous hand, it felt unusually rough. He had secretly palmed a hundred-dollar bill for me and smiled when I slyly pocketed it. As they waved from the car, I blew both my parents a kiss, turned, and walked to the check-in desk, whispering to myself a quote from a positive-thinking book I had read: "Success lies outside of your comfort zone."

Four hours later, the sprawling lights of Los Angeles poked up through the clouds. As I looked down, a nervous sickness poked up in my stomach. "Fasten your seat belts and prepare for landing." The treadmill was waiting for me.

Not long after I returned to LA, a sharp pain that felt like someone snapped a mousetrap on my spleen appeared in my side while I was working at Tower. Was it the stress of my dreams screaming to be let go? At night, with cheap headphones full blast, I danced around like I had as a kid, lip-synching to my favorite songs, imagining a crowd singing along, and it kept me sane and the pain at bay.

No magical record exec ever came into my life like I thought he would. But eventually a famous actor did.

CHAPTER 10

Reruns All Become Our History

One night, I was sipping Dr Pepper and changing the strings on my guitar, when a TV interview with President Bill Clinton was interrupted by a cheap commercial showing a woman running in an alley. Clutching a fake baby wrapped in a blanket, she looked directly into the camera and proclaimed, "Were you adopted? You deserve to know where you came from!" As she ran back down the alley, an 800 number illuminated the screen.

Even as I laughed at the absurdity of the melodramatic commercial, I scribbled the number on the *TV Guide*, then pulled the phone by its cord across the floor to me. I called the number, and a few weeks later, they called back.

A mild curiosity about my birth parents had always been a part of my life, and after all these years, a free service requiring only my birth information used the magic of computers to easily connect me with my biological mother, Charlotte.

"I've been looking for you for years," she said breathlessly through the phone. "I paid private detectives and everything. The detectives promised me you would call me on your sixteenth birthday. I waited by the phone every year for years." I obviously had never called. I had no idea who she was, let alone that she was waiting for me. The private detectives took her money with no intention of finding me.

My biological mother and I talked on the phone regularly from Valentine's Day all the way through to when the stores changed over to Father's Day cards. One day she said, "I think it's time I tell you who your real father is. He's not like other people."

I had to wonder, was he in jail? Or maybe he was in a wheelchair? When someone says "He's not like other people," the mind goes in all sorts of directions.

"Is he okay?" I asked.

"He wears fancy jeans," she replied. I was confused.

"He's an actor. He's the star of that show *Cheers*."

Her stoic voice told me she was completely serious.

I knew the show well. Scanning the cast of *Cheers* in my mind like the Terminator looking for a human, my brain pored over every face, trying to think of one that remotely resembled mine.

I stood up, dropped the phone to my shoulder, and yelled to my roommates: "I'm rich! My biological father is Ted Danson!"

On the line, my biological mother interrupted to correct me: "No, J.T.—he played Eddie LeBec. His name is Jay Thomas."

"Jay Thomas the disc jockey?" I replied. Jay Thomas was a Los Angeles DJ battling every morning for radio supremacy against Howard Stern, who was on the East Coast. Howard had the bigger audience. Jay had the bigger head. Literally.

Outside of my apartment window on the side of a building was a ten-story picture of Jay Thomas, his giant head on the body of a woman in a bra. It read WE APOLOGIZE FOR JAY THOMAS, POWER 106 FM. Every morning, walking to the bus stop to head to Tower Records, I passed under that picture of Jay and stepped over his star on Hollywood Boulevard.

I was in shock. This couldn't be real life. Only a few weeks before that call I'd gone to a movie theater in Westwood for a movie premiere that Prince was rumored to be attending. Elbow to elbow with hundreds of other stargazers, Kirk Gonzales—a Grosse Pointe buddy of mine who was living in LA—and I had stood pressed up against the velvet rope, my demo in hand to give to Prince.

A tuxedoed emcee holding a microphone talked to celebrities as they walked the red carpet. He was reporting for *Entertainment Tonight*.

My buddy and I cracked ourselves up heckling the emcee, mercilessly yelling from behind the velvet rope, demanding to see Prince. Turns out, the emcee was Jay Thomas.

Jay had also come into Tower Records once, reeking of gin and wearing a purple velour suit. He'd wandered in with his friends while I was there and walked the CD racks, loudly calling the Beatles hippie freaks, Elvis a thief of Black music, and Bob Dylan a talentless moron. I had crossed paths several times with my biological father without having any idea of our connection.

It was 1995, and Jay was in his third season of starring on the show *Love & War*.

"Hey, man, well, this is wild, eh?" Jay said to me over the phone after my biological mother gave him my number. "Come down and see a taping of my show. I'll get you set up with parking and a VIP ticket."

What I didn't know at the time was that Jay had sent out one of his buddies to sit next to me in the audience to scope me out. To see if I was some sort of scammer. There was a comedian warming up the audience before the TV taping.

The warm-up comedian's jokes were so cliché I heckled him, shouting, "You should perform on airplanes! That way your audience can't leave." The studio audience was laughing at my jokes louder than at the professional's. I was tearing them up.

Jay's friend didn't wait too long. He went right backstage and told him, "Oh yeah, that's definitely your son."

Jay appeared under the bright studio lights. Walking past his castmates, he moved through the made-for-TV bar and extended his hand to me in the audience. "Hey, man," he said warmly. He leaned his short but stocky frame over the rail in front of the audience chairs, and I shook his hand. His smile was friendly, his eyes curious and maybe a little suspicious. The tourists sitting around me in the audience squealed and waved at Jay. "Hey, darlin'," he said to a senior citizen clutching her purse and gushing over him.

Watching Jay film his show with his perfect timing for jokes and facial expressions was exciting. After the taping Jay drove us to the '50s-themed Ben Frank's diner on Sunset Boulevard. A waiter refilling a glass jar with straws excitedly shouted "It's J.T." when we walked in. Jay and I both turned to him at the same time.

Jay had been known his whole life as J.T. His name is John Thomas, but he changed it to Jay Thomas once he got to Hollywood. When you're an actor you're not allowed to register your name if someone already has it. Someone had already registered the name John Thomas with the Screen Actors Guild.

"In case you're wondering, I don't want any money," I told him between bites of pasta. "I was just curious who my birth parents were. I have a great life—it's just fun to meet you."

Jay replied, "Good, because I don't have any money. I've been divorced three times. One marriage lasted almost as long as this dinner. The woman I married tossed her wedding ring off a bridge. I looked for it in the water the entire next day. What a nut! I told her, 'I've been a lot crazier for women a lot crazier than you.' " I laughed out loud.

Jay smiled. "Use that on someone that breaks up with you. Also, if you like a pretty girl that all your friends are after, ask her if one of her eyes is a little bigger than the other one. Reverse psychology, my friend—she'll take you straight to the bedroom." He flung his hand forward like a referee giving a first-down signal. I laughed harder.

"Tell me about your mommy and daddy," Jay asked sincerely.

"This answers a lot of questions. That's what my mom said when she found out about you. They both are kind of excited about it all," I mused.

"Well, good. Charlotte thinks you might be gay because you have long hair. Doesn't matter to me," Jay told me.

"I thought I was, the first time I saw John Taylor of Duran Duran," I joked.

Laughing in the exact cackling cadence as I did at his jokes, Jay swirled the ice in his glass, even as it was melted, between us.

Jay in a chef's hat next to Robin Williams as Mork had been staring back at me from the cover of the *Dynamite* magazine I read as a kid. A Twizzlers commercial with a Claymation smile saying "I am a mouth" was constantly on TV when I was growing up as well. I would repeat the commercial word for word. The mouth's voice on a licorice high was Jay's. You can YouTube it.

Billboards advertising *Mr. Holland's Opus* with Jay as the football coach were all over Hollywood.

It was as fun as it was bewildering to know him and connect the dots of the times he had wandered into my life via entertainment. We became fast friends.

My parents were very understanding. Lance was worried I wouldn't come home for Christmas anymore, but I didn't see Jay as a father figure. He was more like a wild long-lost fraternity buddy. He was fun and exciting company, but he would never replace my family.

"Do you want a martini?" Jay's wife, Sally, said as she hugged me, welcoming me in from the moment we met. Their two sons, Sam and Jake, not yet five years old, jumped all over me like I was hiding candy in my pockets. I loved it and I couldn't wait to meet my biological mom's family.

Sitting in a car outside a small house on a humid day in South Carolina, I made small talk with my biological mother. The engine hummed as she watched the house like a detective on a stakeout. Jay had generously paid for a plane ticket and hotel so I could go meet her.

A frail man with gray hair and glasses looked out of the house window. Seeing him, my bio mom hit the gas and we shot forward like a racehorse at the Kentucky Derby. "I never told my parents about you—that was them! I never told anyone about you," she said, panicked, rolling through a stop sign before speeding through the quiet suburb.

Over dinner at a Cracker Barrel, her anger at Jay Thomas made her face red as a royal flush. When I mentioned him, she would curse him out like he was sitting with us. After all the friendly phone calls between her and me, I realized it did not apply to him: "I'm going to call *Star* magazine and tell them all about J.T. and how you left him," she told Jay over the phone.

"Please do, I need the press," Jay snapped. Not helpful.

I don't pretend to understand the feelings a woman has after carrying a child for nine months and then giving that child up. It must be very hard. I do feel bad for her. I thanked her over and over for having me. I have such a good life. She has a story to tell and it's hers to tell when and if she wants to. I'm forever grateful to her.

Back in California, "Reruns all become our history" by the Goo Goo Dolls blared from a Jeep's radio as I walked to Tower one afternoon. The lyrics seemed to be directed right at me in relation to Jay.[8]

Meeting my birth parents wasn't the only unexpected development in 1995. On the other side of the country, somewhere between the skyscrapers that make up the Manhattan skyline and the taxicabs darting through the New York City streets below, my yellow demo tape caught the eye and ears of a certain someone.

---

8 Songwriters, your most personal feelings are what people will relate to the most. Think about your all-time favorite songs and how the lyrics make you feel they were written just for you.

=== CHAPTER 11 ===

Smells Like Springsteen Spirit

It's funny, man. I forgot about your CD. It was laying in the bottom of a box full of them and I saw it and I remembered you." It was Brian Koppelman on the phone. The bright yellow label I used to make my CD stand out had worked.

He continued, "I'm not really signing anyone to deals right now, but we are putting out records that need songs. You have any more songs?" "Absolutely!" I responded.

"Cool, I'll be back in LA from New York all next week. I'm staying at the Four Seasons—I'll come by the store."

By this time, I'd traded in my rock 'n' roll roommates for a two-room place by myself in the empty maid's quarters of a nice white picket-fence house in the Hollywood Hills. It was the best-case scenario. A rich couple owned the house, they liked having someone there, and the rent was cheap.

Thanks to leftover money from *Rock & Roll Jeopardy!*, I managed to set up a Guitar Center drum machine and four-track recorder next to my futon. After writing a song, I'd record it on my own in my room. Drum loop, guitar, and vocal. Simple recordings. Brian's call came at a time of great inspiration.

When the taxicab first dropped me off on Sunset Boulevard the day I ran away to LA, hard-rock bands with enough hair spray each to destroy the ozone layer were topping the

Billboard charts. Then a high school pep rally that turned into a riot came blasting into everyone's living room. Via my faithful friend MTV, "Smells Like Teen Spirit," the song and video by Nirvana, '80s hard-rock bands became obsolete overnight. Nirvana and Pearl Jam wrote anthems for a generation of music fans who swore they didn't want them. An endless stream of angsty bands in cargo shorts and flannel shirts followed.

Then tragically, Kurt Cobain killed himself and it was like all the anger of the era disappeared. Softer acoustic songs emerged. Hootie & the Blowfish singing "Hold My Hand," Counting Crows' Van Morrison–flavored "Mr. Jones," and Sheryl Crow musing "All I wanna do is have some fun" began dancing out of car speakers and the VH1 video channel.

At Tower, employees received free copies of new CDs so we could listen to them and, if we liked them, tell customers about them.

Sheryl Crow and Counting Crows released their debut albums at the time. Sheryl's lyrics were deeply visual—images about Las Vegas casinos, folding shirts to keep a lover happy, barflies and tough guys.

Counting Crows packed an emotional punch with their lyrics about winning over Spanish dancers, taking trains to mysterious streets, and being somewhere in the middle of America.

Both CDs had very simple guitar chords. Heavy metal music and its lightning-fast guitar solos were too difficult for me to play, much less write. Grunge was world-changing, catchy, and great. The guitar chords were easier to play, but it was very angry music and didn't come to me naturally.

I was captivated by the sound of the two Crows (Sheryl and Counting), and their work fueled my ambition and songwriting education for lyrics and melodies. Another influence grabbed me by the heartstrings and to this day hasn't let me go. From what I had seen on the streets of LA, it appeared to me that the "City of Angels" brings out the devil in people, but unexpectedly I found religion.

Born Again

A rare nippy wind blew through La La Land. Given a free ticket by a record store regular, I pulled up the collar on my coat, rode a bus with brakes that squealed like a saxophone to Inglewood, and wandered into some kind of Wednesday-night church revival.

As I took my seat I noticed no one in the crowd was sitting down. Looking to the stage, I saw a preacher standing in a blazing bleach-white spotlight. Dressed in a black suit, a white collared shirt with a bolo tie, and sweating from every pore, he stomped his snakeskin boots and sang a gospel song that had tried to reach my heart and soul years before but had made no sense to me at the time. That night it hit me like Zeus's lightning bolt.

Veins bulging from his neck as he sang and gripping a piece of wood like it was made from the True Cross, the preacher looked right at me and I looked right back. He sang about the promised land, belting the words "It ain't no sin to be glad you're alive!" With steam rising from his skin, he simultaneously bowed his head and slowly raised both his hands toward the ceiling in surrender. His congregation of twenty thousand believers, myself now included, raised ours as well. I was converted. Standing in the LA Forum, the preacher had blessed me in the rains of New Jersey, his wood was a guitar, his religion rock'n'roll, his name was Bruce Springsteen.

The next day I beelined to a used record store on Melrose Avenue. Standing between a man shopping in Urkel glasses and a flamingo-pink bathrobe, and the Q-tip-pale male clerk with a safety pin through his lip and hair dyed electric banana blond, I flipped through the Springsteen bin and bought four of his CDs.

With the headphones cranked on my portable CD player, I would lay on my futon on a nightly basis and immerse myself in his songs, riding shotgun as he went "racing in the street," meeting a girl in "the darkness on the edge of town." I learned more from a three-minute song than I ever did in school. In Springsteen's music I saw something I recognized. I saw myself. As a heavy-metal-obsessed Grosse Pointe teen I had never understood Bruce. But now, listening to "Born in the U.S.A." I was born again.[9]

Pop and rock songs rocked me in an emotional way, but where those lyrics were pretty broad and open to interpretation, these new influences were like watching someone's home movies. The lyrics were so detailed, and I wanted to write lyrics like that.[10]

Standing in the shallow end of the empty swimming pool of the house I was renting a room at, holding my black acoustic guitar, I strummed three simple chords over and over. A song called "Kentucky" came to life.

The song was about me on a road trip with a girl. "On the way to Kentucky, we shared a shake at Stuckey's. I made her laugh so hard she fell off her seat," I sang.

Using imagery from my childhood, the lyric took shape. As a kid, my family drove to Nashville from Detroit every summer to visit my grandparents. We would stop to eat at a place called Stuckey's. It's hard to rhyme with *Kentucky*. Stuckey's fit perfectly.

---

9 Bruce came into Tower Records. I helped him and told him I was learning to write songs listening to his. He said "Enjoy, enjoy," his sincere gravelly voice sounding exactly like it does on his records.

10 "Kenny Chesney once texted me from a Springsteen concert and said 'Somewhere With You' that you and J.T. wrote makes me feel like these Bruce songs."—Shane McAnally

Tower employees elbow to elbow in jean jackets and Soundgarden T-shirts, swigging dollar beers, erupted in cheers when I sang the opening line "I quit my job at the record store," premiering "Kentucky" at a show with my band at the club Coconut Teaszer, which was painted as pink as the Pink Panther.[11] Jay Thomas would come to see my band as well, and people would whisper, "The actor guy is here again, he must be attracted to J.T. How creepy." During the show, Jay jumped onstage and over his Zoot suit–style dress pants banged a tambourine from his buttocks to his crotch, swaying like a hula dancer on cocaine. My drummer could barely keep a beat from laughing, and the tambourine has a restraining order against Jay.

I carried a CD with "Kentucky" and two other songs I'd written burned onto it with me every day. I couldn't wait to give it to Brian Koppelman.

Working extra hours at the cash register, I kept my eye on the front door like a thief standing guard during a bank robbery. Eating my lunch on the cement steps in front of the store, I avoided the break room in case he came in.

Like a child of divorce waiting for a parent to pick me up, I regularly hung around work after my shift, but he never showed.

By the end of the week, anxious and disappointed, I knew I had to do something. I had three new songs I'd recorded. Dangling from a plastic smiling broccoli next to the microwave I made popcorn in was a set of Lexus keys on a hook. The car belonged to the owner of the big house I rented my room from. I decided to sneak his car out while he was sleeping and go to the Four Seasons at two in the morning.

---

11 Random song fact: The lyric "a pink hotel, a boutique, and a swinging hot spot" by Joni Mitchell in her song "Big Yellow Taxi" was inspired by the location of Coconut Teaszer.

I turned the Lexus key as gently as I could, thinking that if I started it slow, the engine wouldn't make as much noise.

I moved slowly through the moonlit palm trees of Beverly Hills over to the Four Seasons, where I left my new songs at the front desk for Brian. I wrote a note and hoped he'd receive it. There wasn't texting then. I didn't have his number anyway.

Driving back to the house, I cruised around. The streets were deserted except for a water truck spraying down the stars on the Walk of Fame.

Parking the car carefully, I quietly put the keys back on the kitchen hook. As much fun as I had been having, I was dreading going to work at Tower the next day. I fell asleep with a stomachache.

The alarm clock hadn't gone off but I jumped up startled when I saw it blinking 8:50. My brain thought the numbers on the clock were change I owed somebody at the Tower cash register. Slumping back onto my pillow, I realized my job was really getting to me.

As I brushed my teeth, yellow Post-it notes I'd written to myself and stuck on the bathroom mirror cheered me on: "Don't Give Up"; "If Not You, Then Who??"; "You've come this far, go the rest of the way."

The phone started ringing as I wiped Crest from my mouth with a towel. I had no interest in answering. Hearing my outgoing message on the answering machine—"This is J.T. from South Deeeeetroit"—followed by a beep, I then heard an unfamiliar voice.

"J.T.? You there? Pick up!" a voice gushed.

Picking up the phone, I breathed "Hello?"

"It's Brian. 'Kentucky' is a smash. I'm signing you to a record deal."

Bouncing down the hill to Sunset Boulevard on the way to work, I stopped, arms raised in a V and my chin to the sky. Standing in triumph like the guy who busted out of prison in *The Shawshank Redemption*, but without the rain, I was walking on sunshine.

CHAPTER 12

Subway Cars in Camaro Town

Play it like you mean it, boys," a voice shouted over drumsticks clicking out a one, two, three, four. Holding the drumsticks was Kenny Aronoff, superstar drummer for John Cougar Mellencamp.

Pounding out the perfect beat on all the John Mellencamp records, as well as starring in the videos for "Jack & Diane," "Pink Houses," "Small Town," and a dozen others, Aronoff, with his ear-to-ear grin and a shaved head, was an MTV staple.

Kenny wasn't smiling at me from the TV. He was counting off a song called "Camaro Town,"[12] which I had written. In a recording studio in New York, one block from Times Square, a band of studio musicians blasted into the song they had learned from my home demo recordings as I sang along. Recording had begun for my debut album on EMI Records.

Billy Joel was in the adjacent studio and rock band Warrant of "Cherry Pie" fame passed me in studio halls lined with gold records.

Eating sushi in the studio lounge, Aronoff told me, "John

---

12 On late-night cable I heard a comedian describe his Southern hometown as "Camaro town." I wrote it down and wrote a song around it. Titles are everywhere if you listen for them.

Mellencamp invited me over one day. He was sitting on his kitchen counter and he played 'Pink Houses' for me on his guitar. When John got to the 'ain't that America' part, I knew we were going to be stars." Goose bumps went up my arm imagining the scene.

Things happened fast with EMI. Tapping a Marlboro cigarette over his shoulder, paying no attention to the ashes falling on his dress shirt like burning dandruff, a famous and fearsome white-haired music attorney Jay Thomas introduced me to proudly let me know a huge check was coming my way, before adding, "J.T., never trust a manager who can't pay for dinner, or a backup singer who can."[13]

He handed me a pen, and the attorney and his staff all laughed when I collapsed onto the floor pretending to faint after I signed the contracts. The check from EMI with multiple zeros made quitting my job at Tower a no-brainer.

Koppelman had put together an incredible band, booked the studio, and FedExed me a plane ticket to New York City. The black limo that picked me up for the drive to the LA airport was so big I literally sat on the floor in the middle of it, smiling like I was in a Jacuzzi without water.

Driving down Sunset Boulevard toward the airport, I was caught off guard by the sign above the Tower parking lot. In big black letters it read: GOOD LUCK J.T.

Seeing the sign made my spirit rise as if the prettiest girl in the world was whispering that she liked me. Los Angeles isn't famous for its friendships, but I made real friends working at Tower. The limo driver turned around at my request.

---

13 All kidding aside, never do a music deal of any kind without an entertainment lawyer.

Unwrapping a brand-new disposable camera I'd stashed in my backpack, I snapped a picture of the sign.

In New York, barefoot kids jumped through water spraying from fire hydrants in the summer heat. I passed company softball games and women in bikinis tanning on the emerald-green lawns of Central Park. A fresh slice of pizza burned the roof of my mouth, making it taste like a penny for a few days. Subway cars sped by tattooed in Rubik's Cube–colored graffiti, and mannequins smiled at me from department store windows when I wandered late at night, too excited to sleep. All the sounds and visions branded the iconic "I ♥ NY" logo forever onto my own heart.

For two weeks that July, bouncing from my fancy New York hotel to the recording studio, the future was so bright I had to wear shades.

"I never doubted it," my dad boasted through the phone when I called home to tell him the deal went through and recording had begun.

"Your son is an incredible writer," Brian gushed to my mom as she and Lance sat in the Times Square studio as my songs played back through the speakers. They had come to visit and were put up in the fancy hotel with me. Leaning her head on my shoulder, Mom sighed. "The mom always worries, but I'm very proud of you."

A real-life Jessica Rabbit with fire-red hair, a lip ring, and clear latex gloves peeled meat off chicken wings, placing it in front of Lance in a pile. He paid extra for the service. He was a Hooters VIP. Lance's lips were Papa Smurf blue due to the third Hooterade vodka he was sipping. I had a half of a Corona and was so tipsy I felt like I was standing on a water bed.

"Watching the computer line your voice up with the guitars and everything at the studio, dude, I was thinking this is the greatest thing ever, " Lance said before adding, "I'm stealing books to sell them for beer money, and here you are."

He looked up at a baseball game on a wall of TVs as I politely declined having my chicken wing meat pulled for me. Peeling off her 3 Mile Island sauce–stained gloves, the Hooters girl shrugged as Lance told her, "Don't mind him—the only woman he's ever been in is the Statue of Liberty."

The jumbotron-sized red-and-white Coca-Cola sign in Times Square was flashing above us as Lance and I hopped on a subway back to the hotel. The next morning, I hugged him and Mom goodbye. It felt great to have had them in New York for a couple of days, but my favorite kind of cardio was scheduled for the next day: shopping.

A corporate American Express credit card swiped over and over as shopping bags filled up for me. A stylist hired by EMI took me around shopping for vintage band T-shirts and bright-soled Puma shoes to wear in the pictures for my album cover. It was my own *Pretty Woman* moment.

Pulling open the door to a hip vintage-clothing store in the East Village that smelled like someone's grandma's attic, I felt my heart drop when I saw one of the greatest lost loves of my life alone in the back of the store: A KISS pinball machine. The same one from the roller rink. Playing KISS pinball became my daily after-studio ritual. When the recording sessions were finished, Brian said to me, "John Thomas, you are the smartest, most in-tune-with-America writer I've ever heard." A woman in a dress winked at me as I flew back to Los Angeles. It was the Statue of Liberty.

Every Mistake Imaginable

A twenty-pack of CDs arrived at my house back in California in September. Like John Travolta staring into the magic briefcase in *Pulp Fiction*, I stared at the newly minted *Camaro Town* CDs. Staring out from the cover of the CD, leaning on a powder-blue classic Camaro, was yours truly.

From the Hollywood sign to the Skee Ball slides on Santa Monica Pier, I'd drive around listening to my CD in a car I'd purchased with my own money. The song "Kentucky" sounded as glossy, sparkly, and professional as any song I'd ever heard.

With *Camaro Town* blasting, the only CD in my car's five-CD changer, I imagined myself in the music video. I was on the verge of stardom, once Brian and EMI decided on what the first single should be. On a phone call Brian said, "Getting on the radio and getting a tour will be hard, but we will win!" His confidence in me made me feel invincible. I put together a band, called clubs in cities we could get to by car, played some energetic shows, and waited with a permanent Scrub Daddy smile on my face for the plan to be rolled out.

School buses picked up and dropped students off as crossing guards held up stop signs and umbrellas for the kids running in the rain. Along the Pacific Coast Highway, the beaches were foggy and deserted. *It's the Great Pumpkin, Charlie Brown* morphed into *Frosty the Snowman* on TVs across America as the seasons changed and a new year began. All communication with EMI Records had stopped, and I had no idea why.

Thanks to the money in the bank, I didn't need a day job, but money couldn't pay the rent on the restlessness inside my body and soul aching to get my record out. Pacing around my room at night, I wondered why my calls to Brian's office went unreturned for months.

Trying to catch him off guard one morning, I dialed the main EMI office line.

"Brian's not here, J.T. I'll leave a message," the receptionist at EMI said.

I spent a lot of time in Michigan, and naturally all my friends and family wanted updates. "How's your record, pal?" my dad asked from behind his newspaper as he sat reading on his La-Z-Boy. "Dad, it's so great—just waiting in a line of other releases, totally normal," I lied.

Another day I lay down next to Cooper, my family's black Lab, as she stretched on the carpet. Lance, his face illuminated by his laptop screen, enjoyed the only green food he would allow in his body, a Shamrock Shake from McDonald's. "When are you going on tour?" he asked as his straw squeaked in his cup.

"I hate to say this, but I don't know what's going on," I confessed to him. "Brian used to treat me like a hero, now I'm a substitute teacher."

"You're the greatest. People are gonna figure it out," Lance said as he lowered the straw down to Cooper, her tongue frantically licking it like a kid licking green frosting from an eggbeater.

Heat lightning finger painted the night sky that Fourth of July as I sat alone in the family kitchen. Hootie & the Blowfish were playing a sold-out show live on VH1. Listening along, I lightly plucked my guitar. *If I could write a song with them, it would be a hit*, I thought. I wonder what I would've said if someone had told me, "in the future you will be writing hits with Darius Rucker."

Denial turned to anger. For a few weeks I kept spitting things like "You know what EMI stands for? EVERY

MISTAKE IMAGINABLE" to anyone who would listen. "Screw Brian Koppelman" came out of my mouth on a regular basis for another two months after that, but the moment he finally called, I ran to the phone like Baby finally hearing from Johnny in *Dirty Dancing*.

"Did I do something wrong?" I started.

"No one is asking me about your record here. They're not behind it, so we're not releasing it. Keep writing," he told me. "You'll get another deal."

"What if you get another job. You can sign me somewhere new, right?" I pleaded.

"I loathe the music business—I just sold a movie script that Matt Damon is gonna be in."

When I heard those words, a black hole appeared in my mind, sucking all the light out with it. Everything I had worked for was over before it even began. I was not only heartbroken, I was embarrassed. I shouldn't have been. Walking into parties, I could've bragged, "I had a major record deal. I made a record in New York City with John Mellencamp's band in the same studio Billy Joel was recording in. Thanks to EMI there's eighty thousand dollars in my bank account and they can't take it back."

But that's not how I felt. I felt like I'd been dumped, hard and without warning. I wandered around with a hangover-meets-heartbreak gut-churning nausea. Brian believed in me when I needed it the most, and looking back, I think maybe his hands were tied. EMI Records closed not long after. Maybe he saw the writing on the wall like the graffiti on a passing subway train, but I never understood why he didn't just call me back all those months. I got over it—what doesn't kill you makes your songs stronger. Being in the studio and wandering the city that never sleeps was a magical time. Brian was a good finder of talent. He had also signed David Gray to EMI, who was let go a few years later but released the worldwide smash song "Babylon," which gave me hope. Brian turned out to be a talented writer himself; he made *Billions*.

June Gloom

The Santa Monica Ferris wheel was empty as a keg after a frat party. Zoltar sat lonely in the fortune-telling machine, longing for kids with quarters to run into the arcade, and clouds cement-puddle gray made a ceiling over the coast. *June gloom* is a California term for a weather pattern that results in cloudy, overcast skies with cool temperatures during early summer. It also matched how I was feeling after losing the record deal. I drove around Hollywood without knowing where I was headed, literally and figuratively.

Luckily, interviews I had read with rock stars through the years came flooding to mind, countless stories of my favorite singers and songwriters who had signed a deal, then lost it, but still managed to make it big.

In *Rolling Stone* magazine Sheryl Crow spoke of making a Mariah Carey–esque album that ended up on the shelf. A few years later she made her incredible *Tuesday Night Music Club* album, which charmed the world.

Heavy metal icons (and my personal heroes) KISS were originally called Wicked Lester. In their book *KISStory*, lead singer Paul Stanley explained how they were signed to Epic Records but were then dropped from that label, inspiring them to regroup and become KISS.

Country superstar Kenny Chesney was signed to an alternative rock label called Capricorn. He lost that deal, but as we all know, he persevered and honky-tonked his way to stadium-status superstardom.

Before they were famous, solo artists Neil Young and Rick James were in the same band, signed to and then dropped by

Motown Records. Picturing Neil Young in assless red leather chaps makes me think that definitely wasn't a band that was meant to be.

Fueled by these stories, I knew that if I'd done it once, I could do it again.

Basketball-sized pink paper lanterns hung from the ceiling like electric gumballs. Below them, a family spun a lazy Susan dotted with plates of steaming vegetables and noodles dripping in garlic sauce. A young boy in a booster seat pierced a hot dog with a chopstick and held it up in triumph. Five brown leather booths away, my voice and guitar playing fluttered around the room.

I was at a Chinese-Jewish restaurant called Genghis Cohen known for krispy kanton knish, matzah ball eggrolls, and singer-songwriter nights.

After playing songs to the bartender's polite applause, I unplugged. As I was curling my guitar cord up like a cowboy does with a rope, I heard something unexpected.

"J.T., I love the record you made for EMI."

A tall man with brown hair and an easygoing smile that reminded me of Al Gore stood before me.

I said, "Oh really, you're the one?"

He laughed as we fist bumped and he introduced himself, "Brian Brinkerhoff. I work for Disney Publishing. We should do something together."

Walking Melrose Avenue back to my car, I studied his business card in the streetlight glow as the smell of beef with broccoli rose from my clothes.

Two days later, I was driving the Ford Thunderbird I'd purchased through the security-guarded gate onto the Disney lot. Passing turtle-green hedges that were cut in the perfect likenesses of Goofy, Donald Duck, and Mickey Mouse, as if

Edward Scissorhands was the groundskeeper, I parked the car, and then bounced into the publishing office. The office was two hours north of the real Disneyland, but I was as excited as a kid waiting in line to ride Space Mountain. I had learned that Brian Brinkerhoff had tried to sign Rage Against the Machine and the Spice Girls. Two totally different kinds of music, but both bands were superstars. He had an ear for hits.

"I can give you money to make a record," he told me. "Write a bunch of new songs, and we will make the record ourselves. We will own it, shop it, and we will say take it or leave it."

This new Brian's belief in me had me fired up, and he paid for my record on a handshake. I put together another band, and after a very few short showcases, Atlantic Records signed me on the spot. Months later, they stopped returning our phone calls. Once again, I got to keep the money but didn't have a record deal. Brinkerhoff was furious, but to me it didn't sting as much as EMI because I didn't really know anyone at Atlantic.

I did like my new songs, though. I was using drum loops from computers under my really pop-sounding acoustic songs. I thought, *Well, I'll just take this record somewhere else.* Brinkerhoff and I are still friends to this day.

The universe had my back, but there were a few more steps to go. A hit song that I would write was just around the corner. But to reach that corner I'd first have to walk a mile in high heels, so to speak.

CHAPTER 13

The Man in the Sequin Pajamas

Mike for J.T., Mike for J.T." The walkie-talkie in my hand was barely audible over the heavy metal onslaught blasting through the nearby wall of amplifiers. My face was illuminated by a two-story upside-down star made out of television sets.

"Go for J.T.," I yelled back.

"J.T., there's about fifteen girls by the side entrance asking for you," shouted Mike, the tour manager.

Walking fast, following in reverse the fluorescent orange arrows that were taped to the floor showing the way to the stage from the dressing room area, I made my way through the arena's halls.

Knowing there was always a small crowd trying to get backstage, I replied into the walkie-talkie: "On my way. How will I know which ones they are?"

"Well, the women are topless, wearing thongs, and they all have KISS makeup on their faces." Mike laughed.

For most guys this scene would be a once-in-a-lifetime moment. For me it was an average Tuesday night. I was on a world tour. I had become the personal assistant for a famous rock star.

A month earlier, I'd gone back to square one with the record that Brinkerhoff and I had made. I started taking the new CD all over Los Angeles to different record companies, trying to get another deal.

There were so many record companies back then—because of the internet there are very few record labels now, but in the late '90s the music business was so huge even individual rock stars had their own labels.

Madonna had a record company, Maverick; Bon Jovi had a record company, JAMBCO; even the rock star I started working for had one. One day I dropped off a CD with his manager. He wasn't putting out any records, but I met the star and he offered to take me out on tour as his assistant. "Your CD is like an AM radio that fell out of the sky. The songs are so catchy. I could direct videos for you to help you get a deal. Grab your shit, you're coming with me."

He had colorful tattoos and a colorful personality to match. His fans thought he was the Second Coming. To me, he was the High Priest of Crazy but he was the perfect salesman. He handed me the proverbial apple, and I took the biggest bite I could.

Crisscrossing America and then the world for the wildest year of my life, my main job for him was to hand out backstage passes and make sure there was a themed party after every show.[14] He slept all day, so after I bought chocolate syrup that was put into buckets to be used as fake blood during the show, and set up the night's shenanigans, I would sift through my scrap papers of song ideas, trying them out on an electric guitar and eating room-service fries in my hotel room.

Turning off the engine of his dented Toyota Prius, a

---

14 For those of you that might think all I did was walk around at his shows and talk to beautiful girls, guess again. Being chased full speed through arenas by angry boyfriends whose girlfriends I had innocently approached was also a nightly occurrence.

runner whose job it was to drive me around on errands clicked the unlock button on his door.

"Be right back. We still have to go find some Dippin' Dots for my boss to eat when he wakes up and a little cooler so they don't melt," I said, climbing out of the car. It was noon. We were parked in an empty dirt parking lot somewhere in America.

A hand-painted sign the size of a highway billboard sat above a tin-roof trailer turned bar: THE BOOBIE TRAP. The two o's in the logo were breasts with a bikini holding them up.

A neon Coors sign missing a letter blinked as if it was squinting in the bright daylight. Running my first errand of the day, I knocked on the screen door of the strip club. A man as skinny as Olive Oyl from the Popeye cartoon appeared, wiping his face with a napkin. Orange buffalo wing sauce stained his gray beard.

"We're closed," he barked. A thick gold necklace hung over his flowered shirt. He wore a white sailor's cap over his curly graying hair. His eyes darted from the idling car in the parking lot back to mine. From the car, a Nintendo Game Boy beeped in the runner's hands as I spoke.

"So sorry to bother you, sir," I began politely. "I know this means nothing to you and I'm not trying to brag, but I work for the rock star that's in concert tonight at the arena."

He shrugged. "Yeah, I heard. What does that have to do with the price of eggs?"

Holding up concert tickets in one hand and the small rectangular bright yellow backstage passes in another, I continued, "I have tickets and backstage passes, and I was wondering if any of your dancers would like to come to the show tonight. You're invited as well, of course. I know that the dancers always bring a chaperone."

Pushing open the screen door, he stepped out of the club and inspected the tickets "How much?" he asked.

"How much what?" I answered.

"How much are the tickets, dipshit?"

"Oh! They're free. These are totally free. We want you all to come to the show and to the backstage party."

The 1998 Nokia cell phone in my pocket buzzed. I grabbed it and glanced down, looking at the caller ID: *Sequin Pajamas.*

The rock star's name was entered in my contacts with that name because I'm pretty sure if you say his actual name three times in a row, he'll appear in a puff of smoke, and he only wore sequin clothes. Sending his outfits to be washed in a Ritz-Carlton as the tour began, he explained: "Albert Einstein always wore the same clothes so he didn't waste time choosing an outfit. Einstein only thought about his math theories. I'm no different than Albert Einstein—I don't have to think about anything other than my art."

His offstage wardrobe was sequin socks, sequin shirts, sequin pants, sequin high-heel boots, and in bed, sequin pajamas.

I answered quickly and politely, like Carlton from *The Fresh Prince of Bel-Air*, "Hey, yeah, I'm here. Okay, great—got it." I asked the club owner, with the High Priest on the line, "Everything hunky-dory?" The club owner, feeling the texture of the backstage passes in his hand, nodded yes.

The High Priest of Crazy lost his temper as often as most people lose their sunglasses. His gravelly, hungover voice yelled from the phone, and I listened, then replied: "Okay, sure thing, sounds good then, thanks, sleep tight."

After hanging up, I told Captain Booby as gently and quickly as I could, "By the way, one tiny thing: All the girls should have their faces painted like the band KISS. See you tonight."

Night after night, concerts and the party rolled along, hitting every city in America. At any point during his show, the High Priest would flip me off, signaling there was a pretty girl in the audience he wanted to get backstage. Running along the barricade that separated the fans and the stage like a soldier in wartime, I would scan the audience, then lean over the barricade, trying to hand over the pass or stick it on the girl he'd seen.

Rabid fans saw the pass like it was the One Ring and would grab at me, jerking me by the arms into the crowd, turning me into an unwilling crowd surfer.

Miraculously able to hear my screams for help, tour manager Mike would grab my legs and try to pull me back to safety. I was a human rope in a heavy metal tug-of-war.

Before anyone was let backstage, they would have to produce identification that proved they were at least eighteen. The High Priest was never present for this part. He was backstage—the inner sanctum, as he liked to call it. Once word of these parties spread, girls trying to get backstage became very creative.

One time a pretty girl with a sly smile pulled her ID out of her back pocket and handed it to me. She was topless. One breast was meticulously airbrushed to show a pineapple-yellow sun coming up over green grass and a bird flying in front of the sun. The other was airbrushed indigo blue with a moon similar to Van Gogh's *Starry Night*.

The High Priest appeared unexpectedly, looking over my shoulder like Dracula. Lowering his sunglasses, he pointed his finger at her cleavage and said, "J.T. Experience, do you know what's in between these paintings?"

"No, what?"

"Brunch."

Another night, a girl with strawberry-blonde hair arrived with an older woman with identical hair, pleading to get backstage. The twenty-something girl was bare naked, wrapped in cellophane with a doorknob-sized sunflower covering her privates. The older woman was fully clothed, assuring me the younger girl was of age and handing me two driver's licenses.

"How do you know each other?" I asked, trying to process the cellophane dress.

"I'm her mother," the older woman proudly explained. It was like *Rock & Roll Jeopardy!* was *Rock & Roll Family Feud*. "Things wrapped in cellophane? Survey says—A High Priest of Crazy groupie!"

The parties were expected to be new and exciting on a regular basis, but that wasn't difficult because the High Priest had great ideas. In Chicago, he flew in a lady who was four feet tall with whipped cream–white hair to her waist who sang Christian songs on a knee-high plug-in Walmart karaoke machine.

Some of my high school buddies had been in the crowd, and miraculously the High Priest let me bring them backstage. A proud smile came across my face as they stuck the passes on their preppy multicolored ski jackets and high-fived as I led them back into the party.

In the dark locker room turned party den, the small lady, swaying left to right like the tail of a Kit-Cat wall clock, sang into a microphone the song "The Trumpet of Jesus." The High Priest, fresh out of a shower, his long hair longer, weighed down by the weight of the water, sat in a chair listening intently, the violet gemstone glued on his front tooth competing with the only light in the room, a Lite-Brite in the shape of Smurfs having sex glowing blue on the catering table.

No less than thirty girls sat at his feet, starstruck. The girls huddled together with their jet-black hair, fluorescent fishnet stockings, and safety pin piercings looked like the Bride of Frankenstein's bachelorette party. Two of the fans had scratched letters into their arms with a knife, giving themselves matching scab tattoos of his name.

As my Grosse Pointe friends nervously poured whiskey

and took in the scene, the High Priest threw a handful of Skittles that hit me like rainbow shrapnel, then hooked his finger in a circle summoning me over to him. Undoubtedly, he wanted to tell me "good job" in front of everyone. Wrong. He grabbed my shirt, pulling me to his face so hard our foreheads hit.

"Tell your ugly friends to buy every CD my small friend is selling or I'll stab you in the eyes and tell your mom you caught AIDS."

Somewhere in a Chicago shoe closet still lie three dozen Christian karaoke CDs, collecting dust.

Sometimes it was like passing my own shadow by the backstage door as local bands would be waiting to meet the High Priest, hoping to be discovered. I knew what that was like and I tried to make sure he knew they were there. After a show, I positioned a mohawk-haired singer to meet the High Priest by the tour bus. Handing his CD to him, the young hopeful excitedly proclaimed, "Our band is called Blood Everywhere."

"What's your first single called, 'Used Tampon'?" was the High Priest's reply. At least he took the CD.

Urine Trouble

Dust swirled up from the Oscar-the-Grouch-green–colored cat litter that smelled of lemon and pinecones as I filled a litter box to the rim. Gently, I ran with the ice-chest-heavy litter box down the backstage hallway into the pitch-dark arena as the sound of a haunted house church organ that was the band's intro tape grew louder. I placed the litter box on the ground yelling, "Hold up, hold up!"

Turning around to give him privacy, the High Priest of Crazy unzipped his sequin pants and urinated in the litter box as the intro music faded into a screeching guitar and the sold-out crowd roared like ancient Romans watching a gladiator about to get killed by a lion. The High Priest zipped up, then strutted onstage scowling, with his arms arched up like a werewolf.

The High Priest's manager had called me a few days before, bellowing about the money he was being charged because the High Priest was peeing before the shows behind the drum set on stages all across America like a dog wandering from fire hydrant to fire hydrant in the summer. "Last-minute nerves, I guess," I told the manager from the tour bus as we rolled through the night. The manager yelled through his phone like he was Yosemite Sam and I was Bugs Bunny, "This will be your last minute of the tour if you don't figure something out. If I'm in trouble YOU'RE in trouble. Fix it!"

I'd had enough of mopping at Tower Records, and thinking back to my cat, Pickles, I had as a kid, I went to Target and got a green litter box and some cat litter, and I believe that solution has been a staple of his shows ever since. I wasn't just basking in the glow of the High Priest's fame; I also wanted his management and possibly his record company to notice me as a good worker as well.

Maybe I could get a meeting with them about my music someday. I was eager to please. I had no interest in getting into a pissing match.

Vodka and Kool-Aid

Thanks to the tour, my passport has more stamps than an underage drinker's hand after a summer of hitting club shows. We traveled first class, all expenses paid. We went to so many cool places, all with different cultures and different languages—places like Europe, Russia, Iowa.

"Dad loves bragging on the golf course: 'J.T.'s seeing the

world on someone else's dime,' " Lance told me on a phone call home I'd made from a Ritz-Carlton in Paris overlooking the Eiffel Tower.

A flight attendant squished coffee cups into a small garbage bag with her hand as I lifted my tray table, stowed my new favorite book *The Grapes of Wrath*, and then wiped the dew off an airplane window. Looking down, I saw a city that was glowing in the dead of night, not from lights but because of the fresh-fallen sugar-white snow.

As we circled above the marshmallow world, I noticed that the runway lights were barely visible and that there were three feet of snow on the runway as well. I'm from Michigan, with its cold winters, and I've flown everywhere. If there's one thing I know, it's that a runway should be plowed. But we were not in Michigan—we were not in the USA, we were runway sliding into the old USSR, in Moscow, Russia.

"The runway isn't plowed!" I shrieked to the High Priest over my shoulder in the first-class cabin. Of all the High Priests of Crazy in the world, he's the High Priest-iest. His chipped red-painted fingernails grabbed the back of my seat and started shaking it as if we were crashing. I gripped the armrest of my chair like I was fighting with a Cub Scout for a newly discovered *Playboy* magazine. I laughed, pretending I wasn't scared. We skidded safely into a landing and were ushered through customs very quickly.

We were all assigned our own bodyguard, me included. I wasn't a rock star, I wasn't even part of the band, but when a man in a three-piece suit who looked like the Russian boxer from *Rocky IV* guided me through the airport, I felt like a superstar.

A motorcade of brand-new black SUVs awaited us, as if we were the traveling party of the president of the United States. It was after three a.m. but we were not headed to the hotel. With a police escort cutting our path, we ran every red light in the city, racing to the most popular nightclub in Moscow. In broken English the bodyguard said to me, "It is the new time in Russia, I watch out for you." I figured out he meant since it wasn't communist anymore, everyone was partying and having the time of their lives, but the economy wasn't doing well and the police hadn't been paid in forever. Anyone they stopped they tried to get money from, which is why we each had our own bodyguard in case we were just out and about. It felt like mice were running through my stomach I was so excited to be there.

The SUVs pulled up at the club and we were ushered past the velvet rope. Techno music played so loud I hope I can still have babies. Strobe lights flashed like cameras at a kid's birthday party as we entered the club, which was packed with revelers. A giant spiderweb made of ropes on the ceiling had women in costumes crawling through it like a Cirque du Soleil haunted house. Russian accents yelled the High Priest of Crazy's name, obviously knowing that he had sold-out concerts in the city.

We filed into a back room the size of a nice dance studio with a high ceiling, where the most expensive Russian vodka and caviar awaited us. There was even another DJ back there, but other than that we were by ourselves. "J.T. Experience, go out there and bring as many girls back here as you can," the High Priest yelled over the music. It wasn't difficult. Everyone wanted to meet him and everyone knew that we were in the VIP room. The club was zombie-swaying with the most striking women I've ever seen, as if I'd stepped into the George Michael "Freedom! '90" video starring the world's top models. I politely invited a group of ladies to come back into the VIP room, and they all happily joined us.

The High Priest nodded under his snakeskin cowboy hat, which I understood as "Invite more." I went back out, and next thing you know there were literally fifty girls in there, all of us dancing as the DJ, holding one headphone to his ear, spun "California Love" by Tupac. When a band arrives in a city, the promoter of the concert tries to show them the best time they've ever had. The Russian promoter was trying to do everything to make sure we were having a good time, and a good time had begun. It was four thirty in the morning.

Most of the girls spoke a little English. I was on the sweaty dance floor, sipping Beluga vodka with its invisible shade of honey and a spicy aftertaste, with a smiling girl whose eyes were the color of ice on fire, her body wrapped in a low-cut gold dress. All of a sudden, as if someone had yelled "Hey, Kool-Aid!" on the hottest day of the summer, a giant pink stuffed animal burst through the doors and everyone started cheering. The seemingly Barney the Dinosaur–sized walking, waving stuffed animal wasn't a big red pitcher of Kool-Aid with a smiley face on it, it was someone in a seven-foot penis costume.

We all laughed and cheered except the High Priest. He started chanting my name: "J.T.....J.T.....J.T." Before I could yell *nyet* (*no* in Russian), the penis came right for me like a heat-seeking missile. Everyone on the dance floor formed a wide circle around us like clubgoers did around break dancers in the '80s, so I began doing my best John Travolta poses as I cut a rug with the penis. Suddenly the porno-inspired Disney character started wrestling for my belt, trying to pull my pants down. I fought with him or her, thinking, *This is ridiculous. I'm not gonna be naked on somebody's camera.*

As we struggled, people were egging us on like it was USA versus the Soviets in a "Miracle on Ice" hockey fight, but I knew what no one else knew. I had boxer shorts on.

The chanting rose louder than the music, so the DJ stopped playing the record and was yelling my name through his microphone. Even my bodyguard cracked a Putin-style smile, which was not a good sign. The giant penis was wrestling with me so

Potty like a rockstar!

The South High School newspaper caught this picture of me onstage, standing at the intersection of "who I was and who I wanted to be."

Schoolhouse Rock! AKA: my third-grade artwork.

Dirty Trixx armed with eighth-grade attitude at the Battle of the Bands.

I rode my Huffy to the high school and taped these up in the girls' bathroom stalls.

My grades weren't that good, but my MTV moves got an A+ at the ninth-grade talent show.

Bad hair day? I had a bad hair year!

Sparty like a rockstar!
My superhero dad, Larry,
and me.

My beautiful mom,
Kendra, and me at a
wedding in Mexico.

The breast of times! An
average Tuesday night on a
rockstar's world tour.

Chester to the rescue. Bleeding from the head while opening for the great Linkin Park.

I mustache, who is your biological father? Jay Thomas and me after filming Dr. Phil.

Dropping beats, not bombs, for the troops in Afghanistan.

Kenny Chesney and me at the "Somewhere With You" number-one party.

Keith Urban and me celebrating our number-one song "Somewhere in My Car."

Sipping drinks with Blake Shelton at our number-one party for "Sangria."

After writing a song for them, I had my boy band moment hanging out back-stage with the Jonas Brothers.

Brothers from another mother! Lance teaches Jake how to hold me like a football.

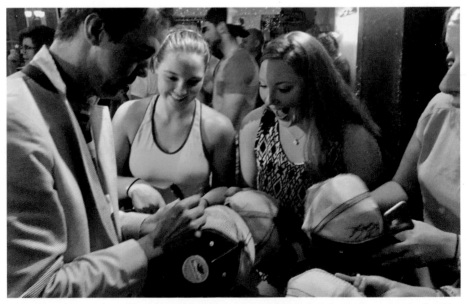

Another day at the office. Meeting fans after a Bluebird Cafe show in Nashville.

hard there was only one thing to do. I unbuttoned my top button as we hit the ground. As the penis pulled my pants down, I could feel my butt cheeks on the cold wooden floor, but luckily I was holding my boxer shorts up so as not to expose my most private area. The penis began bouncing on me, making my legs kick like a baby with a helium balloon tied to its foot.

Like a frat party cheering on a stripper, the band, the bodyguards, the Russian girls, and the promoter were clapping and laughing. I was losing this fight, when I felt a shift in the room, almost a gasp, and then silence.

Unbeknownst to me, the door had opened and an older silver-haired man with a stern face and a scar across his chin had entered the room with four bodyguards of his own. Crossing the room, parting the circle, he stopped above me. With the penis still, but still straddling me, I looked up from the floor right into the man's no-nonsense eyes. He stared at me like I had walked into a bar mitzvah dressed as a Christmas tree. It was Harrison Ford.

I said the only thing that came to mind: "I loved you in *Star Wars*..." Expressionless, he said simply, "I know," before taking a seat next to the High Priest across the room.[15]

The revelry resumed, everyone sipping and swaying. As I pulled my dance-floor-dusty black corduroys up, all I could think was *Everything I've ever heard about Russia is wrong*. No one was talking about the nuclear bomb or the Cold War, they wanted to get bombed on cold vodka.

Standing in front of a church-like building with hot-air-balloon-sized rooftops shaped like the Trolls' hairdos and painted in blue and green stripes, my bodyguard clicked a camera, taking pictures of me posing in front of the Kremlin like I had only seen presidents do. Climbing into a black SUV,

---

15 Ford was real. His response may have been the vodka in me.

I hummed the James Bond theme as we drove to Arbat Street to walk and shop.

Russia didn't disappoint. Strolling, I saw a man with a polar bear, a real live polar bear hooked to a chain on the street. He was trying to sell it. The police were there telling him to get the bear to a zoo. I also passed a woman carrying an orangutan dressed up as a clown in a white polka-dot pointed hat—a real orangutan, not a stuffed animal. Can you imagine if I had those waiting by the Skittles at the backstage party that night?

The High Priest, of course, put on shows of a lifetime. All the shows were sold out, and he had real Russian guards standing not only in front of the stage but on the stage like statues. They had on those cool fluffy ushanka-hats, and I traded the guards guitar picks for the hats to give to each of my brothers back home.

I put so many fluffy Russian hats in my suitcase I had to leave most of my clothes behind because they couldn't fit in the case. When I finally latched it closed, it was practically jiggling like you see in a Bugs Bunny cartoon. But the tour wasn't headed home yet. Our midnight flight was pointed to the land of the rising sun, Japan. A bucket-list wish for me. I was flying but I'd soon be falling.

Sushi with Mr. Potato Head

In Japan, the High Priest said something to me I'd never heard him say before: "Good morning." Since we were halfway across the world, the High Priest's internal clock was flipped so he was actually awake in the daytime, and he took me shopping in Japan. He was truly excited to show me sights and sounds he had already seen several times on previous tours.

A thin street with endless shops on both sides, the Harajuku shopping area of Tokyo was a kaleidoscope of colors. While out walking, we ran into the band Green Day, who were also on tour in Japan. The High Priest bought me an expensive vintage Levi's jacket with Japanese patches on it, and as we walked eating McDonald's fish sandwiches, he moaned as he chewed as if he were eating three-hundred-dollar-an-ounce caviar. "They don't taste this good in America," he announced on the crowded street where we both stood a foot taller than everyone else before he stopped in his tracks in front of a store window.

"I'm buying you that." He had an exceptional eye for fashion. Everything he wears he has designed himself. "You're wearing it and you can open up the show for us tonight." Growing up, I wore out the album *Cheap Trick at Budokan*. Opening a sold-out show in Japan was beyond a dream come true.

"HELLO, JAPAN!" Mike the tour manager's voice ping-ponged through the arena like a monster truck rally announcer's. "Please welcome, from the mean streets of Detroit Rock City, the J.T. EXPERIENCE." The High Priest had given me that name. Cutting up newspaper headlines, then scattering them about to come up with song lyrics for himself one night, he explained, "You're like Jimi Hendrix but you're white with no rhythm." Keyboards and electronic drums blasted through the giant wall of speakers. Mike handed me the microphone, half smiling, half terrified.

The curtain dropped like a guillotine, and ten thousand Japanese faces greeted me. There I stood in the spotlight, in the outfit the High Priest had purchased. It was a full-body, skin-colored zip-up onesie that looked like a cartoon of a naked woman.

On the package of the suit was a Japanese man in the outfit, smiling like he won the lottery. Earlier in the day, the High Priest—in sequin sunglasses and sequin top hat—had pulled out his American Express card, placed it on the counter, and said, "We'll take the Mangina outfit."

The crowd gasped as I began. It was not my CD I was singing along to; it was Britney Spears's "...Baby One More Time," the High Priest's choice. Dancing across the stage, I sang over the track in the naked lady suit. My face, painted by the High Priest, was white with a red circle around my nose in honor of the Japanese flag. I looked like a rodeo clown on acid.

Through the years, Japanese audiences have been rumored to politely applaud sitting in their seats at concerts. Pictures in magazines and tour documentaries of famous bands I'd watched showed Japanese audiences completely quiet and still through hit songs.

They were standing and cheering wildly, unrestrained, as if it were a surprise birthday party for me. Who knows who they thought I was. The more I danced, the more they screamed and reached for me.

The High Priest was on the side of the stage filming me with his video camera. In my peripheral vision I saw his bandmates laughing. The High Priest, like a rabid dog, shoved one of them, screaming, "You don't know a genius performance artist when you see one. Shut up or I'll stab you and drink the blood!" They stood like scolded children as he filmed.

Hands outstretched over the barricades trying to reach me and white spotlights on me made my blood rush. It was glorified karaoke but so what? I was onstage and the fans were going ballistic. They were dying to touch me. Cameras flashed like fireflies in the audience.

I had not seen the High Priest stomping his cowboy boots and enjoying himself like this since we watched his favorite group, Munch's Make Believe Band, at a Chuck E. Cheese on a day off in Poughkeepsie.

Dropping the mic on purpose, I raised my arms. The crowd was in a frenzy, all their hands in the air imitating me. I had never stage-dove before and knew this was my moment to do so. Running toward the edge of the stage, I dove like

Batman taking flight over the crowd, knowing I'd land softly in their loving arms.

Remember the scene in *The Ten Commandments* when Moses parts the Red Sea? That's exactly what the crowd did. With army-like precision they all moved out of the way, half to the left and half to the right in the blink of an eye. Like an airplane without an engine, I crash-landed at top speed face-first on the floor of the arena.

My fake boobs deflated and my knees were covered in grime as a white-gloved Japanese security guard helped me up. The security guard looked at me concerned, like he was seeing a Mr. Potato Head with its nose where the eyes should be, a sideways ear instead of red lips for a mouth. I was in a daze. I did not pass out but my head hurt like when I'd eaten ice cream too fast. The house lights came on and ten thousand people politely clapped like I'd won Best in Show.

Take a Bow

Japanese schoolkids slid coins into a refrigerator-sized, water-filled glass claw machine game, where a live lobster was the prize and not a stuffed *Toy Story* character. Electronic billboards showed Brad Pitt advertising jeans and Eddie Murphy selling cars. Wandering the streets of Tokyo at night while everyone slept was a once-in-a-lifetime experience I wasn't going to miss. The neon streets were blazing every color of the rainbow, flashing on all sides as I walked the crowded streets like I was inside a video game.

In a toy store I bought Ultraman action figures—my older brother, Lee, would've loved it. We watched *Ultraman* on TV as kids but I had never seen merchandise from it. Ultraman has an entirely silver and red body. Every episode ended with Ultraman defeating Godzilla and becoming extremely weak:

Ultraman's Color Timer, which is connected to his heart, starts blinking, alerting him to fly back to his home planet in the nick of time. In an eye-level tent with steam rising from it on a walking bridge, I ate sushi rolls as thick as my wrist, with wasabi so hot it made my scalp itch.

In a Starbucks connected to the hotel, a barista looked at me, puzzled, as I ordered. "Mocha Frappuccino? I'm sorry, I only speak English. It's like ice and coffee blended up, zoom zoom zoom." Spinning my fingers in a circle, I tried to explain.

The sweet Japanese barista didn't understand. Reaching under the counter, she pulled out a plastic menu. It was like a Waffle House menu but instead of smothered and covered egg dishes it had all the Starbucks drinks pictured on it. "Yes, this one. Thank you." I smiled as I pointed at my drink of choice. She smiled back and bowed.

Whispers behind me caught my attention. It was a small group of Japanese schoolgirls pointing at me.

If they thought it was funny that I used the plastic menu, no biggie, I wasn't embarrassed. Two Japanese businessmen holding briefcases joined them and whispered too. I wasn't interested in whatever they were talking about. Pushing the paper off a green straw, I grabbed my drink and headed to the door.

One of the men put up his hand to stop me. "Dude, I paid for this, it's okay," I said defensively. "Mangina!" he yelled. The schoolgirls clapped and hopped in place, overjoyed. One of the girls held up a popular Japanese rock magazine. The magazine's centerfold was a picture of me in the outfit, standing with the monster-mask-wearing heavy metal band Slipknot.

I had not seen the picture. Slipknot were part of the tour and I vaguely remembered them dumping water on my head as a camera flashed, but I was seeing stars after my fall and I thought I might have imagined it all. I autographed the magazine as one by one the girls took my picture and said "Thank you" over and over while bowing.

Everywhere I went near the hotel I was recognized. The next day I mailed a postcard home. On the back of a picture of the Technicolor Tokyo skyline, I wrote, *Dear Mom and Dad, I'm big in Japan.*

We partied like it was 1999, but the year 2000 had rung in and the High Priest was slumped over in the back of his limo like a Muppet without a hand in it. When we arrived at his Hollywood Hills house, he opened his bloodshot eyes. They looked like road maps. The High Priest tour had come to an end, and a phone call the night before let him know that so had his romantic relationship with a famous actress.

He tousled my hair like an older brother would and then spoke, his hungover voice sounding like he swallowed a wasp. "J.T. Experience, you can sleep with the girls you put in your videos, but never put the girl you sleep with in your videos." He disappeared into his house.

The High Priest of Crazy was good to me for the most part, but after twelve months, the tour that for so long had made me feel warm in the glow of this star's fame began to feel like sitting in a bath that had gone cold. The Color Timer connected to my own heart was starting to blink. I wanted to write hit songs, not be an assistant.

Gently placing the High Priest's suitcases inside the door of his house, I locked the door with his security code, which was easy to memorize: #313. He had told me in all seriousness that 313 was the number of the exact frame on the Zapruder film that JFK had been shot in. Lovely.

Smog concealed the afternoon Hollywood sun as I heard the clinking sound of steel tools being picked up and placed back on the concrete in the High Priest's driveway. There, the High Priest's father, who I recognized from pictures, was working on a motorcycle.

The tools sounded just like my dad's tools had when I was growing up in Grosse Pointe. "Hi, I'm J.T. I work for your son," I happily introduced myself. "Sir, I know this sounds funny, but you remind me of my dad." The High Priest's father, tightening a screw with a socket wrench, replied, "Why, is he fucking your mother too?"

A German girl had wrapped her arms around my waist on a midnight scooter ride through the streets of Berlin. Sushi had melted on my tongue like cotton candy in Japan. I had seen the sunrise paint the rocks flamingo pink through a tour bus window in Sedona, Arizona, and the lights over the Kremlin from a seat in a private jet. I had lived a movie. The tour was a fun wild ride, full of bumps and bruises that might have been hickeys, worthy of its own book, but I was done being an assistant. I was worn out. Even my hair hurt, but I was burning with musical ambition.

The High Priest's music is pretty epic. His showmanship was top-notch. His nightly costume and set changes would make any musical director on Broadway envious. But a lot of bands that opened up for him were walking earaches. I kept thinking, *How do these goofballs have songs on the radio and I don't?* Song ideas were purring to me from the universe, telling me to get to work and get my music heard.

Immediately, other famous bands started calling me to work for them. Word had spread about the assistant who threw big parties backstage. I politely declined all offers. There was no way I was going to spend my life working for bands. I wasn't going to sing karaoke as Mangina. I was going to write songs that people sang at karaoke bars.

CHAPTER 14

Linked In

I answered my cell phone. "J.T., it's Mike! Are you in the naked lady outfit?" I heard him laugh. My head hurt at the memory of my concrete belly flop. "No, Mike, I'm not, but you can borrow it anytime." He chuckled. "No thanks, my wife wouldn't approve." It had been months since we spoke—it was good to hear a friendly voice.

"Linkin Park needs an assistant. You're the only person I'm recommending. The tour is sold out and we leave in two days. The money is double what the High Priest paid you."

At the time, Linkin Park were selling millions and millions of records. Their songs were on every radio station. Pop, heavy metal, and alternative music fans alike embraced them. The money didn't interest me. Something else about them was far more enticing.

Like Madonna, Bon Jovi, and other forward-thinking rock stars, Linkin Park had their own record label. Through it, they were discovering artists and sharing them with their gigantic following. Going back to Tower Records was not appealing. My love for Los Angeles had faded. I was living in an apartment complex that was so LA, both ends of the pool were shallow. I took the job.

At our first meeting, the six members of Linkin Park introduced themselves to me with polite confidence. They seemed so different from one another. Chester looked like a punk rocker, covered in tattoos. You would never mess with him in an alley, but he was laughing and friendly. Mike, in a black baseball cap and baggy pants, was serious, focused, and seemed like an East LA rapper. Joe the DJ, a Korean American, had the coolest tennis shoes I'd ever seen. Brad, the skinny guitarist and riff master, with his brown bushy Afro and beard, looked like Bob Ross's son. Phoenix on bass had a shaved head and reminded me of an action movie hero.

Rob, the hard-hitting power drummer, was surprisingly soft-spoken. His mom had dated the drummer of Aerosmith years before. She took Rob to see them in concert as a child, and his destiny was sealed after that.

Linkin Park seemed like they all had such different personalities, but collectively they were six arrows shooting at the same target and hitting the bullseye worldwide. Incredibly focused, incredibly talented. No wonder they were the biggest-selling band on the planet.

They had three rules for backstage: no alcohol, no drugs, and no guests of any kind for anyone. They were all married or in great relationships.

On tour I didn't see them much during the day. They weren't sleeping—they were either at the gym working out, doing autograph signings, or holding interviews. Always working, always promoting.

They were incredibly low maintenance. Going from the High Priest of Crazy to Linkin Park was like a soldier shell-shocked from war returning home to work at a yogurt shop. It was such a change of pace it almost gave me whiplash.

In each arena, unpacking and setting up Linkin Park's Xbox backstage, which they loved playing to relax, was my first task.

Their bedroom closet–sized black road cases on wheels were rolled in by roadies. I'd unlock them so they could access their stage clothes, which happened to be similar to their regular clothes. Local menus, so they could order food in if they were hungry after the show, were gathered from a runner and placed by the Xbox. That's it. It took about an hour. The rest of my day was open.

Grabbing one of their many guitars and a handful of guitar picks with the LP logo, I'd write songs in the empty backstages of arenas across America.

Growing up, I'd often wondered why so many backstage pictures of my heroes Van Halen had metal gym lockers behind them. Now I knew.

"Backstage" was the local sports teams' locker rooms when concerts weren't in town. Despite the sour smell of sweat left by athletes that had competed there the night before, the giant showers had great acoustics. A dozen new songs came to life with me singing and playing guitar standing fully clothed in those arena showers.

Lead singer Mike Shinoda, before a show, would gently slide off his wedding ring and hand it to me to keep it from being stolen or dinged when the band played. Taking the ring in my hand as we stood quietly, I never asked him to listen to my songs.

Chester Bennington had me escort his family with him to his tour bus after the show every night. Walking past all the fans yelling his name, I didn't brag to Chester about my own music.

Linkin Park DJ Joe Hahn, guitarist Brad Delson, and drummer Rob Bourdon ate with me regularly. Out of respect, I never forced my music on them. It wasn't my style anymore and I was there to work.

Strutting into the dressing room before sound check like the Warriors gang, they would see me plucking out a melody and writing lyrics on the back of napkins with the Xbox game *Halo* blinking at the ready. They eventually realized on their own that I was writing songs.

They were intrigued to hear what I was writing and

impressed that I had been signed to EMI. I was laying out a dozen Sharpies on a large folding table for them before their daily meet and greet with fans, when the band asked me if I wanted to open up the show for them.

This was not going to be Britney Spears karaoke in a foreign country. This was me singing my songs in front of a sold-out crowd in the USA, and I jumped at the opportunity. They said I could do three songs.

Linkin Park had a few bands touring with them. Really loud, wild, heavy metal bands would open their shows. One band wore heavy tribal makeup I thought was frightening—until I saw their actual faces and I realized the makeup was an improvement.

"J.T. is on the move," Mike Shinoda informed the entire road crew, who were all connected through their walkie-talkies. A stubble-faced roadie with cigarette breath put a wireless pack on my guitar, telling me, "You can move around onstage freely without a guitar cord, go nuts." He gave me a confident thumbs-up. We were in Kansas, I was going to go on between the makeup metal band and Linkin Park. Mike was talking into a walkie-talkie as if he were my bodyguard.

Black acoustic guitar, black pants, and a thin black jacket zipped all the way up, I was dressed and ready as the band triumphantly led me to the stage like a bachelor about to get married. It was a blast.

The house lights went dark, letting the audience know it was showtime. The stage was pitch black. Twenty thousand people screamed. It was go-time on the biggest stage I'd ever been on. Exactly as I had pictured it countless times in my living room as a kid.

As if God himself had punched a hole in the night sky, a single bright white spotlight from the back of the arena clicked on and shone down on me. The sold-out crowd's hollers of excitement morphed into twenty thousand sad Charlie Brown faces. They all groaned. The crowd thought Linkin Park were coming out. Nobody had thought to introduce me, a simple— but embarrassing—oversight.

"Hello, Kansas! I'm a friend of Linkin Park. I'm gonna do a couple songs that I wrote," I offered into the microphone as it shrieked with nails-on-a-chalkboard–sounding feedback. Strumming a fast rhythm on my acoustic guitar, I sang: "Two motels and a mannequin factory is all this town has to offer you and me…"

The song was called "The Living Dead," a Bruce Springsteen–esque song I'd written one morning on the empty tour bus, about a small-town kid who felt lost in life. Little did I know that I was about to become the living dead. An avalanche of *boos* drowned out my song. I kept strumming and singing. Linkin Park had invited me to play—the audience would catch on.

Thirty seconds in I had the crowd chanting. Have you ever stood on a concert stage and had the crowd chanting along? I can still hear them: "You suck you suck you suck." But I wasn't leaving that stage. The crowd wanted Linkin Park, but I was defiant. "Okay, Kansas, you want to take me on? Then take on me!" My voice ricocheted like a racquetball through the giant arena as I blasted into the poppy chorus of the iconic '80s hit "Take On Me" by a-ha.

It was one of my favorite MTV videos. I'd learned how to play it on acoustic guitar even though it was a keyboard drummachine song. I was ahead of my time—a band not long after did a remake of it and did have a hit with it.

Suddenly what sounded like hail hitting the roof of a car at the beginning of a big thunderstorm—*tink tink tink clink clink clink*—caught my ears. The stage was starting to get covered with bouncing pennies, dimes, ice, Bic lighters, and the obligatory single shoe.

The crowd now was foaming at the mouth for Linkin Park. Anything not tied down was being thrown at the stage, but I kept playing and singing. Something hit me above my eyebrow that I thought was a rogue flying shoestring. Using my shoulder, I kept trying to rub it off my eye quickly in between playing chords, but it wouldn't budge. Like a young Luke Skywalker learning to use his light saber, I used my guitar to deflect the debris being thrown.

Amid the chaos, the crowd miraculously changed gears. They suddenly started cheering with excitement. True rock 'n' roll yelling and cheering. I'd finally won them over.

I felt an arm around my shoulder. Looking to my right, there was Chester of Linkin Park. The crowd was cheering for him. He'd come to my rescue. He was frowning like a concerned parent but he was laughing slightly as well. He wiped my eye with his hand. Turns out it wasn't a shoestring over my eye—it was a trickle of blood as wide as a stick of gum.

This wasn't chocolate syrup left over from the High Priest tour either—it was real blood. My blood. Someone had thrown a quarter at me and slit my forehead on impact. I didn't feel a thing when it happened. Onstage I'm the superhero version of myself. Now, seeing the blood on my guitar, I realized I was human.

"This guy has more balls than all of you put together!" Chester yelled into my microphone like an angry preacher damning his congregation. Pretty girls and frat guys in the front row were screaming, "Chester, I love you!" He didn't have to come out and scold his fans, but he did.

Chester put his forehead on my shoulder as we left the stage laughing like two teenagers drunk on their first beer. Roadies ran out onstage with massive brooms. They were pushing all the debris off the stage, there were literally piles of coins. "Well, if nothing else, J.T. got paid to sing!" they shouted to each other.

A nurse wearing blue gloves pressed a tiny bandage above my eyebrow. Looking at my reflection in the glass of the first aid office and seeing the blood on my forehead, I felt dizzy. My face changed shape as if I was looking at myself in a fun-house mirror. "You'll be fine. Just keep this on it for a few days. You're lucky it didn't hit your eye." Leaving the first aid room knowing I had a job to do, I walked fast to check on the band, who were due onstage. No doubt they would be annoyed I had been gone so long.

The band's faces were red when I entered. They were laughing and rolling on the floor when I walked in. They had unplugged the Xbox and were glued to the big-screen TV glowing in front of them. DJ Joe, who directed all of Linkin Park's award-winning MTV videos, had filmed my performance. In slow motion you could see a shiny object fly from the right and my head flinch to the left. The band kept rewinding it over and over with tears of laughter in their eyes when the quarter struck me. Shiny object from the right, head to the left. Right, left, right, left.

The next day, on the front page of the Kansas paper was the concert review. The last paragraph of the review said, "The opening act was a one-man band called the JT Experience who, despite bleeding from the head, finished a promising three-song set." Over the review was a half page–sized color picture of Chester coming to my rescue onstage.

Squeezing past a maid's cleaning cart full of fresh towels and tiny shampoo bottles, I heard "Follow Me" by Uncle Kracker playing over hallway speakers as I left the hotel that day. Knowing Uncle Kracker was from Detroit, I was impressed to see his "Follow Me" video and hear the song all over the world as I crisscrossed the globe.

"J.T.! J.T.!" young voices shouted as the glass doors of the lobby slid open. Just as I was recognized in Japan by High Priest fans, Linkin Park fans waiting by the tour buses asked for my autograph and gladly accepted copies of my Brinkerhoff-funded CD now titled "J.T. Experience" that I carried with me.

Eventually one of those CDs was played by a teenage Linkin Park fan in a car with her parents. The parents had a friend who worked at the biggest music publishing company in the world and sent them the CD. That friend played it for their boss.

I'd written my phone number in black Sharpie on every copy of the CD. One day in a San Antonio hotel room as I lightly rubbed my finger above my eye, feeling my rock 'n' roll battle scar, my cell phone rang. I was offered a writing deal on the spot by the head of that music publishing company.

"J.T., we are based in LA, but we have offices in London, New York, and Nashville. Your lyrics are like three-minute movies. I'd like to send you to Nashville. You'll be Songwriter of the Year someday, I have no doubt." Linkin Park were gracious as ever when I told them I had landed a deal and wouldn't be their assistant anymore. They told me to let them know if I ever needed advice.

I was still J.T. Harding when I returned to Nashville to write and record, but now I was stronger and wiser than I'd ever been before.

CHAPTER 15

"Party Like a Rockstar"

Tim McGraw's "Live Like You Were Dying" was coming through the radio as surfers floated like bobbers waiting for a wave to carry them to shore outside the window of my car on my drive from Los Angeles up the Pacific Coast Highway to Jay Thomas's dream house in Santa Barbara. The house had a pool that his two sons—my new brothers—Sam and Jake would be in all day playing water volleyball, then after dinner we'd stay up super late playing Xbox in the den.

Over time, my biological father and I had become good friends. It was 2004, girls were melting over the movie *The Notebook*, George W. Bush was about to be re-elected president.

Watching Sam and Jake grow up, I've felt my heart beat in places that I didn't know existed. They are also enamored with my brother Lance. His beer-drinking adventures were of endless fascination to them. I even told them not to call him Lance but by his Native American name, Dances with Budweisers.

Visiting New York City the previous Christmas, all of us were on the subway after dinner. As the subway rattled along under the city that never sleeps, Lance was snoring in his seat. "Let's get off and leave Lance and see what happens," I whispered to Sam and Jake.

The subway closed its doors and pulled away from us,

heading from Times Square to the Bronx late at night. Lance, with his head and MSU hat leaning against the map of Manhattan, was still on it, sound asleep. Jake and Sam looked at me in shock. I was howling.

An hour later Lance walked a few miles back to the hotel in the snow without a coat. Opening the door, Sam said, "I'm so glad you're okay, you must be freezing." Lance belly flopped onto our hotel room loveseat, his football-player-sized body overwhelming it like a butterfly net trying to catch a cannonball. His hair was frozen stiff from his walk in the snow.

"Feels good outside! It's refreshing! You guys act like I've never fallen asleep on a subway before and missed my stop," Lance announced. Sam and Jake *cheers*-ed him with their minibar Dr Peppers.

Jay's amazing wife, Sally, hugged me and offered me the key to their house the day we met. She has been gracious and accepting of me from day one. I spent many weekends at their house working on songs.

Surrounded by empty Slurpee cups, crumpled Doritos bags, and bean dip jars scraped clean, I sat alone one night after Sam and Jake went to bed.

Unzipping my guitar from its case, I started working on a song with a title I had written down on a receipt and put in my sock a week earlier.

Why my sock? So I wouldn't forget it when I put my pants in the wash and it was lost in my pocket. This was before you could make endless notes full of titles and song ideas on your cell phone. Anytime I took off my socks, little pieces of paper would fall out, little ideas that would possibly lead me to gold...or better yet, platinum.

On a date at a club with a girl one night, her ex-boyfriend passed us. As he walked by, she said to him, "Long time no see. What have you been up to?" He didn't stop. He had a

Ryan Gosling–handsome face and the collar of his polo shirt popped up. He smiled as he danced by, raising his drink, and replied, "Just partying like a rock star."

That phrase, "partying like a rock star," stuck in my head when he said it. It sounded like it was echoing over the speakers at a baseball game. Song titles still do that to me. I can't explain it, when someone says something that my brain instinctually knows is a good title, the words they are saying echo in my head. It's otherworldly.

These days the phrase *party like a rock star* is used so much it's a cliché, but at that time I had never heard it before. Picking the guitar on the couch, I started the song as a ballad.

Slowly strumming, sadly singing "got a broken heart again, must be the millionth time, you're out with all your friends, I'm home alone and crying, you said we'd last forever, forever came at noon, tonight there's only one thing to do." Then I BLASTED into the chorus like Metallica with an acoustic guitar: "I'M GONNA PARTY LIKE A ROCKSTAR! HIT A BUNCH OF STRIP BARS, WAKE UP NAKED IN A HOTEL ROOM!" Jumping off the couch, I fist-pumped the air in Jay's den. The melody and words and chords came in one flash. It felt like a hit. I have no idea what made me write it starting slow, then into the surprise up-tempo chorus, it just happened.

Rock star images were needed. Steven Tyler of Aerosmith came to mind. "I guarantee you Steven Tyler doesn't put up with shit like this" was added. Billy Joel had recently been in a fender bender, so "find a telephone pole to wrap around my car" was added.

In "Gin and Juice," Snoop Dogg sings of smoking indo. What is indo? I have no idea, but it rhymed with my lyric "throw my TV out the window" perfectly, and it was another rock star party image, so indo was added. Then at the end of the song, to get my imagined eighty thousand people singing along, I sang "everybody say *party*" a few times.[16] It added a fresh punch at the end of the song that's easy to sing along with.

It's the best feeling when a brand-new song comes together. This was one of the first songs I brought to Nashville to begin my songwriting career. "Party Like a Rockstar" was recorded in a recording studio on my first trip to Nashville on Music Row. Music Row is a typical street you would find in any suburban town, with two-story houses stretching one after the other for a mile between the moss-green lawns of Belmont University and a once-famous five-story hotel now turned apartment building with a swimming pool shaped like a guitar. But there aren't families in these houses; they are now crowded with songwriters working every day.

The once-upon-a-time living rooms are now usually a front office, and the bedrooms hold a couple of chairs and a table and gold albums on the walls. The houses still have kitchens filled with beers, water, and Reese's Pieces, but instead of kids rifling through the snacks about to work on algebra problems, songwriters are thinking of much more pressing issues like "what rhymes with Volkswagen."[17] There's even an old redbrick fire hall that has been turned into a space for songwriters.

In New York and Los Angeles, you can't even get into the parking lot of a publishing company, and there are metal detectors at the doors of record companies. Not in Nashville. In Music City, you can walk right through the front door and introduce yourself like a neighbor asking for a cup of sugar, and it's pretty awesome.

---

16 Adding a new, unexpected, but simple melody at the end of a song keeps the listener engaged. Prince has a similar "party" chant at the end of his classic "1999."

17 If you think of a rhyme for that, DM me on Instagram @jtxrockstar

Myspace was new then, and I had "Party Like A Rockstar" playing on my Myspace page. Taking my cue from the High Priest of Crazy tour, the JTXPERIENCE was my one-man band name.

As I had hoped, the song made people want to party, and people started writing me and sharing the song on their own Myspace pages. A small buzz was growing around the song. Kid Kelly, a high-energy and influential disc jockey on Sirius-XM Hits 1 who talks like he pours Monster drinks on his Cheerios—the most listened-to pop music radio station in the world—added the song to its rotation.

Adjusting the mirrors in my airport rental car on a visit home to Michigan, I noticed the car had satellite radio. I turned the channel to Hits 1 just in case I might hear my song.

Driving out of the lot, I was not even past the yellow ARRIVALS AND DEPARTURES airport sign when a robotic voice came over the station: "THIS IS HITZZZZ ONE AND THIS IZZZ JTXPERIENCE—'PARTY LIKE A ROCKSTAR.'" I almost drove off the road. The song title was flashing across the black-and-orange radio screen like a high score on a Donkey Kong game.

Merging onto the highway as the song played, I had to remind myself to breathe. It was the first time I had ever heard a song I wrote on the radio. My mind flashed to all the people who might be hearing it at that exact moment. Kids cleaning the house or bored in their rooms, teenagers throwing a Frisbee at the beach or driving around their small towns. They could all be staring at the radio and turning up my song. The mystery and magic of music coming out of a radio that had charmed me from earliest memories of singing "Yellow Submarine" and walking around the rock station WRIF had welcomed me in.

Like finding the lost diary of a girl you longed for long ago and learning she felt the same way about you, it was a euphoric feeling, and to this day it never gets old.

Every time I hear a song I've written on the radio, I get that excited feeling like I'm living in a movie. Thanks to Sirius-XM, "Party Like a Rockstar" was added to big pop radio stations in Arkansas, Connecticut, Colorado, Kansas, and two stations in the great state of Michigan—a station in Traverse City and also 89X in Detroit. I shortened the band name to JTX after kids started tagging me in pictures and holding up handwritten signs at my shows that simply read JTX. It seemed like a good logo and surely it was easier to spell.

Arriving in a rented van to an Arkansas nightclub as the sun set on Little Rock, I saw a line of people snaking out the door and all the way down the block past where my new band and I had parked. We rolled our amps and drums through the back door, and the club owner greeted us in the Pine Sol–lemon-smelling backstage. Excited to be playing for such a crowd, I asked, "Who are we opening for?" The owner laughed. "J.T., there's no other act—everyone's here to see you guys."

In Detroit I had assembled a new band. We played as JTX in all the cities where "Party Like a Rockstar" had become a favorite, and the shows were sold out. The power of radio.

The plastic metallic-colored cordless phone constantly rang at my parents' condo. Record companies started calling the house looking for me, but not to offer me a record deal, as I had hoped and dreamed and longed for. They were calling to ask how on earth I was able to get my song on all these stations they wanted their acts on. I had no idea. Luck, talent, some combination of the two? Who knows? All I know is that I'm still writing hits.

The Father, the Son, the Holy…Shit!

"My son J.T., who I gave away as a child, has a hit record on his hands!" Jay Thomas emoted to the listeners who tuned in to his daily talk show on SiriusXM. Jay also filled in every Friday for Howard Stern on the Howard 100 XM channel. Jay had a huge audience. Leaning in close, whispering into his mic like a hypnotist sharing his sage advice with the masses, he added: "So, parents, take it from me. Give your children away, let someone else raise them, and when they are grown and making money, open your arms and welcome them back into your life like I have. Here's 'Party Like a Rockstar' by *my* illegitimate son—JTX!" He would play the song daily. I loved it.

Being that Jay was well known, gossip columns started mentioning his story about me, and then his agent called to report that television shows were interested in interviewing us, and would we be interested? There are two things I never turn down: sex and a chance to be on TV. It was a surefire way to promote my music as well.

People holding handwritten signs displaying their hometowns on them huddled in Rockefeller Center trying to get on camera as Jay and I arrived at the *Today* show with Kathie Lee and Hoda. They were so fun and full of energy, I've been a fan ever since. On the show during the interview, Kathie Lee was talking about the song and pointed to my shirt, which said—what else?—PARTY LIKE A ROCKSTAR. "Kathie Lee, if I gave you this shirt, would you wear it?" I asked. "Of course," she replied, looking flattered.

On live television I pulled my shirt off over my head, revealing underneath a black lacy Victoria's Secret bra over my chest. Every cameraman, TV assistant, makeup person, and Kathie Lee and Hoda went wild with laughter.

People all over America spitting out their Frosted Mini-Wheats, saying "What the…?" was what I imagined in my head. Jay had no idea I was going to do that. As the camera rolled he had his hands over his eyes, shaking his head from left to right, saying a bleeped-out "Holy shit, holy shit." Kathie Lee, popping her eyebrows up and down like Groucho Marx, smelled my shirt on camera.

Now before you think I always wear a bra or have a Victoria's Secret–inspired fetish, no, I don't. To be noticed and remembered and talked about was the reason for the wardrobe change.

Before the show, backstage in the greenroom, one of Jay's fellow employees, SiriusXM disc jockey Madison, was kind enough to secretly loan me her bra. She quietly took it off in the restroom; when she came out she slyly handed it to me and I snuck into the restroom and slipped it on.

Jay was mortified but it worked. When my plane touched down back in Michigan, a voice mail from the *Today* show was on my phone. They wanted me back the very same week.

They flew me back to New York and put me up in a lavish hotel, all expenses paid. This time the bra was gone but my guitar was in my hands. JTX in big letters was written on it so people watching TV would have a visual to remember my name. The segment was a panel about dating advice. They asked me to sing a quick little song about men going on dates.

At some point Kathie Lee's red-bottomed high-heeled shoe came off in my hand as I was crawling and barking like a dog. Yes, on live television. Once again it worked: On the top of AOL and Yahoo! News the next day was my picture with the Guitar Hero video game font, but the headline read GUITAR ZERO.

My phone was blowing up—radio stations, friends, relatives. Everyone was talking about the TV appearances and about "Party Like a Rockstar." Once again it was "wheels up" as another show flew Jay and me back to NYC.

A stagehand wearing a headset with headphones and a microphone by his mouth was standing behind me as I waited in the wings offstage at the show *Fox & Friends*. The stagehand was older than me, he had long gray hair and a handlebar mustache that curled out like angel wings. His hand was on my shoulder as he listened for his cue to cue me.

"My family's from New Orleans. My dad called me the White Tornado when I came home on breaks from college. It wasn't a compliment. I had J.T. then but I was too young to care for him properly." Jay first told his story alone, sitting with the hosts. Ideas ran through my head lightning quick. Slipping off my pants, dropping them on the floor (I had boxer shorts on), I whispered to the stage guy over my shoulder: "Don't worry, I'm just trying to kick it up a notch out there." As if the Woodstock pot was still flowing through his veins, he whispered back, "Do what you have to do, man. Do... what...you...have...to...do."

Out on the stage, the host said, "What an inspiring and touching story, Jay. Let's welcome your son J.T." The stagehand tapped my shoulder to go. I came on high-kicking like a Rockette with hairy legs in my underwear, and the live studio audience of a few hundred mostly women tourists erupted like they were at Chippendales.

Jay was flabbergasted once again. That night, a late-night TV gossip show presented a clip of the hit series *Ghost Hunters*, where the hosts used an infrared camera to investigate a pitch-black haunted coal mine. On the episode they were terrified, breathing heavily, inching through the coal mine.

In the pivotal scene they slowly opened a cobweb-covered door in the mine, then they screamed as from behind the door, out ran...ME IN MY UNDERWEAR! The gossip show had edited my *Fox & Friends* clip into the *Ghost Hunters* scene. I always say, "If you want to be a star you've got to learn how to shine."

Jay and I were interviewed by *People*, *Entertainment Tonight*, and Dr. Phil, who it was a thrill to meet. Leaning into me on camera, Dr. Phil asked, "What did you think when you first met Jay?" I replied, "OH NO, I'M GONNA BE BALD!"

The audience laughed and Dr. Phil put his hand on my arm and in his famous fatherly voice said, "Hey, worse things could happen."

The audience laughed louder. The Dr. Phil joke was innocent. It honestly never crossed my mind that he had no hair. He was incredibly gracious and made a point of asking me on-air about my song and how people could find it. That episode of *Dr. Phil* still plays on reruns and is easy to find on YouTube. People text me often to say, "You're on *Dr. Phil* right now."

Backstage at another show a well-dressed woman with black curly hair stared disapprovingly at Jay from across the room. "Oh shit, that's Casey Kasem's daughter," Jay whispered, emptying some coffee in a garbage can to make room for creamer.

"Wow, she looks mad. Did you get her pregnant too?" I smirked.

"No, I said 'Walk like an Egyptian, smell like an Arab' once on the air. Her dad hated me ever since."

"That was you? I read about that in the paper growing up. I loved Casey Kasem." The past and the present kept on colliding as Jay and I got to know each other.

Being on TV was a blast. Total strangers recognized me on the street or when I was shopping.

By this time Facebook was a thing. My Facebook in-box was full of messages from people around the world who had seen Jay and me on TV and wanted to share their adoption stories with me. The attention reminded me of a quote I love: "When you're smiling, the whole world smiles with you." Well, almost everyone.

"Have you been watching these TV shows? Fuckin' classic, right?" I said, laughing into my cell phone as I waited in a line of cars at an In-N-Out Burger drive-through.

"Uh-huh," Lance replied on the other end of the phone

with as much enthusiasm as a teenager locked out of a strip club.

"What's the matter?" I asked as I sipped a black-and-white milkshake.

He replied, "You are the nicest, most selfish person I've ever known." I could tell he wasn't kidding.

"What are you talking about?" I asked before he sternly said, "Mom wanted to meet Dr. Phil."

"Oh man, she didn't tell me that." I sighed as he cut me off, yelling like Gordon Ramsay looking at subpar grilled cheese.

"She shouldn't have to! You're so caught up in promoting yourself you don't even see what's going on around you!" He yelled a bit more and I listened.

I didn't like hearing these words, but I didn't deny it. I'm lucky to have a brother that calls it like he sees it. I apologized to my mom, and I did contact Dr. Phil's studio, but I couldn't reach anybody. I promised myself if I was ever back on his show, my mom would not be in the audience: She'd be center stage with me.

The Sun and the Moon and My Dad

Water was squeezed out of a ShamWow during a commercial on ESPN. My dad leaned over from his favorite Lay-Z-Boy chair and said, "Guess what the nurse's daughter's favorite song is? 'Party Like a Rockstar'!" holding out the "R" sound for effect. In a T-shirt that read "Help! I've fallen and can't reach my beer," my dad was frail, and skinnier than I'd ever seen him.

The year before Jay and I made the TV show circuit, Larry Harding—my true father and my superhero—was diagnosed with prostate cancer. He never showed any signs of discomfort or pain of any kind. I was in total denial when he told me he had limited time left.

Six months later, as hospice nurses came and went daily from our house, the reality of the situation hit me like a wrecking ball. Doing sudoku from a book, my mom sat close to him as Lance and I recounted our biggest laughs with him and watched TV, doing our best to put on a brave face. As usual, Larry Harding was braver than us all, bringing up my song on a regular basis, his thoughts focused on making sure I knew he believed in me.

Ever the coach, he grinned as he instructed us to have the Michigan State University fight song playing at the party after his funeral. Words jumbled in my mouth and collided with tears trying to tell my dad how much he meant to me. The last time we spoke, he told me he was the luckiest man on earth to have had me for a son.

Our living room in Michigan was filled with all our family and his best friends standing around his bed the night he passed.

Later that night, in the silence that comes to a house when no one can sleep, I got out of bed, walked down to the basement, and dug out smiling pictures of my giant dad when he was a child. In one he is playing with a puppy, in another making a snowman. If only I had five more minutes with him, I would love to have thanked him better.

"My dad died," I breathed into the phone.

"I'm so sorry. I'll be there on the next flight," replied Jay. He was the first phone call I made when my dad passed. We had become closer than I realized. He was on the next plane to Michigan. He said he would speak at the funeral after demanding a puzzled Lance and I do the same. It had not crossed our mind to speak, and I'm glad Jay pushed us.

"I'm here to bury my son's father," Jay said solemnly to a standing-room-only crowd at the local church as sunlight shone through the stained-glass windows. "Larry Harding once caught a touchdown pass in the Rose Bowl for his beloved MSU. But by far the greatest catch Larry ever made was when J.T. slipped through my hands and landed in his arms."

Hearing Jay's heartfelt words, Lance and I, each holding one of our mom's hands, smiled through our tears in the front row pews of a church that was filled to the brim with everyone my dad had ever known.

"The Hardings hired a famous actor to speak at Larry's funeral. What a family—they don't miss a trick," a woman whispered to another person two pews behind us as she held up a tablet to take a picture of Jay. How she had missed the craziness Jay and I were causing on TV, and my adoption story, I'll never know.

It was an unacceptable reality that my dad was gone. I'd never known life without him, he had always been there. There was the sun and the moon and my dad.

Jay and I got to know each other through laughter, and we bonded through tears. Little did I know, anger would soon fracture us.

CHAPTER 16

Letterman, Oh Man

Taxicabs honked as Taylor Swift's "Last Christmas" drifted out of a tiny radio set in the doorway of a Times Square gift shop. A man dressed as Santa rang a handbell, collecting money for charity. DON'T WALK signs blinked orange behind falling snowflakes as Jay Thomas, his two sons, and I walked the crowded streets of Manhattan, tossing a football to one another. Jay was scheduled to do his annual appearance on the *Late Show with David Letterman.* Every year, Letterman would have Jay tell his famous story about meeting the Lone Ranger at a car dealership. Then Jay would throw a football at a meatball on top of the *Late Show* Christmas tree. If you've never seen it, look up "Jay Thomas Lone Ranger Story" on YouTube. It's a classic.

It was a television tradition that happened for years. Jay loved it—it made him feel good to be seen by so many people on such a big show.

In Christmas hats with blinking reindeer antlers we bought from Walgreens, my brothers and I had a skip in our step heading from the marble-floored hotel David Letterman had put us up in to the studio where Letterman taped his show. Sam, Jake, and I danced between the light snow falling and the shopping tourists, singing "It's the moooost wonderful time of the year" in our best old-school crooner impressions.

At Broadway and Fifty-Second, the buttery smell from hot pretzel vendors collided with the energy of enthusiastic men selling fake Gucci purses as they blew on their freezing hands. A long line of ticket holders excitedly waiting to enter the famous Ed Sullivan Theater stood under the huge yellow-and-blue illuminated marquee that read: LATE SHOW WITH DAVID LETTERMAN. Around the corner was the private entrance to the show.

Security guards with thick Brooklyn accents greeted Jay like a conquering hero. "Hey, Eddie LeBec! What was it like to kiss Carla on *Cheers*?"

Jay replied, "I should've got combat pay for that."

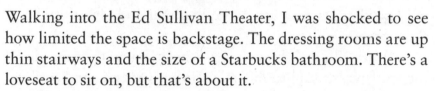

Walking into the Ed Sullivan Theater, I was shocked to see how limited the space is backstage. The dressing rooms are up thin stairways and the size of a Starbucks bathroom. There's a loveseat to sit on, but that's about it.

The greenroom where celebrity guests and their families can mingle isn't much bigger. It has carrots and cucumbers and drinks, but it's as tiny as a college dorm. Alec Baldwin was in there with us one time, holding court. The Letterman band drummer played on a few KISS albums—uncredited, but I knew he did due to my KISS obsession. His hands drumming lightly on his knees, he smiled, surprised when I said, "Loved your work on KISS *Unmasked*." A large-screen TV backstage in the greenroom shows the *Letterman* taping as it happens for guests not sitting in the audience.

David Letterman never came out to say hello to the guests or any of the family members before a show. It wasn't his thing. Jay Leno, Conan O'Brien, and the star hosts of every other TV show Jay appeared on would always say hello. Jay told me Dave wanted it to be spontaneous and electric when a guest sat down by his desk and they met face-to-face during the taping.

Kind of a bummer for those of us wanting to meet Dave or get a selfie, but that was his style. The five times Jay took me to the show, the only time I ever saw Letterman was when he was on the stage interviewing a guest or doing the opening monologue.

When taping ended, all the doors to the greenrooms and dressing rooms were shut so Dave could walk by and go up to his office without seeing anyone.

"Give me some band names I can use to keep my story fresh," Jay asked me as he flipped through notes about his Lone Ranger story in front of a mirror framed by big lightbulbs like on an old movie set.

After Jay had his makeup done, a staff writer for the show in a David Letterman varsity-style jacket would come in and tell Jay what David wanted to talk about and give a little pre-show prep.

"Love all the shows you've been on with your dad," the staff writer said to me, adjusting his glasses and smiling. *Boom!* There's no way Dave hadn't heard about our antics if his head writer was mentioning them to me.

Since Jay and I had been on so many TV shows lately, I thought naturally Letterman would mention me at some point. A Letterman mention would be the cherry on top of the greatest sundae ever. There's nothing bigger than Letterman. People would recognize me everywhere if I was on that show. My song would be played by countless people, I had no doubt.

It was cut-glass-with-your-nipples cold in the theater. You could almost see your breath inside the studio. Everyone in the audience was still wearing their winter coats and hats.

Running full speed across the stage, Dave appeared to welcome the audience before the taping. The audience wildly cheered. The hello to the audience was never shown on TV. It felt special, like a private joke just for Dave and his loyal fans. I feel very fortunate to have experienced all of these behind-the-scenes moments.

"Ya hear about the goof who threw his shoe at President Bush overseas?" Adjusting his tie, Letterman could not stop his famous giggle as he spoke about the incident.

When the actual show began, the audience clapped loud and the cameras were rolling. Dave went down the nightly changing "Top Ten List," which featured a cartoon of a shoe being thrown at Abraham Lincoln.

Paul Shaffer and the band made their wisecracks and rocked out. Mickey Rourke was on as a guest as *The Wrestler* was out and was a huge holiday hit. There was a buzz through the audience.

Later, Jay walked onstage looking great and smiling to huge applause. Jay was confident about the meatball throw. Earlier in the day, we spent an hour in Central Park rifling a football to each other, getting his arm warmed up.

They made some small talk for the audience—Dave poking fun at Jay for this or that. Sitting in the packed balcony looking down at the stage, I watched eagerly, knowing there was a good possibility of my being mentioned. *Who knows*, I thought, *I might even get called down to the stage.*

Not far into the interview, David looked Jay directly in the eye and asked, "How's your son?" Jay replied, "You don't want to talk about that" and waved it off.

Dave giggled. "I don't?"

"No," Jay said firmly, "you don't. That's a different kind of interview."

A rush of heat rose from my chest up to my face as if fire ants had stung me. My tongue felt like ash in my mouth. *How on earth can Jay not mention me on a show of this magnitude?* This was the moment when I knew we had the same blood running through our veins.

I can't explain what came over me next. In one swift beautiful motion like a tennis pro, I reached down, slipped off my shoe, stood up, and threw it as hard as I could at Jay from the balcony. Shoelaces flying like the arms of a tall, skinny inflatable man outside a car dealership, my shoe tumbled over itself midair, over the audience's heads, before landing with a thud, ricocheting off the couch, and bouncing high off Dave's desk, coming to a stop in front of Jay and Dave on the stage.

As the shoe pinball bounced on the stage, I stood up and yelled, "David Letterman is the greatest! I'm Jay Thomas's son and I won't be ignored! Letterman's the king, Dave Lettermaaaaaan rules!" The cameramen with their shoulder TV cameras onstage all turned and zoomed in on me. There was a big gasp from the crowd. Jumping in place, whooping it up in triumph, I knew flattering Letterman would get me on camera—stardom was mine.

A Vulcan grip on both of my shoulders made my knees buckle. CBS security—in the form of two gigantic guys in suits with earpieces, who were most likely formed at birth in the same test tube as Gronk and The Rock—grabbed me and lifted me up and over the shocked family of tourists sitting behind me.

My feet did not touch the ground again until security threw me out of the front wooden doors of the Ed Sullivan Theater and onto the cold, brown-snow sidewalk.

As I hit the ground with a thud, a lady with a clipboard and a headset came running out, yelling, "It's okay, it's okay, it's Jay's son, let him back in." The guards were now confused. They picked me up, brushed me off, and held the door that I had just been thrown out of open for me. The black sock from the shoeless foot was wet from the snow and squished as I walked back up the stairs to the balcony from the lobby.

"Why don't they freakin' tell us when these pranks are

going to happen? They never prepare us for this stuff," one bodyguard said to the other one behind me, adjusting his earpiece.

My two brothers Jake and Sam were still sitting in their seats when I returned. They weren't laughing—they didn't know what to think. As Dave interviewed Mickey Rourke, I whispered to Sam, "Ugh...that was pretty bad, right?"

Sam, the older of the two, who loves a wild adventure, looked ahead without smiling and simply said, "Oh my God."

Far from the Tree

The normal after-show handshakes and pictures with us sitting on Letterman's desk with *Late Show* regulars Biff and Paul Shaffer obviously weren't going to happen. Walking out the front door to the crowded sidewalk, I waited for Jay. Sam and Jake went backstage. I felt nervous. I felt terrible. I knew I had made a mistake. The crowd spilled out onto Broadway in their scarves and coats, starstruck over seeing a live taping of a great show. Thankfully, no one seemed to notice me.

Eventually Jay came out the side door, storming past the paparazzi like a lion released from a small cage. He was screaming at me at the top of his lungs as he approached.

"If I see one word about this on your stupid Facebook or the tweet machine, I'll never speak to you again. What's the matter with you? They're not going to invite me back on again. I am so fucking mad at you, it's like you're really my son!"

Jake and Sam, not knowing if that was a complaint or compliment, muttered, "Sheesh, Dad."

Jay turned around, the snow melting on his burning forehead. "Letterman asked me if I planned this. I said to him I swear to God I didn't and he knows I'm telling the truth because it wasn't funny. I do this for a living. If I had been a part of this plan it would've been funny."

Jay and his sons walked up the street back to the hotel as I shrank into the constant motion of people with shopping bags that is New York City sidewalks during the holidays.

That night in the living room of the hotel suite, a deck of cards cracked as Sam shuffled them over and over. Jake played his Game Boy and Jay watched the interview when it aired at midnight on CBS.

The Lone Ranger story and meatball throw were shown, but my interruption was edited out of the broadcast that night. Hiding out in the lobby of the hotel, I called a girl I had a crush on as they watched the TV upstairs. My drummer, Carey Weaver, texted me too, asking: *Is everything okay? I just saw one of your colorful shoes lying in front of David Letterman on TV.*

Jay refused to let me apologize or contact Letterman, even though I had no idea where to contact him if I wanted to.

At the airport the next day, Jay held up his hand in my face when I tried to talk to him. He just said, "Don't make it worse. Let it all be forgotten." We went our separate ways that Christmas.

My mom missed my dad terribly, and I went home a lot to spend time with her. We would order Chinese food and laugh as she tried to catch me up on her favorite show, *Lost*.

Drawing ideas for future JTX record covers with a black Sharpie late one night, I saw Letterman on TV. Dave seemed especially gentle as he interviewed a much older woman. The woman was the mother of the late comedian Bill Hicks.

Years before, Hicks was on the Letterman show. It was supposed to be the comedian's big break. But Hicks was ahead of his time and more than a little "edgy." He'd done his routine, but it was later edited out of the broadcast.

Hicks passed away from cancer at a young age. Dave

regretted not airing his routine, and to apologize he brought the comedian's mother on the show to say it in person and to acknowledge how great her son was. It was touching, to say the least. It was classy.

Reassured, I began to write a letter to Dave on a blank sheet of paper in my lyric book. Writing slowly in my best handwriting possible, I began:

> Dear Mr. Letterman,
>
> I am Jay Thomas's son, and I wanted to sincerely apologize for interrupting your show. Unlike what you do on a nightly basis my stunt wasn't classy, it wasn't cool, and it wasn't funny. You have worked tirelessly to have a career and you have earned the right to decide who's on your show. What I did was immature. Please don't hold it against Jay. Being on your show is one of the most important things to him. I am truly sorry.
>
> *Your fan,*
> *J.T. Harding*

Without telling anyone, I addressed it to the theater and sent it off in the mail. I figured it would most likely get lost in the thousands of other fan letters sent to the building.

A week later, a thin FedEx envelope arrived for me. The return address was *The Late Show*, New York, NY. When I was little, too excited to wait until Christmas, I gingerly and secretly unwrapped presents under the tree to peek at them. I opened the envelope as carefully as I did those gifts. Whatever was inside was too precious to get ripped, bent, or smeared. To my disbelief, inside the envelope was a letter from Dave:

> J.T., after thirty years in television no one has ever thrown a shoe at me, so at least we have that. I'm a fan of your father's. He's welcome here anytime.

David Letterman had signed it by hand.

Throwing a shoe wasn't right, but that letter is framed with pride among my many gold and platinum albums and gets more attention than all of them put together.

Jay had forbidden me to speak of the shoe incident, then went and talked about it nonstop on his radio show. As Jay cursed me on air, his listeners had empathy for me and began sending me videos of Jay in his younger days interrupting all sorts of TV shows.

There's one clip where Howard Stern is being interviewed on daytime television and Jay walks through the studio audience and sits on the stage, uninvited and unannounced, as Howard says "He's jealous" to the audience. They were both battling for radio listeners at the time. They bickered on live TV, with Jay completely crashing the party, sitting on the floor like he had every right to be there. Outrageous. "The apple doesn't fall far from the tree," Jay responded to his callers before hanging up on them.

It was clear that Jay forgave me when he started calling, asking me to email him funny news articles that caught my eye on the internet that he could use on his radio show. After the shoe incident faded, I knew my relationship with Jay could handle anything thrown our way—no pun intended.

When Letterman announced his retirement, Jay went on one last time the following Christmas. Sam, Jake, Lance, lots of Jay's radio coworkers, and I all had tickets. We all wanted to be there.

After the show, security cleared the hallway as usual so Letterman could get to his dressing room without seeing anyone. Backstage, everyone put on their winter coats as Lance gripped the laces of the football that Jay had thrown at the meatball on top of the Christmas tree. Suddenly the green-room door swung open, and there stood the great Dave Letterman. The whole room erupted.

Dave leaned in and said, "Is this your family, Jay? Which one threw the shoe?" In a rare moment of embarrassment, I looked to the carpet with a half smile, half wince, as everyone pointed at me. Dave reached out to only me and shook my hand, smiling his famous toothy grin and giggling as only Dave does. He turned toward the door. "Merry Christmas, everyone," and he was off.

Exiting the stage door, Jay waved to a dozen cell phone cameras flashing from behind the security fence. We all climbed into the back of a limousine and rolled to Jay's favorite restaurant in Chinatown. Sam and Jake marveled as Lance poked his head out of the limo's open sunroof and howled as he held up his beer, reminiscent of Mufasa holding up Simba in *The Lion King,* as we passed the glowing Chrysler Building. In the limo Jay touched my shoulder and said, "I'm glad you're here."

"Letterman likes me. Were you surprised he shook my hand?" I asked, smiling.

"Not at all," Jay replied as he lit a cigar and spun it, his fingers moving like an octopus swimming as he puffed. "I told him you were mentally ill."

CHAPTER 17

Party Like a Four-Star General

Where's everybody from?" my voice thundered through the speakers of the Army base mess hall with its make-shift stage. Standing on the stage in front of an American flag, telephone pole high and semitruck wide, I pointed my mic to the crowd. Sweat beads dripped from my arm as soldiers yelled out their hometowns. I'd say, "Cool—anybody here from…[then as fast as I could into the mic] Florida, Georgia, Tennessee, Kentucky, Illinois…," naming all fifty states to flashes of cheers from all points in the crowd. Naming every state in one long breath is not easy—try it!—but it was the least I could do. It was a way to honor them all. Just when I thought I had seen the world, I was once again thrown for a loop. My band and I were on tour in the Middle East.

Thanks to the underground buzz and radio success of "Party Like a Rockstar," my manager was getting requests asking if I wanted to entertain US troops in Afghanistan. Talking to my band, we all agreed this was an incredible way to show support and give back to the troops who keep us safe, and bring a little bit of home to soldiers stationed half a world away. We rehearsed a tight blazing ten-song set in my drummer Carey Weaver's basement.

Carey's basement was wallpapered with posters of JTX shows from around the States that we cleverly spiced up with Ferris Bueller's picture over my face or the world's most famous shark swimming up to the word *JTX* instead of *JAWS*. As I'd learned years before, in order to stand out, you have to get creative.

Our families dropped us off at the Detroit airport. My mom, gushing with pride, told all the baggage handlers we were going to entertain the troops.

Our plane lifted off and flew us to Germany, where we boarded a military plane as big as a Home Depot that would take us all the way to Afghanistan. No-nonsense soldiers with high-and-tight haircuts strapped us into the military plane's seats, the band and I smiling like SpongeBob we were so excited. The seats were not in rows. We all sat side by side along the perimeter of the plane. Our weapons of mass entertainment—drums, guitars, and a few small amplifiers— and my suitcase of stage clothes were loaded up and sitting in the middle of the plane among desert-sand-colored Army jeeps and heavy military equipment. The ceiling was so high and the plane so spacious, it was like flying in a warehouse.

There were no movies or snacks on the six-hour flight. Holding their helmets in their laps, a few soldiers shrugged and looked left and right, teasing good-naturedly, as I looked for the plane bathroom. After some searching I discovered the "bathroom" on the plane was a laptop-sized metal vent that opened up at waist level. Walking back to my seat, over the hum of the giant propellers I yelled to my bandmates, "I just pissed in a mailbox."

On the descent into Afghanistan the plane had to spin in tight circles all the way down during landing. That's how they do it for safety reasons, to avoid being shot at. During the Wile E. Coyote roller-coaster landing from hell, my face turned green, purple, then plaid. Running to the "mailbox bathroom" was out of the question.

My fingers gripped my seat as I squeezed my eyes closed.

As the plane spun like water rushing down a drain, I let out a loud "fuck me," pools of cool saliva forming in my mouth, warning me I was about to throw up.

The enlisted men among us were laughing and slapping their knees as if Gomer Pyle had joined their ranks. Hearing them, I had an epiphany. We're not only here to rock them; I'm here to give these soldiers a distraction any way I can. Lyrics or laughter, music or mayhem, I was up for it. If war is a kind of circus, I was more than happy to be the clown.

Once on the ground the blazing desert sun outlined the top of the giant bay door at the back of the Army plane as it lowered. We walked off the ramp onto the runway and were greeted by military personnel saluting us. Soldiers handed us bulletproof vests, helmets, and necklaces with an infrared light to get us to the "outhouse" undetected by enemy snipers when nature called at night. Thoughts of my dad rushed through me. He'd proudly served in the US Army. How thrilled he would be knowing I was here doing my part for America in my own way.

Not five minutes on the ground, we ducked our heads under the spinning rotor blades just like in a movie and boarded a Black Hawk helicopter. Outfitted in my heavy helmet and vest, I felt my stomach drop as we lifted straight up into the sky, and the next thing I knew, the wide-open desert was zooming below us.

Wafting through the open helicopter doors, the warm air felt like a hair dryer all over me. Between seemingly endless stretches of sand, countless yellow poppies blanketed the desert like a lemon river.

A machine gunner sat on either side of the helicopter, looking down over the desert in silence, their helmets, goggles, and headset microphones on. Watching them, I was giddy with excitement. I kept thinking, *How did I get here?*

We visited five bases and at each one our musical instruments would already be set up for us by the time we landed, either on a makeshift basketball court, in recreation rooms that tables had been cleared out of, or in giant clamshell tents with folding metal chairs for the soldiers to sit on.

In Concert: Jtx, Singer Of Party Like A Rockstar posters with my picture on them were hung in mess halls and mobile gyms, on church bulletin boards, in the outhouses, and in the dozens of cubicles where soldiers could use the internet. I felt like Elvis in Memphis. Everyone was anticipating our arrival. Marines in beige camouflage fatigues shouted "JTX" and waved as we walked by, checking out the fascinating scenes.

American soda brands of every kind, but with logos written in Arabic instead of English, sat on ice in our tent. A Kermit the Frog stuffed animal was tied to the front of a military ambulance. Stick-figure family pictures drawn in crayon were taped above GI bunk beds, reading I Love You Daddy Come Home Soon, next to orange leaves that had fallen off a tree somewhere on the East Coast of America.

Soldiers were only allowed one fifteen-minute call home each week. Under the glass at every table that had a phone was a printed sheet of paper: *Do not ask about your boat or jet ski, ask your loved ones how they are and how they feel.*

"I'm giving you and the band permission to use the phones anytime you want," the major in charge of us said, handing me a receiver in a cubicle. As much as I love getting the rock star treatment, I was embarrassed by this. The soldiers deserved the phone lines much more than I did. Punching the USA access code into the phone, I only called home once to tell my mom I had arrived safely. My mom picked up her cell in line at the Kroger in Grosse Pointe. "I'm so proud of you, J.T.," she said over the sound of her groceries being rung up.

Make Music, Not Bombs

Servicemen and women all chanted "Ain't that America" from the get-go as we opened up the show with John Mellencamp's "Pink Houses," then rolled like a tank through ten songs and always closed with a rowdy "Party Like a Rockstar." At some bases there would be fifty soldiers watching us, at others five hundred. Either way, I gave the performances of my life.

Halfway through the concert I'd appear in my pea-green army helmet and bulletproof flight jacket from the side of the stage. It made the soldiers happily lose their minds every time. Ducking out of sight again during Carey's drum solo, I would draw a black star around my eye like Paul Stanley of KISS with an eyeliner pencil, then come running back out as fast as I could. I wanted the crowd to be on the edge of their folding chair seats for the entire hour, wondering what would happen next.

Jumping into soldiers' outstretched arms, I would crowd-surf. Throwing chairs to make sure they knew I meant business got them all riled up. Playing the Black Crowes' "Hard to Handle" mixed with my original material got them singing along. One serviceman got so excited he picked me up and ran around with me in his arms like the Heisman Trophy was on the line.

Pointing at a Canadian flag that troopers from Toronto held up, I said into the mic, "Man, people say there's nowhere to go in Toronto, but I disagree. You can go to Detroit and you can go to Buffalo." The laughter was so loud it echoed through the mountains of Afghanistan for days.

While I scanned the audience as I spun, danced, sweated, and sang, one of my favorite things to do was find someone that did not look like they were there to have a good time. Usually it was a very high-ranking official, who you could tell was not going to crack a smile the entire show. Picture Mr. Clean from TV, his bald head polished to a high shine. His giant muscles. Then picture him in a military uniform adorned with medals and his arms folded, staring at me like a disapproving father. That's what they usually looked like.

I understand that these commanders live in the most dangerous part of the world for the most intense years anyone could ever imagine. They're not just going to crack a beer and have a laugh because a band's in town. Their job is to be alert. Even so, I was hired to do a job. I was selling smiles and I was open for business.

During my performance, I'd don a purple feather boa and a Slash of Gun N' Roses–style black top hat. I'd pirouette in place, then grab the microphone stand, my hands sliding down it like a fireman's pole as my legs stretched into the splits on the stage. Standing back up, I would jump off the stage and run through the audience as my band onstage kept jamming.

Every soldier would be cheering and high-fiving me as I bounced by. Running past the person I had secretly picked out, I would stop on a dime and rub the feather boa over my butt while dancing up behind them without them knowing.

All the soldiers watching would double over with laughter, some using their fingers to let out a piercing whistle through their teeth. Then, draping the feather boa loosely around Mr. Clean's shoulders, I'd zoom my ass back to the stage.

Whoever was the unknowing victim of my Marilyn Monroe dance would usually forgive me and pat me on the back at the end of the night. Playing music, spreading some laughter, asking about their families and homes, it was my hope I could provide a little bit of stress relief from the circumstances they were under. After the shows the outpouring of love was overwhelming and humbling.

Signing autographs until my hand was sore, I couldn't help thinking back to the Battle of the Bands. If someone had told me I'd sign so many autographs one day, I might not have believed them.

My drummer, Carey, brought a case of drumsticks to give away, and he would autograph drumheads for anyone who talked to him. My bassist, Good Time Charlie, snorted Swee-Tarts in protest of the "No Alcohol" rule, which prompted camaraderie and raised eyebrows from many soldiers.

Anyone who asked to strum my guitar was handed it without question. One night, as a soldier quietly played "Crash Into Me" by Dave Matthews Band, I slow-danced with a part-time schoolteacher now deployed overseas who was missing her husband.

Picture after picture of people's children were shown to me. Breakup texts soldiers had received from a lover back home were read to me. A young guy with pimples told me, "I joined the National Guard to serve one weekend a month in order to pay for college. Somehow I'm locked and loaded in the desert." Perplexed, he raised his arms over his head and said, "How did I get here?" For hours after every show, soldiers would talk to me about their hometowns.

Camouflage Bibles, lighters in the shape of grenades, and patches by the dozen with different division names on them soon overwhelmed my guitar case. As we traveled from base to base, soldiers constantly gave me keepsakes to take home. After one show, a lifer, an older man with gray hair and a huge grin, told me our show was "the best thing I've seen since 1969 when I saw a band in Vietnam called Mick Jagger and the Rolling Stones!" That comment is framed on the walls of my heart. Soldiers hugged us, thanked us, and I even kissed a single girl or two (or three or four). This epic footage of us is on YouTube—look it up under "JTX (I'm Gonna) Party Like a Rockstar."

One morning, as the sun spilled like lava under the door into our tent, the band and I were woken and instructed to put our bulletproof gear on. We did as told. We were hurried to the mess hall, where we ate Raisin Bran cereal out of the iPhone-sized Kellogg's boxes I had not seen since I was a kid at a truck stop diner. "You're going to the Afghan base. The Afghan Army is our ally and helping the United States. You're going to meet the leader of the Afghan Army," the commander in charge of us said, nodding proudly. It was a spur-of-the-moment trip.

"We do not stop for anything. Keep moving until we reach the destination. Do not stop for anyone or anything," the commanding officer instructed the drivers of our convoy. Two young female soldiers giggled and nudged each other, staring at me as we climbed into our vehicle.

In a convoy of armored sand-colored Humvees, we passed mud hut villages and waving little kids on donkeys, and I was once again rocketing across the desert. Women dressed head to toe in black burkas floated by like the Ghosts of Christmas Past.

At my feet were boots, bullets, and bottles of water. The vehicles all had a pivoting gun mounted on top, loaded with a belt full of bullets the size of my fingers. A soldier gripped the gun and stuck his head out of the Humvee to look back at a car. "That car behind us is getting a little close," he yelled to the driver before it finally veered away from us. I probably should've been scared, but I was lost in the moment. No regrets about the past, no concerns about writing another hit song in the future. Life was a movie and I hoped the credits never rolled.

Passing wandering sheepherders and tanks with Russian lettering rusted and burned out, left over from past wars, I was filled with a deep sense of humility. Music had brought me here, which was hard to fathom. Over and over I reminded myself to give 100 percent onstage, to use every trick I had learned from MTV, from the High Priest and Linkin Park, and from past USO concerts—every audience deserved the best of my abilities.

"I partied like a rock star before the service. Got arrested fifteen times," a soldier with a square jaw and bitten finger-nails gripping the steering wheel of our vehicle bragged as he drove us. My eyes caught his Jack-Nicholson-from-*The-Shining* smile in the rearview mirror as we were waved through the gates at the Afghan Army base.

Through hallways with cracked walls and chipped paint, the Army major in charge led us to an office in a small build-ing that had seen better days.

Beside a flower-print couch the color of seashells and a 1970's-era TV, the general of the Afghan Army sat behind a mahogany desk. His uniform was a dark forest green, and he wore a ruby beret. He did not speak English. After we were introduced, his interpreter translated for him: "This is a rock 'n' roll band from the United States of America. They're here to perform for the troops." The Afghan leader stood.

With his chin high, his arms stiff to his side, he spoke to the translator, who relayed what he said: "Just what Afghani-stan needs: more noise."

We all laughed as the leader smiled slightly. He reached over to his desk and rang a tiny handheld bell, and that made everyone that worked for him scurry from the room. He sat down behind his desk and motioned for us to sit on his couch. He then rang the bell again. Another person rushed in and clicked a brick-sized 1970s remote control with a button that looked like a red Lego.

The Afghan commander's old TV fuzzily crackled to life and a black-and-white show came on. A man was club-bing another with a bowling ball. The commander said "The. Three. Stooges..." and we all clapped and laughed for the next half hour.

Who would've dreamed that seven thousand miles from

home, literally a world away, we would bond with the most powerful man in Afghanistan, and the international language understood by us all would be Curly skipping in place cockeyed with a "Nyuk, nyuk, nyuk."

When we left, I thanked the commander with a bow, even though I wasn't sure if that was the appropriate thing to do. "Thank you for having us, Commander. We are from Detroit, Michigan." The Afghan leader didn't seem to know of it. So, me being me, I walked over to his huge wooden desk, which had a globe on it, the kind you'd find in an elementary schoolteacher's classroom. The globe was so old the paper was peeling off it. Spinning it around, I found and pointed at Michigan.

His eyes stretched open as big as teacup saucers, then he said *"Chee-kah-go?"*

"Yes! Chicago!"

He clapped his hands with a smile. Who knew he had an affinity for Chicago! Maybe *Good Times* is his second-favorite American TV show.

One hundred Afghan soldiers stared at my band and me curiously as we all ate lunch together on their base. Wandering table to table, I sang "Party Like a Rockstar" on my WRIF sticker–covered acoustic guitar. Many of them laughed and some hugged me. We carried a video camera with us everywhere and filmed as much as we could.

After filming the soldiers, Carey would then show them the video. They fixed their hair as they watched themselves.

When we were back in our heavily armored Humvees, the sun began to set; outlined by the black sky, it looked like a monarch butterfly over the desert dunes. The night sky in Afghanistan has stars so big you have to see it to believe it. They shone down like someone had taken a big paintbrush, dipped it in white paint, and pressed it against a black bedroom ceiling.

I felt like I could reach up and grab them like Lance did with the bubbles that blew out of our Fisher-Price lawn mower as kids. How did I get here?

Pulling through the Jurassic Park–sized metal gates of a US base we had yet to visit, our long day was about to go rocking into the night. Our equipment was already set up, and a crowd was gathering for our show.

"It's seventeen hundred hours, let's go!" soldiers yelled as they pressed up against the stage. Though still decked out in full camo gear, they were off duty and ready to have some fun. At this particular base there were thousands of soldiers from Little Rock, Arkansas, where my song "Party Like a Rockstar" had dominated the radio for months a year prior.

An infrared flashlight path made by the major who had led me on the field trip of my life now led my dusty red Pumas up the metal steps to the stage, clanging as I walked. The sound guy was waiting, my electric guitar at the ready. I slid off my bulletproof vest and exchanged it for my blue suit coat and my cool black sequined scarf. Checking the inside pockets of my jacket for guitar picks, I squeezed them in my slick sweaty fingers as the preshow butterflies started to flutter in my stomach.

Carey counted off a beat to my bassist, Charlie, and they kicked into the fast-paced "Nothing Matters," a new JTX song. I hopped in place from one foot to the other like a little kid. They would play until I came running out. Before this happened, the major offered me a sharp salute. My brother Lee watching *M*A*S*H* years ago flashed in my mind. Leaning close to the major, I shouted over the music, "Thank you for everything you've done for me, sir. Believe me, I know I'm not Bono."

He smiled and replied, "J.T., you are today."

I've Got Soul but I'm Not a Soldier

Back in Nashville, the soldiers' voices were in every song I wrote as summer turned to autumn. The thought *How did I get here?* kept coming back to me.

Flipping the pages of the camouflage Bible I had been given, I set it down and picked up my guitar, its maple body now covered in desert dust and undoubtedly full of stories.

A challenge coin—a thick piece of metal bigger than a silver dollar with military unit symbols on it—is given to a soldier who has gone above and beyond the call of duty. Once, when approaching a unit commander to thank him for allowing us to play, he saluted me, then reached out to shake my hand. As we shook, I felt a cool hint of metal against my palm. He was giving me my first challenge coin.

Half a dozen coins shining like tiny platinum records are on my mantel now from that trip, and I cherish them. American flags, helicopter rides, hellos and goodbyes, filled my head as my fingers found the frets and I began writing a new song.

> *How did I get here, burning in the sun, sleeping with a gun, telling everyone*
> *I really miss you too, I'm coming home real soon?*
> *How did I get here, choking on the sand, my brother in my hand, a million miles away from everything I know? How did I get here?*

I recorded six new songs about my Middle East trip. By this point, I was intrigued by the idea of country artists singing my songs, which is what Nashville is built on. My publisher made CDs to send to country artists looking for songs.

Sweat dripped from the ceiling of Tootsie's honky-tonk, which was packed with tourists bumping belt buckles to the band. A "Nash-elorette" party in matching "Getting Shitty in Music City" shirts and pink cowboy hats hollered from a Pedal Tavern passing by as a John-Deere-T-shirt-wearing band sang, "I wanna check you for ticks." Happy to be back in Nashville after the whirlwind Afghanistan experience, I was dancing with a girl I had asked out, when the phone in my pocket buzzed.

A text from a Michigan area code read: *Yo J.T., where you at? Love the rock star song, thinking we could write one.*

I'm in Nashville, I replied. *Who's this?*

It's your uncle. My date held my glass of Malibu rum as I started to type, *I don't have an uncle in Michigan*, when another text came through: *It's Uncle Kracker.*

The dancing may have lasted a few more hours, but my thoughts had left the building the second I read that text. For the rest of the night all I thought about was the fact that a real-life rock star wanted to write with me. My life would never be the same.

Snowflakes the size of potato chips twisted like little tornadoes in the headlights of a Cadillac that pointed itself north on I-75 in Detroit. Uncle Kracker, in a Bob Seger baseball hat turned sideways and a happy-go-lucky smile above his goatee, had his one tattooed hand over the steering wheel and flicked ashes from a Parliament Light cigarette out the window, which was rolled down half an inch, with the other. I sat in the passenger seat watching the blizzard hitting the windshield as if we were in the *Millennium Falcon* making the jump to light speed to the sound of Kracker's soon-to-be-released album playing in the car. Atlantic Records were dragging their feet on the release, but I liked what I heard.

"They just need a first single to set it up," Kracker explained.

"I haven't had a record out in five years, but royalties and that Kenny Chesney touring money keeps me pretty afloat."

I believed in Uncle Kracker. I had met him after his lawyer Ted Metry dropped off a new demo CD of mine on his front porch. I knew I could have a hit with him. His song "Follow Me" went number one in eight countries. Uncle Kracker has a diamond award, representing ten million copies sold of one record.

Sipping soda from Detroit Red Wings red-and-white plastic cups and eating truck stop beef jerky, we spent the weekend at his cottage writing, and the songs were good, but not great. Packing our guitars and recording equipment up on the last day, Kracker said, "What about a song called 'Smile'?" It was his title and he had the best line of the song: "Cooler than the flip side of my pillow." We wrote it with another writer, Blair Daly, and recorded the demo in the cottage living room as kids ice skated by on the lake.

As excited as a thief who cracked a safe and opened it to reveal priceless jewels, there was no doubt in my mind we had written an undeniable smash hit. Pumping my arms like Tiger Woods after hitting a golf ball, I listened to "Smile" over and over back in Nashville. I knew it would be released as soon as his record label heard it.

Suntans and Subway Rides

Two winters later, no one besides us had heard the song. If they had, they didn't let anyone know. For whatever reason, "Smile" was falling like a tree in an empty forest. I knew in my bones it was magic. Every story has three sides but here's what I remember happening.

My mind went into overdrive like a robot overheating and spazzing out in a movie, but I was doing it with purpose.

Maybe we needed more songs. Maybe Uncle Kracker needed a new producer? I had to be smart and figure out how to assist and get this project going.

High fives and laughter filled the Linkin Park dressing room when I visited them at their sold-out show in Nashville. After giving their new assistant some helpful pointers, I asked Linkin Park's DJ, Joe Hahn, if he would be interested in producing Uncle Kracker. He said that would be fun but nothing came of it.

As I looked at Kracker's career, ideas hopscotched around in my head just like they had as a kid, and at Tower leading to my record deal, trying to connect the dots that led to success. I remembered Uncle Kracker sang on the six-week number one country hit "When the Sun Goes Down," written by Nashville hitmaker Brett James.

If Patrick Swayze and Dennis Quaid had a baby, it would be Brett James—always with a just-back-from-the-Bahamas tan, an easygoing smile, and a champion of up-and-coming songwriters. Brett, I learned, had never met Uncle Kracker, so I set up a write with the three of us. I had never written with Brett either, but I knew saying Uncle Kracker was joining us would improve my chances of getting in the room with him.

Framed Dolly Parton and Willie Nelson album covers decorated the walls of Brett's wood-floor writing room. As we talked and sipped Starbucks around an antique table, we tossed song ideas back and forth like a Hacky Sack game. Kracker had a T-shirt that said FEELS GOOD TO BE A GANG-STER. Inspired by that, the three of us wrote "Good to Be Me," which Kid Rock produced.

Once again, nothing from Kracker's label. Months passed. I felt the clock spinning like at the beginning of a *Twilight Zone* episode.

"Think positive, you've always figured it out before," my mom reassuringly said over P.F. Chang's noodles, which we ate regularly during my visits home. Despite the success of "Party Like a Rockstar," my publishing deal had run out. My mom was my savior, giving me a place to stay as funds were dripping from my bank account like a leaky faucet.

During those visits home in Michigan, I started showing up at midnight poker games that Uncle Kracker's brother Mike invited me to. Kracker was always glad to see me if not a little surprised. I lost money I couldn't afford to lose, often in the first hand, but I couldn't afford to lose touch with Kracker either. Handing me crisp Benjamins under the table like a schoolkid passing a "check yes or no" love note, Uncle Kracker would slyly pay for me to stay at the table. My nose runny and my eyes Netflix red from all the cigarette smoke, I bluffed my way through the games as I bluffed my way into his life.

Knowing he was a fan of good food, I started dropping off expensive meat and cheese at his front door. His daughters stared at me through the window, yelling, "Billy Ray Cyrus is creeping around on our porch." I wanted to stay in Kracker's orbit. I didn't want him to forget about me. We had "Smile," a bona fide winning lottery ticket. We just needed someone to recognize it and cash it in.

With my knee pressed against the steering wheel to guide my Ford Escape, my free hands air-drummed to "Sad But True" by Metallica as I drove through the hockey rink–slick icy streets of my youth. Inflatable Santas waved from snow-covered lawns as I spun the radio dial and was suddenly hooked by an infectious song pumping out called "Shake It."[18] I slid into a church parking lot and googled the writers of the song on my phone. One name stood out—Sam Hollander. I had read an interview with him.

"Kracker, this song sounds like you. We should write

---

18 A catchy part of a song or the best phrase of the lyric is called a "hook" because it hooks you in when you hear it.

with this guy. Let's go to New York!" I said excitedly, standing in Kracker's heated garage-turned-game-room on Christmas night. I played the song on my phone to the sound of his friends slamming the spinning Golden Tee ball, crushing Miller Lite cans, and staring at me confused like I was the North Pole elf who wanted to be a dentist. Kracker is smart and ambitious. As Tony Soprano smiled at me from the side of a blinking pinball machine, Kracker texted someone to set up the write.

Sam I Am, But Who Are You?

SUBWAY POLES ARE NOT FOR STRIP DANCING signs hung above our heads as the crowded train jolted to a stop. Kracker and I hopped off and walked up the steps into the police-spotlight-bright sunshine of a crisp Manhattan day. We passed I ♥ NY T-shirt stands and men playing chess for money, as a group of construction workers hollered "Uncle Kracker!" our way as we made our way across Union Square to the high-ceilinged loft offices of Crush Management. It's fun to hang around someone famous; anyone who says it's not never has or they are lying.

Platinum albums by Fall Out Boy, Panic! at the Disco, and Train glowed on every wall like polished hubcaps as we passed songwriters working with Avril Lavigne in one room, and one of my songwriting heroes, Stephan Jenkins of Third Eye Blind—six feet two inches tall and dressed head to toe in black, looking like Darth Vader's doppelgänger—in another. Kracker raised his eyebrows at me, impressed or planning his escape, I'm still not sure.

"What's up, fellas?" Sam Hollander asked, his calm voice as low as he was tall. Wearing a Liam Gallagher of Oasis–style Kangol hat, he bro-hugged us, welcoming us into his racquetball-court-sized writing room.

Vinyl records stacked like pancakes kneecap high sat around the room. Eighties movies and break-dancing VHS tapes filled the shelves, bookended by a Vanilla Ice doll and a vintage *Happy Days* lunchbox. Framed gold and platinum albums with Sam's name on them covered every inch of the wall like I'd covered a balloon with papier-mâché newspaper squares in second grade.

Sam was already a much sought-after hitmaker and in recent years has written the worldwide smashes "High Hopes" for Panic! at the Disco and "HandClap" with Fitz and the Tantrums. I knew that Kracker and me writing a song with him would help Uncle Kracker's chance of getting back on track to put a record out.

With Fonzie giving me a thumbs-up from the lunchbox, I pulled up a chair close to Sam, his face illuminated by his laptop. As certain of myself as Stephen King about to tell a ghost story, I began talking about song ideas. I had no idea Sam was thinking, *Sit on it, Potsie*. Let him explain…

SAM HOLLANDER: Tommy Valentino was a music lawyer I knew from his days at BMI.[19] Great guy. We also played under the same unpleasant high school football coach a decade or two apart! This was the sort of random bond that one has in the music business that supersedes all of the usual bullshit. One day after much coercing, Tommy connected me with his client Uncle Kracker, who I had been aggressively attempting to write with for the previous half decade. When Kracker finally arrived that day, I noticed a few things: (1) He didn't really want to be there. He just seemed out of sorts in New York. (2) He looked

---

19 BMI and ASCAP are performing rights organizations. They collect money for songwriters when their songs are played on radio, on TV, in bars, etc.

like he had imbibed the entire Lynchburg, Tennessee, Jack Daniel's factory the previous evening. (3) He also brought a "handler" with him. Now the term handler is a tricky one. I mean a plus one, with no context added other than procuring food (or marijuana, etc.).

In all honesty, I was somewhat new to the handler thing. Beyoncé had dropped by the studio once and she had a few minions along those lines, but it just felt very out of context for an artist of Kracker's stature (don't get me wrong, he was coming off a few big hits, but it still felt like a stretch. Pop rock guys tend to run solo and stay salt of the earth). The handler in question's name was J.T. Harding. Kracker introduced him to us as his boy, but had him run out to the store to grab some candy and soda within minutes.

When he returned, J.T. and I began to small talk while Kracker sent some texts to his management (probably hoping to escape the session!). I learned that J.T. had been signed as an artist to EMI. When the dream died, he met Linkin Park, who he ran around with for a few years before linking with Kracker. I loved this kid. We were around the same age and had identical influences. He was both charming and whip smart.

So there we were, about thirty minutes into writing, when Kracker began to officially nod off. He was shot. He explained that the previous evening, he had arrived at Detroit's Cobo Arena to open up for Bob Seger when a stranger in the aisle yelled to him, "Kracker, you wanna have a beer in the parking lot?!" Kracker replied "Yo, yo, yo!" and left the show before Seger's curtain parted. The end result was that he was completely banged up on this day after. As his eyelids crumbled into nothingness, he actually muttered the words "the acoustic guitar makes me sleepy" before crashing out.

The day was devolving swiftly, but I did realize something in those moments of snore. J.T. Harding was fully listening to me messing around with some ideas, and he began to chime in some zingers. Why was the handler throwing out ideas? That's a stellar question, but honestly, at least it was something. Eventually the caffeine kicked in, and Kracker began to really bring it as well. He was also a really fun fella. I had a blast. By day's end, we got two songs out of the session, for one of which J.T. threw a couple of killer punchlines into the mix, even though it was a very odd way for a handler to act.

A few months later, one of my closest friends, Jonathan Daniel from Crush Management, who we shared our studio space with, came back with an advance of the Uncle Kracker record. I guess my song had made the cut. Then Jonathan said, "Look at the credits on this record closely." As I surveyed the sleeve, it seemed J.T. Harding had written five songs on the record. I was beyond puzzled. Then Jonathan said, "I don't think this kid has a publishing deal. Maybe we should sign him?"

Within twenty-four hours, we partnered with Songs Music Publishing and created the joint venture Mighty Seven. J.T. was our first signing (of eventually fifteen writers) and went on to scribe several chart-toppers, including the four-million-selling "Smile" with Uncle Kracker, "Somewhere in My Car" with Keith Urban, "Somewhere With You" and "Bar at the End of the World" for Kenny Chesney,

Dierks Bentley's "Different for Girls," Jake Owen's "Alone with You," and Blake Shelton's number one smash "Sangria." He was the spark that launched a ten-year run for Mighty Seven that included songs for Sia, SZA, and Joey Badass. It was an incredible stretch, and we owe it all to J.T. Someday he'll probably two-step into the Country Music Hall of Fame. Lesson learned. Never underestimate the guy procuring the 3 Musketeers candy bars and Mountain Dews. He might just be a one-in-a-million meal ticket of brilliance.

CHAPTER 18

Songwriting Is My Love Language

Here are the stories behind a few of my hits, although I have to say, songs are like sausages—don't watch them being made; just enjoy them when they're done. (That would make a good T-shirt.) It's not super glamorous, but if you're still reading, I know you're serious about writing hits of your own, so you'd better keep reading. Songwriting is definitely magic. You never know how it's going to come out, you never know where the ideas are going to come from, and that's what keeps you in love with it: the mystery of how it happens.

I've noticed a lot of my biggest hits tend to lean on the heartbreak angle. My heart gets broken, I write a song about it, it becomes a number one hit, and checks get put in my mailbox.

"Somewhere With You"

Driving the I-75 freeway back and forth from my mom's in Detroit to Nashville, wondering if "Smile" was ever going to be released, I faked a smile trying to get something going. My apartment was gone—it had been unexpectedly condemned months prior. Never one to let a good crisis go to waste, I actually filmed my music video for "Party Like a Rockstar" there and had full permission to smash the place up, since it had a date with a wrecking ball anyway. Shane McAnally, who is now one of the biggest writers in Nashville, was at the time sleeping on his sister Tiffany's couch. I was sleeping in my car sometimes, trying to save money myself. Shane is a chiseled-chest, always-smiling, ginger-haired Texan—he had already tried to become a country star in Nashville years before. He wanted to be the new George Strait, but as he told me once "my name isn't George and I'm not straight." It didn't pan out, so he moved to California. One night in 1998, Shane went to a party, and he didn't come home from the party until sometime in 2003. He went to rehab and decided to come back to Nashville for another try, and I'm so thankful he did.

There's a phrase that songwriters have used to describe country music for decades that goes: "three chords and the truth." That phrase sums up "Somewhere With You." The song has only three chords, and the lyrics are the absolute truth. With all the drum machines and computers used nowadays, I like to call country music "three chords and a loop."

Carrying our guitars into a two-story-house-turned-office on Music Row in Nashville, we sat across from each other in leather chairs in a writing room on the second floor where the Kings of Leon had scribbled their names on the closet door before they were famous.

For the first twenty-five minutes, Shane was feverishly texting. He finally looked up from his phone and apologized. "I'm sorry, I wasn't gonna show up. I'm going through a breakup. I don't think I can write a song today."

Funny thing was, I was going through a breakup as well. Shane and I talked for a while, swapping stories and heartbreaks, and I realized we had the same philosophy about relationships. We both agree you cannot make someone love you, you can only stalk them and hope for the best.

We started laughing and he picked up his guitar. Other

country writers I had written with were intrigued by me, but a big writer said, "You're not country, you're a rock guy." The same writer didn't want to write with Shane because Shane didn't have any hits yet. He pawned us off on each other, and it was by far one of the best things to ever happen to me.

I sat with Shane as he played three simple chords over and over, and the fast chorus lyrics in "Somewhere With You" just came out of us. Excitedly, Shane egged me on, "Yes, yes, that's great!" He liked what I was singing, and it felt good. When someone likes what you're doing, it makes you better. Shane knew that and he pushed me creatively.

When writing songs, I try to keep the guitar chords very simple so people can sing along. For me, the fewer the guitar chords, the better the melody. That way, the lyrics can shine. His simple guitar-playing style was such a good fit for me.

Together we wrote the lyrics totally unfiltered. "I hate my life, hold on to me." "Call up an ex to rescue me, climb in their bed." We didn't overthink it, just wrote about our lives.

We also sang three different melodies without changing the chord structure. One melody was the verse, one melody was the chorus, and the third was the bridge. Same chords, but three different emotional earworms for the people listening. Third Eye Blind are masters of this. Taylor Swift's song "Lover" is another great example.

After two hours of writing, Shane and I walked through the graffiti-hickeyed back alleys of Music Row over to a diner called Fido. "I'm going to move back to LA, nothing seems to be working," Shane told me between sips of an Arnold Palmer. Shane's talent was as evident as the spray tan staining the edges of his robin's-egg blue Aviator Nation hoodie. "Well, let's write as much as we can together until you leave. People are going to interview us in magazines about this song one day, I know it." I said those words out loud and I believed them with all of my broken heart.

Another unique thing about "Somewhere With You" that I didn't realize at the time is that the chorus is actually a lot of words being sung at a rapid pace. Choruses at that time in country songs didn't do that. A hit country chorus usually had one note that would lift. Think of "Breathe" by Faith Hill or Lee Ann Womack's "I Hope You Dance." Shane told me recently, "I don't think we could even write a song like that again, because at the time we didn't know any better."

These days, when you turn on country radio you hear fast singing all over the dial, but I believe we were the first to do it.[20] Shane and I weren't doing it to be different, we were just writing what felt good to us, not what we thought other people would like. We knew we had a surefire hit! We knew we'd be rich in no time and hearing the world singing along to our song.

Seven hundred sunsets later, every country star and every record label had passed on the song. People told us over and over: "It's not a country song." Then Kenny Chesney decided to record it and everyone got out of his way as if he were driving a tank through Mayberry. "Somewhere With You" was a three-week number one hit, and the first Kenny Chesney song ever to sell one million copies.

Kenny was given the song by a great publisher named Robin Palmer. Robin was a freelance song plugger at the time. In Nashville, a song plugger listens to songs written by anyone and everyone, and the ones they feel are hits they present to record labels, artists, and managers, hoping to get them recorded. Kenny had recorded an entire record that he felt wasn't right. He had a meeting and told the three dozen publishers there they could each present him one song. Robin Palmer chose to play "Somewhere With You."

Kenny responded to it because it was different. If we had

---

20 My editor pointed out that the Charlie Daniels Band did it first, but why let that ruin a good story?

written a song about a tractor or cowboy hats, we wouldn't have had a hit with him. If we had tried to copy what was on the radio at that time, we wouldn't have been noticed. We turned our most personal feelings into a three-minute movie, we sang it in a way we thought was cool, and it caught the whole world's ears. I urge you to do the same. Be yourself.

A hit song wasn't the only good thing to come out of my meeting with Shane and Robin. They now work together exclusively at his company, SMACK.

"Alone With You"

As tourists slowly passed in a van with Johnny Cash painted on the side, Shane McAnally, Catt Gravitt, and I sat together in a room on Music Row and wrote "Alone With You," my second number one song. Catt is a blonde firecracker of a woman. She looks like a rock star and her incredible melodies and lyrics are sure to appear in any writing session with her.

Shane brought in the title "Running With Scissors" from a book he'd read. We wrote the entire song around these words.

The way Shane plays guitar chords always brings something out of me. It happened when we wrote "Somewhere With You" and it was happening again, like a spark that lights a match. That's what it's like for Shane and me. Lyrics start pouring out of me. I don't know how else to explain it. The way he plays brings something emotional out of me that is unique to us. He might have that with a lot of people, but it's something I only have with him. It's as if my heart is wide open for the whole world to hear what I'm thinking and feeling.

We finished "Running With Scissors" and we felt great about it. As Shane was clipping closed the gold flaps on his guitar case, Catt said, "Guys, we're talking about someone coming over late at night you can't be alone with, but then you end up messing around. I'm just not feeling it—we need people to *feel* it."

"In what way?" I asked.

Catt stood up and proclaimed, "I want them to *feel* it!" as she started gyrating like a Deja-Vu stripper and pointing between her legs. She was not smiling. She meant what she was saying.

If this was a TV show, the camera would have panned over to Shane and me. Shane would've been in my arms sucking his thumb like a scared child. We were both completely freaked out by this display of passion, but she was right. We rewrote the chorus, adding the lyric "Don't slip your hand under my shirt and say it's okay." It made all the difference in the world. That's the power of co-writing.

Jake Owen heard the song and decided to record it with megahit producer Joey Moi. After the studio musicians recorded, Jake stood in the vocal booth and sang the song. At some point during recording, Jake decided he didn't like a line. He said he felt uncomfortable singing it. He called Shane from the studio and Shane called me so we could rewrite the lyric on the spot.

"No way. We're not changing anything, this is our art," I said, certain that Jake wanted to change the "hand under my shirt" line that I loved. I was not budging.

"No, he wants to change the 'running with scissors' line," Shane replied. So, me being a writer with integrity who doesn't compromise, I immediately said, "Of course, let's change it! No big deal—he's the one singing it." And just like that, the words that inspired the entire song were no longer in the song at all. "Running With Scissors" became "Alone With You" and was a number one, million-record-selling giant hit.

"Sangria"

Great ideas equal great songs was a text my publisher Rusty Gaston sent me that I've never erased from my phone. When my friend and fellow writer Josh Osborne came up with the title "Sangria" for a new song, I knew it was great.

I loved it from the moment he said it. New York City is the sexy pierced belly button on the body of America, and I visit often. In the summertime in Little Italy, all the cool sidewalk cafés have chalkboard menus advertising homemade pasta dishes and fresh cannoli, and sangria is always on them. Beautiful girls sit outside, Gucci bags at their feet, sipping sangria in the sun reflecting off skyscraper windows. It's like living in a movie when I'm there. "Sangria" immediately struck a chord with me as an eye-catching title. Josh said, "What if it was about a person who came over, drank all your sangria, and you tasted it on their lips?"

Trevor Rosen of the band Old Dominion wrote it with us. He and Josh thought out loud, "What if it had a vibe like 'Wicked Game' by Chris Isaak?" "Wicked Game" is a sexy, mysterious song. The guitar notes bend and echo like a train passing in the night. Isaak sings in a low Elvis Presley voice as if he's whispering in someone's ear. Trevor came up with the sexy guitar riff that starts our song.

We all wrote the lyrics together. What Josh and Trevor were picturing I don't know exactly, but I was thinking of an abandoned motel in Malibu, California, I have driven by countless times.

The weather-beaten motel is right on the beach on the Pacific Coast Highway. You can see curtains blowing in the windows. You can see the shell of an old tiki bar. I imagine in its heyday it was the kind of place where you could fall madly in bed with someone.

That's where that "You're crashing into me like waves on

the coast" lyric comes from. The forgotten motel I can still picture so clearly.

We knew we needed a bridge for the song. Now, what I like to do in a bridge is re-explain the title in a way the listener hasn't heard yet, to give them more information about the story. Easier said than done, because the verses and chorus already had a lot of lyrics about sangria.

Sitting under his gold record for Kacey Musgraves's "Merry Go 'Round," Josh asked the room, "Where is sangria from?"

Confidently, I replied, "It's a drink from Italy." I knew that because I'm a smart guy who travels a lot, obviously.

Josh did a quick Google search on his phone and looked at me. "Actually, it's from Spain." And that's how we came up with the lyric, "Only thing I wanna do tonight is drink you like a Spanish wine"—explaining the title with words we had not yet used in the song. Pearl Jam do this in the bridge to "Jeremy": "Try to erase this from the blackboard"—new lyrics about how Jeremy spoke in class today.

Little-known fact: Kenny Chesney recorded "Sangria" before Blake Shelton did. For whatever reason, Kenny decided it wasn't right for his new album. We were all bummed when he didn't release it, of course, but I never questioned it.

Chesney is a superstar and that doesn't happen by accident. He knows what he needs for his albums—he's the guy standing in front of eighty thousand people every night, after all. He knows how to make the right decisions for himself.

Thankfully, Robert Carlton, Josh's publisher, got the song to Blake Shelton's producer, Scott Hendricks. Funnily enough, a memo was going out all over Nashville to all the songwriters. In big block letters it read: BLAKE IS NOT RECORDING DRINKING SONGS. He had done enough of those, apparently.

But the line "Your lips taste like sangria" kept getting stuck in the head of Scott Hendricks, Blake's producer, so he sent it to Blake, who recorded it. I can't say it enough—write your own story and write it from the heart. Special songs find their way to the radio.

"Different for Girls"

It was midnight in Nashville, the Food Channel was on mute, and I was sitting alone in my apartment. Struggling for space next to empty sparkling water bottles, Xbox controllers, and a Freddie Mercury biography, I put my feet on the coffee table and plucked around on my guitar with a pick that had a heart eyes emoji on it.

People have asked me if I got the title "Different for Girls" from an episode of the show *Friday Night Lights*. I did not, but TV shows, movies, and books are all great places to get ideas for song titles. Like most of my songs, it came from a real-life experience.

The basic idea for the song appeared after I met a girl on a flight from Florida to Nashville. The girl was cool, full of life, and one exam away from securing a real estate license. I liked her from the start. We talked a few times on the phone before I ran into a friend of hers in line at Starbucks. The mutual friend told me that the girl I liked was going through a really bad breakup. That was news to me. The next time my crush called, I told her, "You seem so together—I'm surprised you're going through a breakup."

"What am I supposed to do? Just let everything in my life fall apart?"

"I mean, that's what my buddies and I do. We play video games all day and don't shave for weeks after a breakup," I responded with a laugh.

A friend of mine had been dumped around the same time. He finally got off the couch when I agreed to be his wingman one night on the town. He picked a fight at the bar we went to. After we escaped the bar, he started texting every ex he ever had, trying to put a Band-Aid on his loneliness. Combining those two stories as Guy Fieri loudly fawned over tacos on *Diners, Drive-Ins and Dives* on the TV, I came up with "Different for Girls."

The calendar in my phone showed a meetup with the name of friend, and now–Grammy Award–winning songwriter, Shane McAnally. Shane and I had a few hits together already and he makes me laugh like no one else. So I saved the idea to show him.

Gordie Sampson, a recording artist from Canada who has made a stellar career writing in Nashville, told me when I first arrived in town that he'd saved the title "Jesus, Take the Wheel" for the two best writers he knew in town: Brett James and Hillary Lindsey. The three of them wrote the song, it became Carrie Underwood's first hit, and they won a Grammy for it. Sometimes it's good to save a great idea to work on with great writers, and I do that a lot.

Writing at his SMACK office on Music Row in Nashville, I told Shane the concept of the song as he texted his husband, Michael. Loving the idea, Shane excitedly chimed in with "I know what you mean! And you know what you mean, but we have to make sure the audience understands what we're talking about." Shane quickly came up with the line "When the going gets tough, guys can just act tough." That line was the glue that brought the whole concept together.

When I sang him the lyric, "She don't text her friends and say 'I gotta get laid tonight,'" I followed it up with, "We probably can't say that."

Shane, being Shane, replied, "Why not?" So we left it in. We sang our truth without worrying about if it was too risqué for radio stations.

I always think of two songs that have stuck with me: "A

Girl in Trouble (Is a Temporary Thing)" by the band Romeo Void and another by Madonna called "What It Feels Like for a Girl." I've always wanted to write a song from that point of view.

Our song didn't sound anything like those songs, but I think subconsciously it was an idea that had been brewing in me for a while. Those songs stood out to me as a teenager because, being a guy, I'm always focused on how *I* feel after a breakup—angry, jealous, what have you—not really knowing it was different for a girl.

The actual thought of how different it is to go through a breakup when you're a girl was such a compelling song idea, but I just didn't have an experience to write a song about it on my own until I got to know the girl from the airplane.

Another thing about "Different for Girls": The last chorus has completely different lyrics than the previous choruses. Shane and I did not do that on purpose—the lyrics just came out, once again showing that there aren't really any rules in music, as long as the end result is catchy, I'm happy.

Most hit songs have the same chorus throughout. You want the listener to be able to sing along without hesitation. You want the chorus to be stuck in their head like a bill they can't pay. That's why I repeat my choruses verbatim in most songs.

Many songs have different lyrics in the second chorus to forward the story, but very few have a totally new chorus at the end. But that's what we did. Just goes to show you rules are made to be broken.

"Somewhere in My Car"

"I'd like to write a song about looking back on a past relationship. I haven't done that in quite a few albums."

That's what Keith Urban said to me when we met up to write at Blackbird Studio in Nashville. Keith knew what he wanted the lyrics to be about, exactly how he wanted the drumbeat to feel and the guitar parts to sound. He had an entire blueprint of the song already in his head before we wrote it.

Surrounded by black road cases on wheels with KEITH URBAN stenciled on them in white letters, equipped with a state-of-the-art soundboard and more guitars than a Guitar Center, we sat alone in the giant high-ceilinged studio and, struggling to hide my excitement, I calmly picked up my guitar. Then Keith picked up one of his. I put mine down again. This was Keith Urban, after all. Keith started chipping his pick against the strings, making four catchy chords, and every lyric I could think of rolled off my tongue like I was speed dating.

There's an unspoken motto among songwriters: Dare to Suck. You have to be totally vulnerable in a co-write and sing whatever you're feeling, to hopefully get to a magic lyric. What you might think is really stupid might make your co-writer drum on the table and yell "Fuckin' brilliant!" And if they don't, that's okay. Dare to suck.

Nashvillians love to talk about Keith Urban sightings at a local Starbucks. With this information as inspiration, lyrics about coffee spoons on the counter and lipstick on a coffee cup kept coming out of my mouth. Keith stopped playing and laughed.

"Man, you have something for coffee, don't you?" he said.

"Oh no, I was just trying things out," I replied sheepishly.

Sitting in chairs facing each other eye to eye, we both sang whatever came into our heads. Some lines about Guns N' Roses on the radio were sung, leading us to the lyric "In my mind we're somewhere in my car." Keith stopped again and said, "Man, I love this stuff about the car." We had a song concept and we were off to the races…no pun intended.

Verse after verse we sang louder and the strumming got faster. Keith pulled an old cassette recorder out of a square leather bag filled with tapes. He pushed the record button and taped himself singing to capture the idea. Most other writers record on an iPhone or their computer—I loved his old-school cassette vibe. We wrote the first verse and chorus. By the end of the day we knew we had the emotion, feel, and lyrics for a cool song.

"Good on ya. Let's go eat."

We climbed into Keith's car from the future. I'm from Detroit and I've never seen, much less ridden in, a car like Keith's. Driving through Nashville with the biggest country star behind the wheel of a sleek inky-black sports car, I felt like we were Batman and Robin.[21] Pretty Vanderbilt students pointed at us from street corners as I tried to mouth "Hit me up on Facebook" as we drove past them.[22]

Over chicken salads we talked about our lives and Keith gushed over his wife, Nicole Kidman, and their kids. Keith might not have noticed every waitress and customer staring at us, but I did. It's fun to be associated with a celebrity.

A couple of weeks passed and Keith was calling me on the phone. "J.T., mate, we need to finish these lyrics. Let's get together. Come to the studio so you can hear the track." By *track* he meant the music—he had already recorded it. Like an architect plans a building, Keith had the song in his head ready to go before we'd finished the lyrics.

Melting into a leather sofa in the back of the dimly lit studio, I was dumbfounded as the speakers bumped and our song filled the room. Even without lyrics, the song sounded

---

21 I was Robin, obviously.

22 Wearing a bright suit coat and pants, I told this story onstage to a thousand people in Sundance, Utah. My brother Lance, who was in attendance, yelled out, "In that outfit they should've called you the Joker!" The crowd roared as if Dave Chappelle himself had said it.

amazing. Keith and his producer Dan Huff were laying down a banjo on the finished track, and it sounded incredible. Keith put the banjo down after a few takes and waved me into another room, and we finished writing the lyrics. We both wanted the chorus to really pay off, and to do that you need to set it up with a scene that makes sense.

"Keith, in your song ''Til Summer Comes Around' you say, 'I'm frozen in this town 'til summer comes around.' Let's set up our chorus like that," I suggested. He sang, "I know you're with someone else...but in my mind...we're somewhere in my car." The falsetto "a woo hoo" in our pre-chorus is a Keith Urban trademark. Keith's songs are all over the radio every day, and I love how he sings. I lobbed the falsetto part into our song and his ice-blue eyes lit up.

With the lyric finished, he played and sang it top to bottom on his acoustic guitar. As it got close to the end of the song, we added "whoah oh oh! whoah oh oh!" Standing up, I yelled over the chords, "Eighty thousand people will be singing this part at the end!" He laughed. "Damn right!"

Adding something catchy and new before your song fades out is a surefire way to keep the listener engaged all the way to the end. Think "Let It Be," "Ain't Talking 'Bout Love," "Purple Rain"...

There's a lot of things I love about "Somewhere in My Car," but I really love how the song pertains to my life. In high school, a white station wagon with rust-stained doors and one blown radio speaker was my rock star ride. It wasn't a chick magnet, but it saved me from myself. On lonely Friday nights, make-out Saturday nights, and—most boring of all— "you should be studying" Sunday nights, I drove around and escaped with music. No matter the mood or what was happening in my life, the radio in that car was there for me.

I'd drive around listening to the radio, imagining I'd written the great songs I was hearing and singing them. On the way to a dance with my buddies, we would blast the car radio, pumping ourselves up. When a new song by a band I loved came out (there wasn't iTunes then), driving around and waiting for it to come on my favorite station was the only way to hear it.

Cruising through Grosse Pointe, singing along and daydreaming of having my own songs on the radio, was my only hobby. To this day, I drive around and listen to music for hours somewhere in my car.

"Bar at the End of the World"

One of the most important things I've learned as a songwriter is to take breaks. You cannot be on output all the time—you have to have input. You can't be creating all the time if you're not having experiences and badass adventures to write about. See movies, read books, listen to a lot of music, fall for people with more red flags than a circus tent. Traveling is also a great way to recharge.

"Captain" Greg is a dive instructor and Kenny Chesney fanatic who lives in the Virgin Islands. Imagine Matthew McConaughey if he wasn't an actor and dressed in flip-flops, a T-shirt, and a "you wish you were me" smile as he drives a boat all day. That's Greg. Greg and I have been as close as R2-D2 and C-3PO since grade school. He moved from Michigan to the Virgin Islands after college.

Visiting Greg one year, the last thing on my mind was writing a song. As you may know, in the Caribbean there are bars on islands you can only get to by boat. You cruise across the Slurpee-blue bay and drop anchor close to shore. You jump in the bath-warm water, swim to the beach, and leave a trail of footprints in the sand on your walk to the bar. One of the best bars is called the Soggy Dollar.

With soggy money in my bathing suit pocket, I waited as a braided-hair bartender mixed drinks and flirted with the tourists. Her shirt had a pirate skull with an eyepatch and read DEAD MEN TELL NO TAILS. There were dollar bills stapled to every inch of the walls of the tin-roofed bar by first-time visitors. The two dozen boats on the water looked like a floating parking lot. Bob Marley songs drifted out of a speaker hung up in a coconut tree.

All these images instantly hit my creative muscle as the bartender's tart pineapple Painkiller cocktail hit my tongue. I knew an incredible beach song could be written about this place, but I didn't have a title. There are a million beach songs already. Nashville is full of good songs. How could I make mine stand out? Without a strong title, I put the idea on the back burner and enjoyed my stay.

My tan lines long faded, while visiting Lance, now happily married and living in Boston, we passed a place called Tavern at the End of the World. Seeing the sign was like Edison seeing his first lightbulb turn on. I knew I had my title for the beach song. (I changed it to *Bar* instead of *Tavern*. People want to party like it's 1999, not 1599!)

Following one of my own rules—"Save a great idea for a great co-writer"—I saved it for David Lee Murphy, who was on my calendar. David Lee Murphy is a doorway-tall, long-haired, cowboy-hat-wearing badass. He is a hit country artist and has a dozen number one songs he's written for other people. Kenny Chesney has recorded so many of David's songs I call David "the Kenny whisperer." Aimee Mayo, who co-wrote the gigantic hit "Amazed" for Lonestar with Marv Green, was the third writer on our song. She has a great spirit and adds a lot of energy to group writing sessions.

"Hell yeah!" David said, adjusting his hat when I told him the "Bar at the End of the World" idea, and we wrote it quickly. Explaining all the Soggy Dollar images and the bars around it on the carless island, David sang, "A little tin roof bar down a path you have to follow," then we talked about pirates and modernized the image with "a treasure map where the edge is burnt from a few too many beers." The beautiful bartender with braids in the pirate shirt and the dollar bills on the walls I had seen became our chorus.

The bridge is fun: We threw my friend Uncle Kracker a shout-out by name-dropping one of his biggest songs. "They're playing 'Drift Away'...back up in that little bay." When we finished, Amy emailed the song to Kenny and he released it as a single. How ironic that the biggest Kenny Chesney fan I know, Captain Greg, inspired me to write a song about our island adventures together, and Kenny Chesney recorded it.

"Beers and Sunshine"

Tornado sirens louder than a thousand saxophones whined through the night as a storm rolled over Nashville, lifting up trees and scattering them like a kid pulling out golf tees playing a Cracker Barrel triangle peg game. My power went out and was out for five days. The TV wouldn't turn on, but I didn't mind missing a few episodes of *Ozark*. It was the peak of quarantine, so I also didn't mind missing some Instagram posts, but there was something I was not going to miss: a first-time writing appointment with Darius Rucker. "Hootie and the Blown Power" was definitely *not* going to be a chapter in this book.

Zigzagging my Jeep through the Nashville streets in a game of real-life *Frogger*, I drove slowly, trying to avoid downed wires, fallen trees, and men waving orange flags. I tried a Starbucks, but no luck there: no power. I stopped by a hotel, but it was closed due to quarantine. I then headed unannounced to my publisher Rusty Gaston's house and knocked.

His son in a Hulk costume made faces at me through the front window as his daughter enjoyed a SpongeBob-shaped Popsicle.

"Get your daddy, please," I begged.

Being the hero he is, Rusty found a safe place for his family to go and let me Zoom-write that day from his house.

Darius, Josh Osborne, Ross Copperman, and I wrote "Beers and Sunshine" that day, and I'm so glad we did. It's a gigantic hit.

I brought in an idea called "Bikinis and Sunshine" and we were going to call the song "BS" but Darius, Ross, and Josh thought it over, tossed the idea around, and came up with "Beers and Sunshine." I remember Darius saying it was a little more universal, and he was right. Josh added with a laugh, "I knew there was a problem when I didn't want to call the song the actual hook we were singing," meaning he didn't want to call the song "Bikinis and Sunshine."

The power was out in my house, but I had the power of co-writing. Someone hears your idea and makes it even better with their own twist. After hearing Darius on the radio for so many years, it was a thrill to hear his voice bringing the *boom boom* to the Zoom room, singing back lyrics we were all coming up with. Be careful what you wish for. I always wanted to be on *The Brady Bunch*, and thanks to COVID, I now spend my days with other songwriters, writing virtually, our heads all floating in the blue squares of the Zoom.

"Smile"

"What about a song called 'Smile'?"

Funny how these simple words Uncle Kracker said to me one afternoon turned into my biggest hit song so far. After a weekend of sipping Crown Royal and orange Faygo in his Northern Michigan cottage, we were sitting around a knee-high table crowded with empty soda cans, and somehow we caught lightning in a bottle.

There was easily four feet of snow outside. No exaggeration. After driving up from Detroit, Kracker's Cadillac got stuck in the driveway. As I was running from the car to the warmth of his cottage, one of my boots came off in the snow. I don't even remember if I ever got it back.

We wrote by day and haunted the log-cabin-style Long Lake Bar at night for chicken wings and beer and to brainstorm song ideas.[23] Uncle Kracker is so popular in Michigan, the bar literally had menu items named after him. The other songs we wrote were okay, but the last one, on the last day, was "Smile," and I knew it was a hit.

Emptying a cigarette-butt-filled black ashtray made to look like a Goodyear tire, Kracker said, "I'd love to write a song my daughters think is cool that my mom can dance to as well." Oh, is that all? A song that is easily embraced by three generations of music fans—no problem. Maybe we should join NASA and go to the moon while we're at it.

It seemed like mission impossible, but we managed.

Another writer, Blair Daly, was with us and he had put together a ten-second piano loop.[24] We started writing lyrics and melodies over that. Kracker came up with "Cooler than the flip side of my pillow." That was a saying I'd never heard before—I love those lyrics when you immediately know what they mean even if they're brand-new to you.

"Buzz like a bee" was my line, and I had to fight for it. The guys thought it was too light, but I knew it would be perfect on the radio. It had an innocence to it. The sun set through the

---

23 An illuminated sign behind the bar says ENJOY YOURSELF—IT'S LATER THAN YOU THINK. We loved the sign and used that line in another Uncle Kracker song he's releasing this year.

24 A "loop" is a tiny section of music that plays over and over repeatedly as if going in a circle.

big bay window overlooking the snowdrifts on the lake as we recorded the demo in the mobile studio we'd brought. Kracker kept singing "Crazy on a Friday night." I corrected him: "It's crazy on a *Sunday* night. You're crazy about this person in the song. You're acting wacky, you're going crazy on a Sunday night. Anyone can go crazy on a Friday night."

Shaking his wrist as his expensive watch rattled, Kracker thought about it for a second, then replied, "Good stuff." The Sunday night lyric was kept. We finished the song and never thought to write a bridge—we put in a cool violin solo instead.

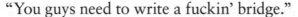

"You guys need to write a fuckin' bridge."

Rob Cavallo, the megahit producer, was instructing us in his *Star Trek* control room–style Los Angeles recording studio as we recorded "Smile." Rob was hired by Kracker and has the energy and the mannerisms of Quentin Tarantino, and I mean that in a good way. He's produced Green Day, Alanis Morissette, Dave Matthews Band, the Goo Goo Dolls—you name it. "Fuckin' A, you want to write the bridge on the very guitar the Goo Goo Dolls wrote 'Iris' on? It's right here!" he said at one point, pointing at an acoustic guitar on the wall.

On his enthusiastic advice, we scrapped the violin solo and wrote the bridge. I can't imagine the song without it now. I've heard it takes a village to raise a child—it also takes a village to tune a banjo and to write a song. It took three writers and a producer's advice to bring "Smile" home.

It's my favorite song I've been a part of and it's my biggest. As much as I love the rebellious hotel-room-trashing rock 'n' roll bands, I'm proud I've written a song that makes people feel good. A song that kids and adults can sing along with too, just like Uncle Kracker wanted. My dad had recently passed when we wrote it—maybe I was thinking of him.

Couples walk down the aisle to it at weddings. People

make "get well" videos singing it for people in the hospital. When Regis Philbin retired, they played "Smile," showing clip after clip of him on TV. As a songwriter you can't really ask for more.

"Smile" has sold four million copies and it's still selling. It was a pop hit and unexpectedly a country hit as well. It's on many TV commercials, most notably for Cold Stone Creamery ice cream for the past three years. It's in movies too. I hear it on the radio constantly and in stores when I'm shopping. Taylor Swift played it during one of her concerts, setting YouTube and my ego on fire.

Playing it live at my songwriter shows inspires a sea of cell phone lights to be held up above people's heads. Best of all, after the worry I caused her by moving to LA many years ago, my mom would get in the longest line at Kroger just to have more people to brag to about "the song my son wrote with Uncle Clunker."[25] Royalty money poured in, and I made sure my mom's bills were covered. After her believing in me for so long, it felt amazing to do stuff for her like that.

Tip-toeing as if I was walking on glass, my silver thousand-dollar Givenchy shoes were plummeting in value with every step I took on a muddy path leading from the backstage area across a field at the Faster Horses Festival. Faster Horses is a country show attended by about eighty thousand fans at a campground in Michigan. Between the superstar acts the promoter invited me to sing a couple of my hits on acoustic guitar, not only was I on the huge stage, I was being beamed around on jumbotrons set up all over the massive Woodstock-sized tent-filled property for all to see and hear. After my solo performance, a girl with sunburned shoulders wrapped in an

---

25 That's not a typo—she thinks his name is Clunker.

American flag tank top and Daisy Duke cutoff shorts took my hand, saying, "I have to show you something" and walked me toward an endless line of green-and-white porta-potties that stood like robot soldiers from a space movie. Ms. Small-Town American left me outside and went into a porta potty, closing the plastic door. An awkward minute later, I heard three short bursts, then one long burst of water.

She yelled, "Can you hear that?"

"Um yeah, why?" I said as concertgoers sloshed by.

She joyously replied, "I'm peeing the melody to 'Smile'!"

Heaven's Playlist

People often ask me which artist I wish would record a song I've written. There are a ton. Luke Bryan, Adele, Jason Aldean, Katy Perry... The ones that I truly wished for were Prince and George Michael, two of my all-time favorite singers. If you're a big music fan, I'm sure you know those two geniuses wrote their own songs. They didn't need help writing, but my friend Allen Shamblin wrote the song "I Can't Make You Love Me," which Bonnie Raitt recorded, and both Prince and George Michael sang versions of it. Can you imagine? That is beyond inspiring.

Maybe Allen and I can write the millennial version: "I Can't Make You Love Me (But I Can Stalk You on Social Media and Hope for the Best)."

Hey Hey Hey, Where My Party People?

A massive bodyguard was slicing his index finger across his neck, signaling at me to get my brother Lance away from Nicole Kidman. Lance's arm was around her as beer spilled over the rim of his red Solo cup. Lance told her how great the parties at MSU are and invited her. In Nashville, when you get a number one hit, the record company and the artist throw a party and you can invite all your friends and family and music business peers. It is special beyond belief. Speeches are made, awards are handed out, and people drink the free booze like they're going to the electric chair.

Every party is different. Keith performed a magical version of "Somewhere in My Car" on piano with a cello player accompanying him at this party. Keith and I had a press conference where we spoke about writing the song. I felt like the vice president sitting with him in front of a sea of cameras and reporters. Nicole Kidman was beyond sweet to all my friends and family, spending time talking with them all.

The party for "Somewhere With You" was so crowded you could not move in the Nashville restaurant, Cabana, where it took place. Standing on a small stage, Shane, myself, and Kenny Chesney in a baseball cap each gave a speech. Kenny spoke softly into a microphone. Most of us had never been in such proximity to Kenny before, and we all hung on his every word. "I'm real lucky to be able to sing this song the rest of my career. When I play it and the intro starts on guitar, eighty thousand people cheer at once. It's an unreal thing. I hope Shane and J.T. get to experience it this summer," Kenny said sincerely. Shane, holding another microphone, said into it, "Can you get us tickets?" Not knowing it was a joke, Kenny swung around and in all seriousness said, "Oh, for sure, let me know, I got tickets."

My mom stood beaming in the audience surrounded by all our friends from Nashville and Michigan who attended the party. I told the crowd how I wished my dad was here and how much he loved country music. I finished with the story of my dad spraying the hose on the crazy neighbor who sped her car up our driveway as I sang in the backyard as a kid.

Kenny laughed and I overheard Shane say, "Damn, that was good."

Following the "Alone With You" number one party, my mom's Facebook was flooded with comments on how good-looking I was. Old friends, neighbors from our Berkshire Road house in Grosse Pointe, girls from high school I had lost touch with, you name it—everyone was commenting on the picture of my mom and me she posted. The brown-eyed, brown-haired, movie star–looking man smiling in the picture with my mom was Jake Owen, not me.

Team Blake

Blake Shelton was having so many hits he had a number one party for "Sangria" and four other songs at one gathering. It was on the patio at Losers, a sticky-floor bar in Nashville. There were fifteen speeches. Every writer was given the mic. It was 100 degrees out. The government channel on cable is more exciting than most of the speeches that were given that night, it was so brutal.

When Scott Hendricks, Blake's producer, handed me the sweaty mic, I raised my fist to the air and yelled, "Thank you for recording 'Sangria,' Blake Shelton for president!" I passed the mic to my co-writer Josh Osborne as the crowd cheered. As I stepped back in line next to the other writers, Blake stared at me hard, clapping fast. The armpits of his shirt were dark circles of sweat. Leaning into him, I said, "I did a short speech on purpose." He yelled back at me over the crowd's noise, "I know, why do you think I'm clapping?!"

Dierks Bentley had a very small party for "Different for Girls." Italian food and expensive wine for everyone. Dierks wore a Detroit shirt that made my day. Elle King, who sang with him on the track, was a thrill to meet. We were allowed only two guests, so I invited my dad's brother Butch Harding and his wife. Butch lived in Tennessee and texted me every time a song I had written was released or moved up a spot on the charts. Butch had attended every party so far and was so starstruck when he met famous singers. Butch loved country music. My dad would have been happy to know Butch was at the party.

Sitting at one end of a long table, Shane and I were interviewed by the press after the party. A dozen cameras flashed like strobe lights as rapid-fire questions were shouted at us like we were Paul and John at an old-school Beatles press conference. As we laughed and talked about writing "Different for Girls," and the Grammy nomination it received,[26] I truly felt like a superstar.

"Different for Girls" and "Sangria" were both awarded "Song I Wish I'd Written" at the Nashville Songwriters Association International (NSAI) awards the years they were released. The award is voted on by my peers in the songwriting community. If my house ever caught fire (heaven forbid), those two would be the awards I would save first.

---

26 When someone says "I was nominated for a Grammy"...it means they lost.

CHAPTER 19

If a Hit Song Falls in the Forest, Will Anyone in Nashville Hear It?

J.T., how do I get my songs heard? How can I get my break?"
The people asking are always polite. They are sincere. They are anxious. They are yearning for the answer. They want guidance. They'll do anything to make it. "You need to move to Nashville," I say. Their heads go back and they roll their eyes like I had told them elephants can fly. They say things like "Oh, come on, I can't possibly do that."

This is my advice: If you're looking to do country music, if you want to write country songs that a country artist will someday record and use to make a hit, you have to move to Nashville.

What Hollywood is to making movies, what Detroit is to making cars, what Arizona is to senior citizens who carry hot sauce with them everywhere, Nashville is to songwriting. That's why it is called Music City.

Megahit writer Brett James once said, "Songwriting is a full-contact sport." If you meet him, don't be fooled by his island-life tan—he's in Nashville writing every single day. I cannot think of one person who is a successful country songwriter that doesn't live in Nashville or spend an incredible amount of time there.

People say Nashville is a ten-year town, which means it takes ten years to make it there. But even then, there's no guarantee. It could take longer. But you have to be there. You have to be in it to win it.

I saw that heartbeat-stopping lifeguard at the local pool when I was seven years old and I've been writing ever since. I wish it had only taken me ten years. Let the work drive you, but don't let it drive you crazy. When you follow your dreams with confidence, you will experience great things when you least expect it.

Go South, Young Man

During a recent visit to California, aspiring writers spilled like marbles into a ballroom at the Loews Hotel to listen to me perform my hits, then asked questions after. A guy raised his hand and said, "My girlfriend would break up with me if I moved to Nashville."

"Well, tell her you'll miss her," I replied, making the crowd laugh.

It's tough advice, but it has to be: There wasn't a girlfriend, there's wasn't a job, there wasn't a family member, there wasn't anything or anyone that could've kept me from following my dream.

If you're not willing to put music first, then you're already in the back of a very long line.

Think of any country star and connect the rhinestones of their journey. Garth Brooks moved to Nashville from Oklahoma. Luke Bryan and his writing friends, the so-called "Peach Pickers," all moved to Nashville from Georgia. Kacey Musgraves came from Texas. Keith Urban came all the way from Australia.

They are as different from one another as you can imagine. But they all share a common trait. They all lowered the number on their hometown population sign by one. They moved to Nashville to write, record, and perform country music.

People from all over the world send me songs they've written, or write to tell me that a friend or a daughter or son or a neighbor has written a song and they'd like to ask for my help. It's flattering, but keep in mind that there is a school in Nashville called Belmont. Every student there is an up-and-coming songwriter. Vanderbilt University is here as well, and it too is filled with aspiring songwriters.

Then there are thousands of other songwriters here, humming an idea they have as they shake the fryer at Chick-fil-A. Young people putting lyrics in their phones as they work their valet shift at the Opryland Hotel. Bands on Broadway playing six-hour-long sets with sweat dripping off them like holy water, praying to be discovered. They work seven nights a week, singing to bachelorettes holding up penis-shaped squirt guns, working for tips and trying to sneak in an original song between covers of "Jessie's Girl" and "Friends in Low Places." Every dog is a lion at home. Get to Nashville.

Working 9 to 5…Then Go Make a Living

So you get to town, then what? Then you have to outwrite everybody else. Get a job that allows you enough time between waking up with coffee and going to bed with Netflix to write every day.

Struggling writers have said to me, "I'll write every day when I get a writing deal!" That isn't how it works. Music publishers sign writers to deals and help them get their songs recorded. Publishers are looking for people who are already writing every day, doing the work to make it happen on their own. Publishers have offices in the houses up and down the famous Music Row in Nashville. The publishers find out who is making records and when. They get your songs heard. They give you advice on songs you're working on. They pay for your demos. A lot of publishers give you a small advance so you can actually write songs for a living. The advance can be one large lump sum or a "draw," where money is given in monthly payments similar to a bank loan.

When they hear songs you've written that impress them, they will set you up with other writers they like, most likely during office hours, long before they sign you to a deal themselves. Write every day.

Meeting other writers is so important. Playing open mic nights at the Bluebird Cafe and every hotel lobby, coffeehouse, and bar is one way. Belcourt Taps, a bar by the Vanderbilt University campus, has singers and songwriters seven nights a week grinding it out. The Listening Room Cafe is another great venue built around shows featuring songwriters of all levels. You have to go out and meet people. You have to dive in and write songs like you never have before.

There's a mural painted on a wall outside of the coffee place where I'm writing this very book that reads SPREAD LOVE—IT'S THE NASHVILLE WAY. Nashville is a nurturing town; there are people here whose job it is to help you.

There's an incredible organization here called the Nashville Songwriters Association International (NSAI). They'll set you up with co-writers. They have seminars all the time with hit writers you can talk to and learn from. It's a real community of great people. Nashville loves songwriters. All creeds, all colors, every level of talent. NSAI has chapters all over America too, small groups of people working together and writing together in lots of cities. Get online, look them up in your area, see if you can find a group. If you can't find one, *start one*.

As you make your way, are you going to meet some flakes and weirdos who couldn't write a song if Paul McCartney and Beyoncé were in the room with a rhyming dictionary? You bet, I wrote with a new band recently, and it was like putting underwear on a kangaroo. But eventually, if you're persistent, positive, and hardworking, you will meet people you'll connect with, and magic will happen. And if you work at it and your songs are good, they will eventually get the attention of a music publisher.

Are you still reading? Good, you're a diehard and I like you already. Continue. Here comes a bucket of cold water on your head: Songwriter Marv Green took the best songs he'd ever written in his life and got a publishing deal. Then his publisher said, "Now you really need to write some *great* songs. The songs I signed you for show potential, but they're not hits." Tough to hear, but it worked. Marv went on to write "Amazed" and dozens of smashes.

If you absolutely positively can't move to Nashville, then find a band or some singers who are doing country music in your town and try to write with them. Maybe when they get discovered you will have written songs with them that they can release. Record companies do look for singers and bands that have big local followings, huge social media followings, or tour a lot on their own.

Eventually though, those hometown heroes you know and love will come through Nashville. When they do, they will be presented with amazing songs written right here in Music City. Ed Sheeran, Bon Jovi, Lady Gaga, and Jay-Z have all come to Nashville to work with writers here. You cannot deny this is the place to be as a songwriter.

If you absolutely can't travel, put videos of yourself

singing on Instagram and YouTube. Let people know about you. Try out for *American Idol* or *The Voice*. You have the world at your fingertips with the internet. Use it to connect with people.

Be Yourself—Everybody Else Is Already Shakin'

Should you move here and start writing, don't forget where you came from.

One major key to my success, I realized after I had a few hits, is that I was being myself and telling my own story. My publisher Rusty Gaston calls it "Writing your truth."

My motto: What's Most Personal Is Most Universal. The things that are happening in your life that you think no one is going to understand, that's what's going to affect people the most.

Take "Somewhere With You," for example: That song is so personal to me, and the melodies were so different no one thought it was a country song. But people stop me on the street to this day to talk to me about that song. Grammy winner Tom Douglas, who wrote "The House That Built Me," once put his hand on my shoulder and in a studio full of people said, " 'Somewhere With You' was a seminal moment in country music."

I was so flattered I had to leave the room and catch my breath. I also had to google the word *seminal*. It means *influencing the development of future events*. In Tom's mind, that song changed country music. I was being myself and that's what set it apart. Writing a country hit isn't easy, although a lot of people I've met on my travels talk about country music in a condescending way. (*Condescending* means talking down to someone because they're not as smart as you.)

People who imagine they can quickly write a "country"

song about a dog and a Walmart and think it's no different than an actual country hit probably think drinking antifreeze is okay because it's the same color as a Slurpee. Country fans are smart and they want what's real.

I'm from Detroit. I'm not going to outwrite those people from Georgia that grew up with driveways made of red clay. Writing songs about being in the backwoods with the crickets and frogs isn't my specialty. To me, camping is a hotel and a hair dryer.

Here's the cool thing though: The people who can (and do) write those songs are not going to write "Sangria" like me. Those writers are not going to write "Somewhere With You" or "Different for Girls." There's room for everyone, so be yourself. I'm not saying you have to have lived every lyric you write. Bernie Taupin wasn't really in outer space when he wrote "Rocket Man" for Elton John, but the longing for love was real, and judging from his autobiography, Elton was probably high as a kite on drugs. I'm saying: Make sure the details are authentic. Let your lyrics be your story. Write your truth.

From Your Lips to Pod's Ears...

Here are some tips to make your songs stand out:

Whether it's words rolling off your tongue as you play your guitar, being typed by your thumbs in your phone, or scribbled in a notebook, your lyrics are expressing yourself but also expressing the feelings of the listeners. Not everyone knows how to say what they feel, and even if they do, a lot of people don't have the courage to say it. When a person can't explain how they feel, they'll find a song that can.

No one's as tongue-tied as I am when a beautiful girl is standing in front of me. The hardest thing for me to say to a person is that I'm falling for them. Equally difficult is when someone hurts my feelings. That's why I'm a songwriter. I write when I feel alone, I listen to music when I feel alone—so always remember, your listener may feel alone too. Write for them. They need songs about heartbreak as much as they need songs about joy and romance. They need you to put into a song how they feel, because it's hard for a lot of people to put matters of the heart into words.

To me, one of the cleverest things to do with lyrics is to say something simple that people can instantly relate to but that no one has said in a song before. It's similar to hearing a comedian tell a joke, and you think, "That's me!" It's not easy, but dig deep and you can wow the world.

The lyric in that Alison Krauss song "When You Say Nothing at All," written by Keith Whitley, says, "Old Mr. Webster could never define what's being said between your heart and mine." How many times have you looked at a dictionary or heard the term *Webster's Dictionary* but never once thought to put it in a lyric? It's so simple and yet so universally understood.

In the song "Bette Davis Eyes," Kim Carnes sings, "Her hair is Harlow gold." Jean Harlow, the original Blonde Bombshell, started the trend for bleaching hair in the 1930s. Ask a hundred people to name a hair color, no one will say "Harlow gold." That's why it's such a stellar lyric! It also reinforces the song's title, singing about another feature of a person with "Bette Davis Eyes." In "A Woman Like You" recorded by Lee Brice, writer Phil Barton came up with "I probably never would have heard of yoga"—so straightforward but so smart in describing living with a girl.

Show, Don't Tell is the motto in Nashville. Show how you're feeling with imagery. In "Sangria" we say "wrecking ball dancing down the hallway." Our description is so much better than simply saying "we were tipsy." Use lyrics like Michelangelo used a paintbrush to paint the Sistine Chapel.

In "Heartbreakers," a song I co-wrote on the latest Kenny

Chesney album, the lyric is "Jenny had the devil in her smile and a cross on her neck, first girl I ever saw smoke a cigarette." Once again, the imagery is so much better than a simple "Jenny was a girl I liked." In "Sweet Child o' Mine" Axl Rose recounts his childhood: "Her hair reminds me of a warm safe place where as a child I'd hide"...he's imagining a wheat field or bushes to describe his lover's hair, and it's really brilliant. Show, don't tell.

When thinking of a song title, imagine seeing it on a T-shirt. Ask yourself: *Would this make a good T-shirt to sell at concerts?* YOU MAKE ME SMILE is a great T-shirt; YOUR LIPS TASTE LIKE SANGRIA is a great T-shirt. Blake Shelton sells wineglasses and decanters with that printed on them now. The song I wrote with Darius Rucker says, "The only BS I need is beers and sunshine." I can picture that as a bumper sticker *and* a T-shirt![27]

On the come-up in LA I was playing a lot of shows, and I learned that people looked up from their dollar beers and people they were flirting with when a song I sang had a cool lyric in the beginning. It's something I now try to do in every song, and you should too. Try to grab the listener's ears like a single girl grabbing a flying bouquet at a wedding. Get a lyric in the first line or two that makes people stop and turn up the radio. Make people look at their friends and say, "Whoa, did you hear that?" In "Different for Girls" I wrote "She don't text her friends and say 'I gotta get laid tonight'" in the first few lines. It caught people's attention. Country radio even bleeped it out on some stations. Double win!

In "Smile" Uncle Kracker sings "Cooler than the flip side of my pillow" two lines into the song. People mention that line to me all the time.

---

27 Darius Rucker now sells drink tumblers with that lyric written on them.

When the Verses Are Loaded, You'll Hit a Home Run

A silver aluminum baseball bat rested on my right shoulder leading to my fingers squeezed tight around the red grip tape. With my left hand I tossed a baseball straight up, my eyes following it above my head, and as it came back down I swung the bat and hit the ball as far as I could. Running the bases in my imaginary sold-out ball field after school, I told myself I had won the Little League World Series.

In reality, I never hit home runs like my brothers did. On the field, I was wagging my tongue like Gene Simmons and using a Louisville Slugger for a guitar, but the baseball analogy is a perfect way to explain how to set up the lyric leading up to your chorus.

The words before the chorus should be like that baseball, lobbed up, waiting to be hit out of the park. What I mean by that is, at least in country music, the lyrics that lead up to the chorus should set it up as a perfect, easy-to-understand payoff for the listener. In "Beers and Sunshine" we say: "Nothing spinning in the blender, the only thing on my agenda is...beers and sunshine." Why do you need a blender for beer? Exactly—you don't. Going into the second chorus we wrote, "Flying high like we'll never come down, we're gonna go until we run out of...beers and sunshine."

Use that trick at the end of a chorus as well if the title doesn't come until the end. "The only BS I need is...beers and sunshine." See how the lyrics feed our title.

In "Somewhere With You" Shane and I set it up like this: "Call up an ex to rescue me, climb in their bed when I'd much rather sleep...somewhere with you." Examples from incredible songs I did not write: Carrie Underwood singing "She threw her hands up in the air...Jesus, take the wheel." Tommy

Tutone's "Jenny I've got your number, I need to make you mine. Jenny don't change your number—867-5309." "Dirt," written by Chris Tompkins and Rodney Clawson for Florida Georgia Line, uses every single lyric of their song to feed the title: "You get your hands in it, plant your roots in it, dusty headlight, dance with your boots in it...dirt."

Hitting the baseball, feeding the chorus like a monster, call it whatever you want, but it works and will take your songs to the next level in terms of writing.

The Wizard of Ahhhs

Melodies are mysterious. A melody is probably the most basic element of music. String a series of musical notes together, one after the other, and you have a melody.

My biggest piece of advice when writing a song is: Keep the Melody Hummable. Standing in line waiting for a register to open at Target, no one "hums" a screaming frantic guitar solo. When people walk their dog at night, no one hums a machine-gun-fast full-tilt drumbeat. We all hum simple nursery rhyme–type melodies, no matter if they are on an instrument or someone's voice. The simple songs get stuck in our heads.

Think of "True" by Spandau Ballet. The best part of the song is the "ah ha ha haah ha" that goes throughout the song. It's almost a lullaby.[28]

If you want to write a *hit*, ask yourself: *Can I whistle the*

---

28 "True" also contains a brilliant lyric: "With...a pill on my tongue...listening to Marvin all night long," referencing a Marvin Gaye song. So personal but so universal.

melody? Is it stuck in my head halfway through writing it, when I take a lunch break?

Another way to write a simple melody is to put your instrument down for a bit when you are writing it. Go for a bike ride or drive around and come up with a melody first, *then* put it to music.

Use long notes and short notes as you sing, mix it up. Just like I've described a song going up and down like a roller coaster with the instruments, do that with your melody. "Somewhere in My Car" uses held-out notes in the top of the chorus, then fast singing at the end of the chorus, and I did the same thing in "Different for Girls." Country music is famous for having the verses in a lower melody, then the chorus soars a bit higher, but that's not a rule that can't be broken.

Songs by Bruno Mars or Train come in full of energy with the singing high and raring to go right from the start.

Jay Thomas told me comedians start out writing jokes alone in their bedroom, then they try them out at open mic nights and see if people like them. Songs are like that as well. You have to work on them and see what happens.

There's no magic button, but I do believe if you listen to songs you like and see how they do it, you're seeing behind the Wizard of Oz's curtain, so to speak, and you will find inspiration.

When writing a song, another thing that's difficult but very effective is to use the same chords throughout the entire song but to change the melody. The song has different melodies for the verse, chorus, and bridge, and yet it's basically the same four guitar chords. Example: "Free Fallin'" by Tom Petty and Jeff Lynne, and "Lose Yourself" by Eminem do this as well.

"Born in the U.S.A." by Bruce Springsteen is basically two chords but there are different melodies going on to keep it exciting.

The same goes in reverse. If you're using a lot of guitar notes and very complicated chords, let the melody over it shine with longer notes and fewer words.

Remember: Always keep it simple. If you're looking for a hit, make sure you can sing along to it easily. Don't take my word for it. The '80s metal band Ratt has a song called "Round and Round" that's been on the radio for almost forty years. Doug Morris, the president of Atlantic Records at the time, heard his nine-year-old son walking through the house singing the song after hearing the unreleased album. Based on that reaction, Doug thought it must be a hit and told the band, "This is going to be your single." Several parents have held up their phones to show me videos of their kids singing along to "Sangria." It's a huge compliment in my book, even though their kids are running around singing about being drunk.

The hardest part is making it look easy. Simple melodies are hard to write but they are easy to listen to. Sometimes it almost seems boring in the writing room when we sing something that's really simple, but don't overthink it, don't complicate your song if you want the world to sing along. Here's a test: If you have doubts when you're writing a melody, see if you can sing it by just clapping along with no other instruments. Most hit songs work very well just like that.

Writing Under the Influence

Tower Records wasn't only a great place to meet record company employees—it was an endless well of inspiration. The long racks of CDs for sale, weekly new releases being played over the store sound system, and the free promo CDs we were given as employees were a goldmine of discovery for me.

Coming home from work every night with all that music

in my head pushed me to spend nights writing on my acoustic guitar. So many of my buddies since grade school can to this day sit down and easily find the notes and figure out how to play famous songs on guitar they've only heard on the radio. Not me.

Figuring out other people's songs to play "covers" isn't a skill I have. In reality, I only know how to play a few chords, but that limitation has helped my songs stay simple and catchy.

One of the best songwriters around is Diane Warren. She has written dozens of hits, including "I Don't Want to Miss a Thing" for Aerosmith and "If I Could Turn Back Time" for Cher. Another great writer is Desmond Child. Desmond—who wrote the giant Bon Jovi songs with Jon and Richie Sambora, as well as "How Can We Be Lovers" by Michael Bolton, cowritten with Diane Warren—had his own solo album out, which I discovered at Tower, and I studied the Desmond Child and Diane Warren songs on it like the Goonies studied One-Eyed Willy's treasure map.

Sidenote: One day at Tower, cutting open a cardboard box of new CDs to be displayed, I noticed someone with brown curly hair standing one aisle over in a leather jacket—it was Desmond Child, shopping. I could not believe my eyes. I recognized him from his album cover.

Taking a deep breath, walking slowly, I approached and said, "Excuse me, just wanted to say I love your music and have learned so much from listening to your CD. I work here but I'm a songwriter."

A huge kid-eating-ice-cream smile came across his face as he said slowly, "Wow, not many people know I put an album out." Balancing the stack of CDs in my left hand, I wiped my sweaty right palm on my jeans, then put it out to shake his.

"I'm J.T. It's an honor to meet you."

His strong hand gripped mine as he said, "Frank Stallone.

Great to meet you." I felt dizzy with embarrassment as I awkwardly smiled. It wasn't Desmond Child at all—it was Sylvester Stallone's brother, Frank. They had the same hair and look. Frank Stallone had released an independent CD on his own, a coworker told me a minute later. Frank left the store walking on air while I went to the break room to hide.

Hair Metal to Pedal Steel

At Tower, the boss put me in charge of the "country" section, giving me permission to listen to any CD so I could tell customers my thoughts and be able to answer their questions. It was there I first heard Vince Gill's voice, which sounds like Christmas snow falling and charmed me with the song "Tryin' to Get Over You." Garth Brooks's "The Dance" was so heartfelt and simple, country music was like rain to my thirsty ears.

"Took your mom and the whole office to see Shania Twain. The old man loves her." I can still hear my dad's excited voice over the phone, telling me I should write country music. I rolled my eyes but how right he turned out to be.

Shania was a superstar. Scanning the credits on her CD *Come On Over* revealed she wrote her songs with her producer, Mutt Lange. Lange's name was as familiar to me as Joey's was to Chandler—Mutt produced the heavy metal–pop perfection Def Leppard albums. Mutt's songs stay in your head; so much so, you'd need an exorcist to get them out.

The pre-choruses to his songs are catchier than chicken pox. Listening to them, I thought his songs had reached the chorus. Then, like Bugs Bunny dropping a piano on my head, the chorus would hit and it was better than the pre-chorus! Listen to "When" by Shania Twain for an example of this. It's Def Leppard with pedal steel guitar instead of fuzzy distortion.

Learning to play those songs on my guitar wasn't the goal. Trying to make my songs feel like those songs was the goal.

Analyzing other writers' songs and learning from their arrangements after a day at Tower, just like I had done in my bedroom back home in Michigan, was like finding a new prize in an old box of Cracker Jacks.

It's a great way to learn how the songs are arranged. How the sections of a song change from one to the next like an expensive car smoothly shifting gears. How the melodies lift and drop, making your emotions lift and drop with them. How the catchy part repeats over and over and over.

I'm not the only one who's been majorly influenced by records spinning in their room and the radio up loud. Kurt Cobain famously said he loved the band Pixies. He loved how their verses were quiet and the choruses would explode. Those songs' dynamics were the template for Nirvana songs. The iconic guitar riff in "Smells Like Teen Spirit" sounds to me a lot like the Boston song "More Than a Feeling." Nirvana drummer Dave Grohl even alluded to that fact in an interview.

As I connected the dots myself, that Boston guitar riff sounds like it could have come from the old classic song "Louie Louie." "Love in America," a song I released under the name JTX, was the number one most played song on SiriusXM Hits 1 in 2012. My guitar riff was influenced by "Louie Louie."

Daryl Hall of Hall & Oates once told *Rolling Stone* magazine that Michael Jackson approached him during the recording of "We Are the World" and admitted stealing from a Hall & Oates song for his song "Billie Jean." Listen to the bass line in "I Can't Go for That" by Daryl Hall & John Oates and "Billie Jean" by Michael Jackson and decide for yourself.

At a Bluebird Cafe show we did together, Jonathan Cain of Journey told me he received a call from Prince in the 1980s. Prince was concerned a new song he'd written was too similar to "Faithfully," which Jonathan wrote for Journey. Prince played Cain the as-yet unreleased "Purple Rain" over the phone. Jonathan told Prince it sounded great and he hoped it would be a big hit.

"Faithfully" was already a smash on radio and in heavy rotation on MTV. I'm guessing the Journey song made its way into Prince's purple house, into his pierced ears, and out of his cloud-shaped guitar, eventually morphing into "Purple Rain."

Listen to the chords on the two songs: very similar, both great.

In Nashville it's very common to see a dozen young people at The Pancake Pantry in a circle reading the Bible out loud. I respect that, but there's no immaculate conception in music. All songs, I believe, are influenced by other songs.

What does that mean? Be influenced by your favorite songs, but make your songs your own. Focus on the arrangement— the way the verse and the chorus and the bridge happen. The dynamics of how and when the drums drop in and out and when the guitar solo comes in—or maybe there isn't a guitar solo at all! Adam Levine told Howard Stern during an interview that his Maroon 5 song "She Will Be Loved" used the same chords as "King of Pain" by the Police. Adam didn't copy it on purpose; it was just subconscious.

Be a fan of current music. Don't be the person that says, "Music was better in my day." How are you going to ever charm the crowds if you don't know what they like and what they listen to nowadays? My colorful friend Craig Wiseman, writer of twenty-two number one hits, says: "I think one of the reasons country is so popular now is because part of pop songwriting has come into it. You hear repetitive hooks in songs by Florida Georgia Line, by Luke Bryan. It can be so simple and so fun. It ain't friggin' rocket surgery, man, it's just popular music!" And just know that if you've written a great chorus, you are halfway home.

Listen to the songs you like, and let them spark your

imagination. Take, for example, John Lennon, one of the greatest songwriters who ever lived. He was influenced by others. In an interview he said he heard "Crazy Little Thing Called Love" by Queen and it inspired him to get back into the recording studio after years of not making any records.

Be inspired by songs that make the hairs on your arms stand on end, or in Freddie Mercury's case your mustache, and keep it simple.

CHAPTER 20

All Write, All Write, All Write

Pulling my Jeep into a dark, rain-soaked, empty parking lot one night in Nashville, I thought I'd come to the wrong place. I texted my publisher, who assured me I was at the right address. I knocked on the door of the house turned studio, it opened, and there stood a smiling producer named Busbee, visiting Nashville from LA. Like kids on an awkward first date, we shook hands and made small talk in the glow of his computer as he ate a chili dog.

"Jonas Brothers need a theme song for their TV show *Jonas L.A.* Listen to this track," he said. Wiping mustard from his lip, he then pushed the space bar on his computer and an infectious groove started.

I pulled out my iPhone and googled Jonas Brothers. I learned they are from New Jersey, and that became the spark for our song "Feelin' Alive." The lyrics describe their journey to superstardom, "From Jersey town to the LA crowd they're hearing us all over the world." We were pumped when the Jonas Brothers chose our song to release, and Busbee and I became friends. This song proves that a co-write isn't only about music; Busbee had info about the Jonas Brothers needing a song, and he was happy to share it with me.

Busbee recently passed away, and he is dearly missed. The

Jonas Brothers dedicated "Feelin' Alive" to him at a concert in Tulsa.

One of the most valuable things I've learned in Nashville is the power of co-writing songs. Ninety-nine percent of all the Beatles' songs were co-written by John Lennon and Paul McCartney, "sitting eye to eye," as Lennon told many journalists.

Elton John wrote countless iconic songs with Bernie Taupin. Bernie wrote all the lyrics and Elton wrote the music. Mick Jagger and Keith Richards wrote the biggest Rolling Stones hits together. Producer RedOne wrote all the first big Lady Gaga hits with Lady Gaga. Billie Eilish and her brother, Finneas, write a lot of Billie's songs together. The list of great songs written by more than one person could be an entire chapter, but if those don't convince you co-writing is a great idea, go be a lawyer, because you must like arguing.

Here's what's so great about co-writing: You can bring in a title or an idea, and the other person sees it completely differently than you do. For instance, my song "Sangria"—Josh Osborne had the title, and he wanted the song to say "You came over and drank all my sangria," but it didn't sound that manly for a country dude to sing. (Sangria is a delicious drink. I love it because I have the same taste as college freshman girls.)

We talked it over and flipped the idea around to "Your lips taste like sangria." Josh had the title but together we brought the song to life.

Another great thing about co-writing is that your co-writers can introduce you to music business people you may not already know and vice versa. Their managers, their publishers, their friends who also write, will find out about you, expanding your network.

Your co-writers have their own teams that will send the

song you write to artists and record companies your people may not know.

Another writer on "Sangria" was Trevor Rosen of the great band Old Dominion. Trevor's publisher, Robert Carlton, sent "Sangria" to Blake Shelton's producer, Scott Hendricks. Co-writing helps you in so many ways besides writing the song.

Simply talking for a bit with a co-writer can inspire things. I once sat down with Rick Springfield in a backstage room at the Wildhorse Saloon in Nashville. I was set up to write with him before his sold-out show. I was prepared with titles, but as a teakettle steamed we got to know each other. Rick, kicking back on a couch holding a guitar, looked as cool as he did in the video for "Jessie's Girl," which was filmed forty-one years ago. He told me, "I go to the gym a lot. I hate walking in, but I love walking out."

Boom! "Rick, that's our title. You love walking in to see your lover, and hate walking out. Let's put a relationship spin in it." We wrote the song as his band sound checked, and Rick recorded "Walkin' In" on his next album.

Uncle Kracker had the title "Smile." That song wouldn't even exist if we weren't in the room together. All my hits are co-writes and I wouldn't have it any other way. Plus, calling a co-writer on the phone and holding the phone up to the speaker when you hear a song you wrote together on the radio is part of the fun.

Success, I've learned, is best spent shared.

Life Is Like High School

Speaking of co-writing: Brand-new writers come to Nashville every day. They see me perform a songwriter show and they ask to write with me. I'm flattered. Truly I am, it is a dream come true to be respected as a writer, but writing a song with me isn't going to get you an instant hit. That's not how it works. You need to find people, your own peers, your own group of writers who are at the same level as you, and write together and rise together.

New writers are the hitmakers of tomorrow and I sympathize with them. Starting from the bottom isn't fun. When I arrived in Nashville, I wanted to write with any writer with a roomful of framed awards and number one plaques. Knocking on every door, trying to get in the room with all of them, I didn't get in the room with any of them. Simply put: I hadn't earned it yet.

Not that I don't pay it forward. I write with beginning writers if it's at a songwriting workshop through a school or through the NSAI, but my writing calendar is booked for months in advance by my publisher. Maybe this is the tough love of the songwriting business, but trust me: Find your own tribe and you will rise together.

Jeff Carlton, one of the best music publishers ever (who unfortunately has passed away), once said about Nashville that "the freshmen always want to write with the seniors." It's a great high school analogy.

Find people with a hunger like yours. People you meet at open mic nights, the songwriters that you meet standing in line waiting to get in the Bluebird Cafe. Songwriters who post on Instagram. The musicians you know at your high school or your college or at a bar where you go and play with your local band. Find people around you that are talented. Write with them and come up through the ranks together. Make a noise so loud that I'm the one asking to write with *you*. It'll happen—just write, write, write.

Wanted, Dead or a Write

It was noon when the gold-numbered door to a fancy hotel suite in Downtown Nashville opened in front of me and standing there smiling was Jon Bon Jovi, the man who's seen a million faces and rocked them all.

For the week leading up to the day, my mind was in overdrive, pinball bouncing from one idea to the next. I couldn't sit still in a movie, couldn't sip Bloody Marys with my friends, too excited to sleep at night, so I was prepared. Walking into my first write with Bon Jovi, I was loaded with six ideas ready to go, right off the bat, with lyrics and a title for each.

My preparation did two things. One: It gave me confidence and relaxed me. Two: Hopefully my coming in ready to work showed Bon Jovi how much respect I have for him. Writing with Jon Bon Jovi is not something you take for granted—I was taking it very seriously.

Sitting on a plush velvet couch plucking my guitar for New Jersey's favorite son, I had started my sixth idea when Jon smiled, put up his palm, and said, "Hey, it's okay! It's okay. I can tell you're very, very talented." Then, rubbing his hand through his silver hair, he said, "I have an idea. What about this?..." We wrote an idea he had that was great. He came prepared as well. That's why he's a superstar.

"Bon Jovi told me to never take a day off and all these years later you get me a co-write with him!" I was excitedly talking on my phone to Jonathan Daniel, my then-publisher, my forever friend, and one of the smartest people in the history of music. Jonathan has had more hits than Snoop Dogg's bong. He manages Fall Out Boy, Green Day, Train, Sia, and so many more.

"The smartest thing you ever did was not get bitter after

your EMI deal. Bitterness has ruined a lot of careers," Jonathan mused.

"I should write a song called 'I've seen a hundred faces and I've rocked them all,'" I bragged.

Jonathan quietly laughed, not unlike Yoda listening to Luke Skywalker, then hung up on me.

Another bonus of co-writing is the friendships it creates. What's pretty amazing about this work is that you can meet a total stranger and by the end of the session, because you're trying to write a no-holds-barred, guaranteed number one hit, you'll know everything about each other.

After deciding on a title and working on lyrics for a couple of hours, we always go to lunch. We talk, laugh, give relationship advice. No stone is left unturned.

Our deepest secrets, our biggest heartbreaks, our happiest moments; ups and downs we've had with family; closeness or frustration with parents—it's all on the table. All of the details people keep close to the chest and hidden in other walks of life or at other jobs are all right out in the open in songwriting.

Imagine walking into your job at a dentist's office or a meeting at Ford Motor Company and announcing over a vanilla latte, "Morning, everyone! I slept with a guy last weekend and he gave me a venereal disease."

Sound fake?

A black raindrop of mascara ran down the cheek of Grammy-winning writer and artist Emily Weisband when she told a roomful of strangers, "I'm crying because this song was inspired by a boy who may have given me an STD."

Emily, along with hit writer Matt Jenkins and me, was doing a songwriter's round, where we played our hits on acoustic guitar Bluebird Cafe style for a few hundred people at Robert Redford's dazzling Sundance Resort in Utah. As Emily caught her breath, I leaned up to my mic and said, "Pay attention, everyone—chlamydia is a really tough word to rhyme." The audience cried with laughter as Matt slapped his Dallas Cowboys hat on his knee guffawing.

Emily then explained how she wanted to write about the awful experience, and the other writers in the room that day were very nurturing and understanding.

"In a completely unexpected twist, this song is now being used by CVS in their pharmacy ads," I joked into my microphone as the audience again went from shocked empathy to loud laughter.

Sitting between Matt and me, Emily gripped her guitar and said, "For your information, one in three people have had chlamydia."

"One in three people...on this stage have had chlamydia," I replied, raising my eyebrows with a sideways glance. The crowd howled.

Emily rolled her brown catlike eyes and played "Consequences," an incredible song recorded by Camila Cabello and inspired by Emily's heartbreak with that guy. This shows us two things: (1) Awful personal situations can be turned into great songs; (2) Never trust a person who can spell *gonorrhea* without autocorrect.

Be prepared. Have a title, a melody, a few lyrics, or even a crumb of an idea ready to get the energy in the writing room going. Being totally open with strangers about your life can be scary and uncomfortable, but boy, it makes you feel close to people quickly. Plus, it can lead to great songs and it's cheaper than therapy.

Bart Herbison, who runs the Nashville Songwriters Association International, asked my opinion on the question he gets asked the most: If a new writer brings an idea to a co-write and it doesn't turn out how they expected, can they rewrite their idea with someone else?

My simple advice would be to tell the person you started it with that you want to rewrite with someone else from scratch. Whoever has had any part in writing it, it's best to give them writing credit, but chances are they'll give you their blessing to rewrite it. Honestly, if a song is a hit there is plenty to go around when it comes to the royalties, and if it's not a hit, at least you did the classy thing and kept everyone informed.

New Kids on the Writer's Block

Walking into a room to write with Keith Urban or Jon Bon Jovi or anybody without a few ideas is something I don't dare think about.

Writer's block is something I work hard to avoid because it's a luxury I can't afford. How embarrassing to meet up with a superstar and expect them to carry the weight when they can write with anyone in the world.

If a new writer on the scene walks into a room with me and says, "I don't have any ideas, what do you have?" I leave. It's an insult when it happens. Don't be that person. Here are a few tips to avoid being that person.

Titles are everywhere, waiting to be found. You just have to shake them out. Read books, watch movies. Eavesdrop on people at bars going through a breakup or on their first date. Listen to your friends and listen to your heart. The world is overflowing with ideas and stories begging you to put them into a song. People who say they are bored have lost all sense of curiosity, and the same goes for songwriters. Saying "I can't think of a song idea" is like saying "I haven't seen any teenagers on their phones."

Olivia Newton-John had a number one song that stayed at the top of the charts for ten weeks originally called "Let's Get Physical," which came out of a moment when one of the writers saw those words written on a billboard advertising a gym in Los Angeles. He knew instantly that he had a hit title.[29]

Songwriter Connie Harrington heard a dad talking on NPR about losing his son in a recent war. The heartbroken dad spoke of "driving his son's truck to remember him." Connie, with tears in her eyes, explained what she had heard to her co-writers, they wrote "I Drive Your Truck," and country star Lee Brice recorded it. Song ideas are everywhere.

"Inspiration exists but it has to find you working" is one of my favorite quotes. Or as author Stephen King says, "Amateurs sit and wait for inspiration, the rest of us just get up and go to work." Start on something and it will come. If you sit around and wait for inspiration to drop in your lap, you might as well play the lottery. Start working on something. The answers are in the activity.

Bruce Springsteen tells the story in his autobiography about the day he received a film script in the mail called *Born in the USA*. Seeing the script lying on his table, he knew it was the perfect title for a song about Vietnam veterans he was in the middle of writing.

"Meant to Be" by Florida Georgia Line was inspired when the singer's wife said "Well, if it's meant to be, it'll be" as the two discussed an upcoming co-write with the pop artist Bebe Rexha.

Passing a bar in their hometown, songwriter Chris Tompkins's wife said to him, "I bet there's a girl in there singing Shania Twain karaoke and wearing a Tweety Bird shirt." Sound familiar? Chris took it to Josh Kear and they wrote the Grammy-winning song "Before He Cheats" for Carrie Underwood.

"Heartbreak Hotel," Elvis's first single with RCA, which

---

29 "Let's Get Physical" was turned down by Rod Stewart and Tina Turner. Whoops!

literally changed the world, was inspired by a suicide note the songwriters saw in the obituary section of the newspaper. The note read "I walk a lonely street."

Years before Axl Rose became the fiery superstar he is today, he was wandering through the most dangerous area of the Bronx on a trip to New York. In an interview, Axl talks of crossing paths with a homeless man who yelled to Axl, "Do you know where you are? You're in the jungle, baby!" That encounter became the seed that would eventually grow into "Welcome to the Jungle."

"Wake me up up before you go go" was a note on Andrew Ridgeley's refrigerator, a reminder for his mom. Andy's best friend, George Michael, saw it and said, "That would make a good song title." This story and the actual note are displayed in Ridgeley's autobiography about his days with George and their band Wham! My favorite Detroit band, the Steve Taylor Three, have a heartfelt song about the day Tom Petty died, called "The Day Tom Petty Died."

"Mony Mony" was a hit for several different artists, including Billy Idol. One of its songwriters, Tommy James, said in an interview in *Hitch* magazine that the music to the song was done but it lacked a title, which was eventually inspired by his apartment view of the Mutual of New York building in Manhattan with its big red sign illuminating the skyline: M.O.N.Y. Imagine if he had looked the other way. It could've been called Nom Wah Tea Parlor!

Speaking of New York, "Empire State of Mind," the first Jay-Z song to top the *Billboard* Hot 100, was inspired by his rise from the Marcy Projects in Brooklyn to an expensive SoHo apartment. Jay-Z mentions living near Robert De Niro now and gives shout-outs to his favorite basketball players in the lyrics. His life influenced his songs.

Sitting next to me at his keyboard, Jonathan Cain told the audience at the Bluebird Cafe: " 'Jon, don't stop believing'—that's what my dad said to me when I was really struggling to make it in the music business. I wrote 'Don't Stop Believin'' on the piano, then showed it to Journey when I joined the band."

It's not only rock, rap, country, and pop—Lin-Manuel Miranda was inspired to write the musical *Hamilton* after reading a biography about Alexander Hamilton while he was on vacation. As he said in an interview with MSNBC, "I knew he was on the ten-dollar bill. That was enough for me to pick up a book off the shelf...I just wanted a big book to read."

Good news: Now, thanks to technology, anytime you think of a title you can put it in your phone somewhere. No more having to carry a spiral notebook around, no more scribbling titles on stained or shredded napkins, then stuffing them in your socks, like I did, so you won't forget the idea. Use technology to your advantage.

Once you have a title, start working on a song. Don't get frustrated if it doesn't come really quickly. One of my favorite songs, "Teenage Dream" by Katy Perry, took Katy and her co-writers four months to write. "Body Like a Back Road" by Sam Hunt sounds nursery rhyme simple but it took Sam and his cowriters a year to finish that song.

Sometimes you get lucky and the lyrics come quickly and you have a masterpiece in your hands, but if it doesn't, don't give up. Keep chipping away at it. Just as a muscle in your body gets stronger when you use it often, so will your creative muscle, so work it. Write, write, then write some more. And don't be afraid to write bad songs—your next one may be great.

Chasing Old Ghosts in New Orleans

Jazz trumpets that whined like the teacher talking on Charlie Brown bounced from Bourbon Street bars to the open-air patio of Café Du Monde. A fresh-from-the-fryer powdered-sugar beignet melted on my tongue with its chalky sweetness. Pumped on sugar and coffee, a few of my coolest co-writer friends and I jumped onto a ringing-bell trolley that rolled from the French Quarter with its gas lamp–lit doorways and NOT HAUNTED for-rent signs, past author Anne Rice's white two-story mansion, before we hopped off at our rented house.

On that weekend getaway, we wrote "Party People" for Florida Georgia Line, "Feel Good Summer Song" for Scotty McCreery, and a song with Sam Hunt called "Vacation" in two days. The change of location was as intoxicating as the Mudslides that poured from blenders all over the city. Old ideas and titles suddenly seemed as tantalizing as the beignets in the shadow of New Orleans.

We take writing trips all the time. The smell of salt water and the breeze over the beach do wonders for creativity after you've been in Nashville, smelling hot chicken and hearing construction workers hammer for months on end. Co-writers and I will go down to Mexico and write on the balcony of a hotel or fly to New York City. Wandering the winding paths of Central Park on a foggy morning or past the punk rockers and colorful characters in the East Village always inspires me to write songs.

If your guitar suddenly sounds boring and uninspiring, put it down, jump over to a piano, or pick up a bass guitar. Go to the park and play songs surrounded by the trees. It's amazing when you go to a different instrument or a different writing room how new ideas just float in the air. A change of scenery brings different energy. If you're always writing in the same place in your bedroom or in your basement, switch it up. AC/DC used a cannon for a musical instrument in one song! Light the creative fuse any way you can on your way to becoming a songwriter.

If you go on a road trip with your friends or on a family vacation, take your guitar, take your lyric book. Everyone in Michigan has cottages "up north." That's where Uncle Kracker and I wrote "Smile," up north at his cottage. A change is as good as a rest. Change your scenery if you need a boost creatively. In an interview, Freddie Mercury of Queen said he wrote "Crazy Little Thing Called Love" sitting in a bathtub with an acoustic guitar.

Let yourself be loud. At one point when I was living in LA, a friend pointed out I kept writing ballads. He was right, but I couldn't figure out why until I realized that, being a night owl, writing songs at two a.m. when my roommates were asleep was keeping my songs slow. I didn't want to wake them up. Even if you're inside, write where you can use your outside voice.

Writing trips can bring unexpected results in the best way. My band's experience overseas with the troops, which inspired me to write songs about the war, led to something beyond magical. Peter Zinn, an award-winning playwright and director based in New York City, wrote an entire musical around my song "How Did I Get Here" after hearing it one night on the CD player at a party. He contacted me via Facebook for more material and ended up using fourteen of my songs.

Our musical, *Music City*, debuted to sold-out audiences in the New York Musical Theatre Festival off Broadway. Sold-out shows in upstate New York, Texas, and Pennsylvania followed, leading to a world premiere and a three-week run of shows in Fayetteville, North Carolina, near one of the biggest Army bases in America.

Country fans sipped McDonald's coffee on the way to work to the sound of my voice in dozens of cities thanks to country stations having me on their morning shows to discuss the musical. Clippings from magazines and newspapers flooded my kitchen countertop like a scattered deck of cards as entertainment reporters from the cities where the musical was showing interviewed me about the process.

Thanks to *Music City*, I finally got interviewed for *Rolling Stone*, just like I had dreamed about, walking down Hollywood Boulevard years ago. Talking on the phone from the parking lot of the Bluebird Cafe, I told the *Rolling Stone* writer proudly, "Green Day has the musical *American Idiot*, ABBA has *Mamma Mia*, rap is brilliantly represented in the *Hamilton* musical, it's time for a country musical that isn't a throwback or a comedy. *Music City* is a real story about this generation and the songs they are singing."

Watching a full cast of actors sing songs I'd written on a stage with a huge set made to look like a Nashville honky-tonk in one scene and the Grand Ole Opry's big red barn backdrop in the next was the most unexpected and thrilling thing that had ever happened to me. Peter Zinn is a brilliant writer and I cannot wait to see where the show goes from here.

You Complete Me

Sometimes songs come out all at once, like a sneeze. It's a rare and awesome thing when it happens, so what happens when you have a song you absolutely love and you're sure it's a hit but it's only half finished? You're stuck on the second verse. Been there a million times. Here's a simple trick: Finish the thought. What I mean is: Keep explaining the story or your feelings in the lyric in the second verse.

In "Different for Girls," Shane and I were stuck on the second verse for a few days, so we "finished the thought" by asking ourselves: Okay, so *how* is it different for girls? We thought out loud. Guys after a breakup sleep all day, don't shave, they play video games, leave the house a wreck, punch the wall. We made those examples the second verse:

She don't sleep all day and leave the house a wreck.
She don't have the luxury to let herself go.
She won't call just to cuss, find a wall she can
punch.

Bruce Springsteen sometimes makes his third verse an entirely new thought that works with his chorus and/or title. In his song "57 Channels (And Nothin' On)" the first and second verses are about old Rambo movies and satellites beaming images to his TV, but there's "fifty-seven channels and nothin' on." Unexpectedly, in the third verse he says his lover has left and the note says "Bye-bye, John, our love is fifty-seven channels and nothin' on." That's why Bruce is called "The Boss." Not easy to do, but very effective.

"Dreaming With a Broken Heart" by John Mayer is a great example of finishing the thought. Near the end of that song he comes in with a totally new lyric that supports the title brilliantly: "Do I have to fall asleep with roses in my hand?" To me that means so he can give them to his lover in his dreams. So simple yet so clever.

Check out Elvis Costello's infectious song "Everyday I Write the Book." In the second verse he sings about "chapter one" and "chapter two," using images about an actual book. In the third verse he's still at it, singing "Even in a perfect world where everyone was equal, I'd still own the film rights and be working on the sequel." Every verse finishes the thought and points at the title with fresh images. It's no surprise to me that it's one of Elvis Costello's biggest hits.

Songs about love, love gone wrong, love that got confusing, are my favorites. When I'm confused about life or love, I write about it, trying to figure it out, spinning my thoughts like the *Wheel of Fortune* wheel. That's why people gravitate toward songs that are written well and from the heart. They are trying to figure it out themselves, and music is there for them when no one else is. The Beatles and Taylor Swift, for example, I imagine feel the same as we do: They write about love to navigate through it in their own lives. That's why so many fans respond to their songs.

Also, in case you didn't know, some people only write lyrics and not music. Some people write music and don't write the lyrics. Some people only write melodies—they don't play an instrument and they don't write lyrics. So, if you want to be a songwriter, it can be any of these combinations. Neil Peart, drummer of the band Rush, was arguably the best drummer in the entire world *and* he wrote all the lyrics for all of their songs. Nikki Sixx is the bass player of Mötley Crüe and writes most of the songs. Pete Wentz is a bassist as well and writes a lot of the lyrics for his band Fall Out Boy. Multi–Grammy Award winner Liz Rose, who co-wrote many Taylor Swift hits, comes up with great melodies and life-changing lyrics, but she does not really play an instrument. Liz also didn't start writing songs until she was thirty-seven years old! If you're not inspired by that, check your pulse: You're probably not alive.

The Unwritten Rule

If you want to be an artist and get a record deal, find the best songs available. Find great songs other people have written and record them. You don't need to write every song.

Country superstar Tim McGraw has forty number one songs and he didn't write a single one. He has a gift for finding great songs like "Live Like You Were Dying," which was number one for ten weeks. Garth Brooks did not have a record deal when he heard "The Dance" played at an open mic by an unknown songwriter named Tony Arata. Garth asked Tony if he could record it, and the rest is history.

Do you know who Michael Jackson wrote "Man in

the Mirror" with? No one—he didn't write it. The audience doesn't care one way or another—they just want songs that resonate with their own lives. When Tom Petty is coming through my car speakers singing, "You don't know how it feels to be me," I'm not sitting at a red light wondering what it's like to be Tom Petty. I'm in my car saying, "Yeah, no one knows what it's like to be *me*!" Listeners imagine themselves in your songs no matter what.

If you hear an unknown song played at a songwriter round, or on a friend's demo, or played by a local band, and it sounds like a hit to you, ask them if you can record it. Great songs make great artists.

CHAPTER 21

Hey, Alexa, Pay Me My Royalties

How much did Kenny Chesney buy that song from you for?"

It's a question I get a lot from music fans and aspiring writers as I shake hands and sign their Hatch Show Print posters after shows at The Bluebird Cafe. It's a fair question, but recording artists don't buy a song from you; they license it. Imagine that one of my songs is a movie. Hollywood makes the movie, then sends it to theaters, and they show it, and people buy tickets or watch it on a streaming service—but Hollywood still owns the movie.

I own my songs forever. All the songs I write are called my "catalogue." People do sell their song catalogues, and I could as well if the offer was too good to refuse (but in a "life-changing money" way, not in *The Godfather* way). Every time a song I've written is played on the radio, at a concert, in a bar, on TV, used in a commercial or in a movie, bought on CD or vinyl, downloaded or streamed, I get paid.

Music has a healing effect on me. I feel physically better when I hear a song that I like. A breakup is made much easier, a Saturday night party is improved, road trips feel like you're in a movie, all because of songs coming through the speakers. A lot of hard work goes into making a hit—musicians playing in recording sessions, producers, record company employees, and radio people all coming together to bring it to the world—but it all starts…with a song. These songs come from hard-working professionals called songwriters.

People don't buy many CDs or cassettes anymore, and yes, vinyl is coming back, but as we all know, music these days is consumed via our phones and through the countless streaming services available to us. What you might not know is that because of streaming, songwriters are not getting paid fairly. Songwriter royalties are not set or negotiated in the free market. They are set under a law Congress adopted in 1909 and two World War II–era Department of Justice consent decrees.[30]

I'm not saying listeners are doing anything wrong. When you're working out in the garage or popping the cap off a Corona in the kitchen and say, "Hey, Alexa, play some music," how are you supposed to know that the songwriters on that album are not getting paid fairly? Well, I'm telling you: Songwriters are not getting paid fairly.

Unlike some other creatives, songwriters don't have a union. Our record labels, publishing companies, and performance rights organizations (like ASCAP and BMI) that collect our money have operated at the mercy of government regulations.

Marshall Mathers, aka Eminem, sued Spotify for billions in alleged unpaid streams. A company representing the Black Keys and Neil Young sought damages for the infringement of ten thousand songs.

Taylor Swift famously took her music off Spotify because the payments were not fair. People respond with things like, "Isn't she rich enough?" Well, okay, if you're a car manufacturer, can't you give us the cars for free? If you're a lawyer,

---

30 A *consent decree* is an agreement or settlement that resolves a dispute between two parties without admission of guilt.

can't you put your years of late-night coffee-guzzling studying aside and work on everyone's lawsuits for free? If you held the patent on the Cheesus Christ cheese grater that has Jesus' picture on it for when you're doing the Lord's work and making mac and cheese, would you just give it away free on TV? No!

JT/DC

My black guitar that I had covered in Pepto Bismol–pink electrical-tape zigzags in homage to Eddie Van Halen disappeared into the moving airport-style metal detector as a man in a suit with an earpiece waved me through security. My shoes echoed through the halls of power as I walked confidently past flags from every state in the union on my way to an office to plead my case to members of Congress.

In Nashville, there's a cool old recording studio with a waterwheel on the side of it that now holds the offices of that great organization, the Nashville Songwriters Association International. Bart Herbison, who runs NSAI and deserves a statue of his likeness put up in Music City for all he has done for songwriters, had flown me to Washington to play my hits in senators' offices and for congresspeople, and it is a rare thrill.

In one office I calmly told a congressman and his staff, "If I made this table in front of us, someone should pay to own it, yes?" Bart slammed his fist on the table as if it was a championship Whac-A-Mole game at Dave & Buster's, and yelled, "Bullshit! Anyone can make a table! J.T., you have a special skill! Now play a little 'Sangria.'" I quickly began to sing as interns and the congressman swayed beneath a framed picture of President Reagan smiling at me from the wall.

To understand how songwriters get paid and what we are fighting for in Washington, DC, here's the short version:

It all started with piano rolls in 1909. A piano roll is used to operate a player piano—a piano that plays by itself. Piano rolls are continuous rolls of perforated paper. Those little holes represent note control data.

Mechanical and Performance Royalties

One of the most important streams of income for a songwriter is mechanical royalty. Mechanical royalties are payments to the writer of a song whenever that song is reproduced in some form. The term "mechanical royalty" dates back to "Piano Roll" Copyright Act of 1909 that established a composer's right to control and distribute their original works. The law wanted to protect consumers from being overcharged by writers and publishers so the public had access to the music, and also wanted to compensate creators to encourage them to create. This is when the government took over the rates we get for our songs and created the "compulsory license," which meant that once a song was released, anyone else could release/record it as long as they paid the statutory rate.

Obviously they didn't see records, radio, and streaming coming in the future, and songwriter publishing rates have always been artificially low, lagging behind technology like a lonely corner pay phone watching people walk by taking selfies and texting on their cell phones. In the days of platinum albums, the business paid songwriters pretty well. That's not the case with streaming.

Performance royalties are paid to songwriters and their publishers in exchange for the right to broadcast or perform a copywritten musical composition in public. In 1941, Congress issued consent decrees over BMI and ASCAP (known as PROs, Performance Rights Organizations) because they controlled so much of broadcasting and performance that they were viewed as monopolistic.

In 1972, "sound recordings" got their own limited copyright protection, which was extended in the 1976 Copyright Act. The key element is the master, the actual recording. If you record an album in your basement or a studio and pay for it all yourself, you own the master. So the master and artist shares are not under government control and can be negotiated in a free market.

If you have a record deal, the record company owns the master. They pay for you to make the record, so to me that seems fair. It's expensive to make a great album in a studio with a producer and musicians. They also promote it to radio, online services, and so on. The master is what a record company makes all the copies from, which they then sell to the public. That's why the master/artist side of streaming royalties has been paid as much as seventeen times what the publishing/songwriter copyright earned for streaming music services in the digital era. The record labels get to negotiate their mechanical royalties in a free market while songwriters have judges set theirs, until recently, under very unfriendly rules.

In 2018, the Music Modernization Act changed what judges who set such royalty rates must consider. The new rules are fairer and should result in royalty increases for songwriters.

Steve Bogard, president of NSAI, and Bart Herbison worked tirelessly with congresspeople and senators, like Hakeem Jeffries, Marsha Blackburn, and Doug Collins, to pass the Music Modernization Act, which will give songwriters an equitable set of rules when the Copyright Royalty Board (CRB) sets them.

Even before the MMA was adopted, the NSAI and music publishers faced off at the CRB against Apple, Amazon, Google, Pandora, and Spotify and won the largest mechanical pay raise for songwriters from streaming services in history, 43.8%, starting in 2021. The verdict is facing appeal by all of the streaming companies except Apple.

Tim Hare, a composer, recently wrote in *American Songwriter* magazine: "Ironically, these streaming companies actually need music to exist, so refusing to fairly compensate the creators that help them generate millions in revenue is likely to cause major issues."

Or, as hit songwriter Lee Thomas Miller posted on Facebook about the appeal, "Not only is this horseshit, it's ground we've already earned. The court granted us this money. Everybody remind Spotify and Amazon Music that these songs don't write themselves. We will never stop fighting for our fair share of that which we create 100% of out of thin air!!"

Streams Come True

Hundreds of songs sit in my computer that I've written and that no one will ever hear. I've written hits but I've written misses as well. I don't expect to get paid for the songs that sit in my computer collecting electronic dust, but the songs I've written that people download and stream one billion times? Absolutely. Shouldn't I get paid by the streaming services that are making millions in advertising and monthly subscribers' fees from using *my* music? Not paying songwriters for their hard work is unfair and it's un-American. I want you to know how important it is that songwriters get paid when a song they write becomes a hit.

The songs people throw Frisbees to at the beach, the songs people sing along to when they're stuck in traffic, the songs people put on before a first kiss or after a last—songwriters should be paid for those. Songwriters work very hard, and if songwriters don't get paid, then the job of songwriting will disappear.

You don't want to imagine a world without music. You can't imagine it. For fun, try for a second. Imagine your favorite sports team running out on the field, busting through the big paper circle, and there's no music. Imagine the movie *Jaws* without those two iconic notes as the shark comes closer to the unknowing swimmers.

How is Bradley Cooper going to fall in love with Lady Gaga without "Shallow"? Imagine a birthday party and no one singing "Happy Birthday." People sat down and wrote these songs.

Every song you listen to, someone or a group of people took their time, they worked very hard for years and years on their craft, and they deserve to be paid. I can't say it enough: I'm very lucky, I've done very well, but the future hitmakers, like most of the people reading this book, deserve a royalty that's fair.

People all over the world can hear a song I've written by simply pressing a button, and I love that, I truly do. When I was a kid, the only way to get a new record was by mowing lawns for a few weeks as my tennis shoes turned green, then convincing my babysitter's boyfriend to drive me to Harmony House record store, then home again. If I wanted to share the record, I had to dig out an old *Sesame Street Fever* cassette with Grover on the cover posing like John Travolta and put tape over the spine of the cassette to cover up the holes that prevented accidental erasing of the cassette. Then I'd pedal to the playground on my black-and-yellow Schwinn Predator Nighthawk and see if anyone wanted to take home my secondhand copy of an album and listen. I delivered songs like a human iTunes. No wonder I was such a skinny child.

People are hearing and sharing all kinds of music instantly that years ago they wouldn't have been exposed to. We live in an exciting time with technology, but songwriting is a real job and it's long overdue that the royalty rate for songwriters is where it should be when it comes to streaming services. In Nashville, there are stickers on guitar cases that say, IT ALL BEGINS WITH A SONG. I love those, but I'd like to print some new ones that say, SONGS START WITH A SONGWRITER.

CHAPTER 22

Is This the Real Life, Is This Just Fantasy?

S now fell like white sparks on the wet streets of Kansas City as people ducked into diners and drove slowly through stoplights as the city came to life on a Friday morning. The night before, the low hum of a tour bus engine and the smooth ride from Nashville to Kansas had rocked me to sleep like a baby in my bunk.

The smell of hazelnut coffee and a tour manager in a Hawaiian shirt, shorts, and flip-flops despite the snow talking on his phone woke me up. "TV interview is at eight a.m. We need to get him to the station at least fifteen minutes early."

After brushing my teeth, I sat on the bus's plush couch wiping condensation off the window with the sleeve of my suit jacket. A sign on the sidewalk outside the club read TONIGHT'S SHOW—SOLD OUT. On an abandoned feed building across the street, a painted mural on a wall, barn door high, showed Dorothy and Toto from *The Wizard of Oz*, accompanied by the words I DON'T THINK WE'RE IN KANSAS ANYMORE.

A car pulled up to the bus, put on its hazard lights, and an excited college student climbed out. She was wrapped in a scarf and Sock Monkey mittens, and you could see her breath as she let the tour manager know she was the person driving the star of the show to the TV station. It wasn't the High Priest of Crazy, Linkin Park, or a country superstar she was driving—it was me.

A twenty-five-city sold-out tour starring yours truly sponsored by Soggy Dollar Rum in the Virgin Islands, raising money for schools affected by Hurricane Irma, was under way, and I was loving every minute of it.

"Different for Girls" came on the radio's country station as we waited for coffee in a Starbucks drive-thru.

"What's it like to hear your songs on the radio?" she asked, turning it up.

"It never gets old," I responded with a laugh.

"So freaking cool." She Instagram-storied the radio playing my song and then turned the phone camera to me sipping my Blonde Roast.

Honestly, it's incredible and funny how life changes. I'm lucky enough to say that I hear a song I've written playing on the radio every single time I get into a car. Instead of being someone's assistant, I now travel on private planes and on top-of-the-line tour buses to play songwriter shows. My friends and brothers can ride with me without having to ask anyone's permission.

When the cameras rolled at station KSHB 41 Action News, newscaster Cynthia Newsome complimented me on my white suit with Star Wars stormtrooper helmets on it. Looking into the camera to a city of viewers, I said, "Don't adjust your televisions—I'm really dressed like this." Off camera, all the camera operators and a meteorologist who favored Jennifer Aniston laughed out loud. "I know my hair looks like I combed it with a pork chop, but I slept on a tour bus last night."

The ever-classy Newsome asked about the charity for schools as the ticker tape under us on the screen scrolled news about President Trump's reelection plans for 2020 keeping viewers abreast of the news. She sang along as I played

"Smile" on live TV. I could see the scrolling news feed change to another story. It read: THE COLD WEATHER IS BRINGING OUT THE SCAMMERS, flashing on the screen under my face.

"They're on to me!" I yelled, and pretended to drop my guitar and run.

Playing hit songs I'd written on the biggest TV news show in Kansas City was a thrill, and proof of how far I have come.

Smiling Without Lip-Synching

As the stars blinked to life above the city, the lights inside the club lowered and wild Kansas City country fans all started hooting and hollering, waving their cowboy hats and pounding on their tables. The infectious ear-candy keyboard melody of Van Halen's number one song "Jump" blasted over the speakers. The tour manager instructed the soundman at every show to play intro music I had picked out to pump the crowd up. Come to think of it, I should've played "Somewhere Over the Rainbow" for a laugh.

Strutting onstage into the spotlight like a game show host, I yelled into the microphone, "Are there any country music fans in the house?"

The audience erupted. Letting the cheers sizzle, I scanned the audience with one eyebrow up before calmly adding, "It would be a long night if you weren't." The laughs turned to excited gasps as I opened the show with "Smile."

"I'd like to dedicate this second song to the nice lady outside who told me the song I wrote for Blake Shelton is her five-year-old daughter's favorite song. It's a perfect song for a five-year-old—it's about drinking too much." I tilted my head sideways in puzzlement, the crowd laughed, and I blasted into "Sangria."

Pointing, pouting, singing, and head banging through all

of my number one hits just like I'd always dreamed of doing, I gave people a show they'd never forget. I know, because the audiences always told me so.

Standing in front of the stage after every show, the tour manager started calling me Bill Clinton as I shook more hands and signed more autographs and took more selfies than I ever thought possible.

" 'Smile' got me through chemo with my husband. We played it all the time in the hospital," one teary-eyed woman said as she hugged me.

"J.T., man, 'Different for Girls,' I play that for my teenage boys to let them know how to treat girls. What a song—thank you so much," a father in a camouflage jacket said as he firmly shook my hand.

"During the worst heartbreak of my life I heard 'Somewhere With You.' I played it constantly. I cannot believe you wrote that song," a girl with a blue streak in her hair wearing a faded David Bowie shirt gushed as she nervously cracked her knuckles.

By telling you these stories, I'm preparing you for all the stories people will tell you about the songs YOU write. Someone is going to have the number one song on the radio every single week until the end of time. It might as well be you.

Fight for your dreams so they know you care about them. If you get rejected—which you will—then you're doing the right thing. You've begun your journey. If you don't have problems, you're not in the game.

I climb back onto the fireplace-warm tour bus with my fist raised in triumph like John Bender at the end of *The Breakfast Club*, and the bus door closes. The tour manager, seeing me, counts by hand the Soggy Dollar Rum merch people on board, the publicist, then announces "all in" to the driver and we roll forward to the next show in Chicago. When we get there, Rich Waller, my childhood buddy from Battle of the Bands, will join me onstage for a few songs. His two grade-school sons will be in the audience watching.

As Ozzy Osbourne barks at the moon from the MTV Classic channel on the giant-screen TV in the tour bus lounge, I sip a tangy and creamy delicious Soggy Dollar Rum Painkiller that takes my taste buds to the islands as we drive. Highway streetlights blend together like a finger painting out the bus window as I think about my childhood. My mom and dad, my brothers, Jay Thomas and his wife, Sally, my friends, talented co-writers, and all the love and support I have been so fortunate to have had and still have.

Checking messages on my phone, I noticed it was two a.m. Excited thinking about Chicago, and still pumped from the show, I just knew there was no way I was falling asleep. I might not be the biggest songwriter in the world but I'm having the biggest time.

A hit song can change your life. Everyone I write with starts off by saying, "Let's write something huge like 'Smile,'" which is such a compliment.

Instead of kissing a girl as Bon Jovi sings on the TV in the background, I have now sat face-to-face with Jon Bon Jovi, singing with him, writing a song.

Years ago while living in LA, I mailed a cassette home to a girl in Michigan I liked with the Goo Goo Dolls song "Iris" on it.

Johnny Rzeznik, lead singer of the Goo Goo Dolls, heard my Jake Owen song "Alone With You" and asked to write with me. Rzeznik and I wrote in a studio overlooking the electric wonderland that is Times Square. Our song "When the World Breaks Your Heart" is on the latest Goo Goo Dolls album.

Times Square now has a new musical memory attached to it, pushing the ghost of my EMI Records heartache back to the grave. In my house in Nashville the hallway walls are covered in framed shining gold and platinum discs presented to me for all the sales my songs have achieved.

Jim Vallance, who co-wrote all the classic Bryan Adams songs I sang along to and studied, came to see my musical, *Music City*. After shaking his hand without letting go like he was Mother Teresa, I complimented him on a dozen of his songs. Adjusting his Ben Franklin reading glasses, he said to me with a lopsided grin, "Wow, you remember songs that I've forgotten I've written." Jim complimented our musical and came to see several performances of it. I even went to dinner with him, the man who wrote the soundtrack to my youth sipping wine a chair away from me.

Peter Zinn, the musical's scriptwriter, startled a server as he yelled out loud, "Jim, when we were teenagers J.T. learned how to write songs listening to 'Summer of '69'!" I replied, "It's true! And Peter learned how to unhook a bra listening to 'Heaven.' "

Only one thing in my house shines brighter than my gold albums on weekend nights: A 1977 vintage authentic KISS pinball machine, given to me by Crush Management's Jonathan Daniel, Evan Taubenfeld, and Sam Hollander for a recent number one, that sits in my bonus room. No quarters needed to play, no roller skates on my feet needed to reach the bumpers.

To anyone reading this book, I can't wait to hear your songs on the radio and meet up with you in a writing room someday. Work hard, be nice to people, and don't bore us—get to the chorus.

Your songs will touch the masses. Your music will be the soundtrack to the butterflies in someone's stomach, the anxiety of a first kiss, the thousandth "I love you," and the voices of eighty thousand people singing along in a stadium. Father-daughter dances need your songs, as do the beer-soaked high fives at parties and tailgates. Stay positive. Keep going, keep writing.

All it takes is one person to believe in you, even if that person is yourself.

Shadowed from the sun by a towering Dutch elm tree, our brick house at 1151 Berkshire was as pristine as ever. The smell of fresh-cut grass and kids passing on bikes made it seem like time had stood still all these years. Another family lives there now, but I sat for a few minutes before pulling my rent-a-car from the curb for a drive through Grosse Pointe.

I passed the War Memorial, where my band won the Battle of the Bands, and the breeze from the lake rushed through the car window, hugging my neck like an old friend. As I pointed the car toward the freeway, my song "Somewhere In

My Car" came on the country station 99.5 like I'd dreamed about when I was growing up.

It was summer 2019 and I was back in Detroit to be interviewed on Channel 7 News by the popular newscaster, and country superfan, Stephen Clark. The Channel 7 studio is in the exact same building where my dad worked and that a radio station still broadcasts from today. Pointing at my guitar and wearing a South High Blue Devils shirt, I told Stephen, "I owe it all to my babysitters, the Keelan sisters," for all of Detroit to hear.

After the interview, Stephen and I went into the same cafeteria my dad and I ate lunch in. I had not been there since I was a kid and I got a little misty-eyed. Stephen handed me a tray as a lady in a hairnet served chicken and gravy from behind a shiny steel counter and we ate on checkerboard tablecloths. The decor had not changed in three decades, it was exactly the same, but everything seemed smaller.

I wished so bad that my dad was here so I could've called him. I would have told him, "Dad, I'm back where it all began. I'm being interviewed at the radio station you worked at. Interviewed about my songs and my gold and platinum records that fill the walls of my house!"

I know exactly how he would have responded too.

"Tell them Coach Larry sent you."

Acknowledgments

The sold-out crowd was still cheering and banging beer bottles as my black-and-yellow ASICS Tigers led me off the stage into the sweaty greenroom at the Listening Room Cafe in Nashville after playing a songwriter round.

As I took off my guitar, my talented friend Bobby Hamrick excitedly held up his phone screen, saying, "Dana Perino posted about you on Instagram!" I had noticed Dana Perino in the audience—I recognized her from TV, and I knew she had worked at the White House. I "liked" the photo and commented, "Thanks for coming!" Dana sent me a message: "Your stories are great. You should write a book."

Dana is the smartest person I've ever met. I'm proud to now be friends with her and her husband. This book happened because of Dana. She introduced me to my editor, Sean Desmond of Twelve books. Thank you, Dana: I'm forever grateful.

Thank you, Sean "Sophomores" Desmond and rock 'n' roll Rachel Kambury for your enthusiasm, ideas, and superb editing skills.

To my brother Lance, and my brothers from another mother, Sam and Jake, thank you for being my best friends. Thank you to Sally Terrell, my second mom. How lucky I am to have had Kendra and you.

Cheers to Steve Taylor and Carey Weaver for being my

sounding boards as I molded memories into 3-D movies on these pages.

Shout-out to Randy Peleaz and the KISS Claptons.

To my friend and mentor Jonathan Daniel: You'll forever be my electric angel.

Thank you, Lorie Hollabaugh, Music Row's best reporter.

To the man whose positivity could power all the lights in Las Vegas, my friend and publisher, Rusty Gaston, thank you for guiding me to the winners' circle not only in songwriting but also in life.

Thank you, Evan Taubenfeld and the "21 hit wonder" Sam Hollander. My CRUSH has never faded.

Thank you, Stacey Reid and Rick Ball, for additional editing, and Jarrod Taylor for the epic cover art.

Sending a hand-drawn heart in the Santa Barbara sand to Taylor Wolf and Winnie: love you both.

Thank you, LeAnn Phelan, for guidance in Nashville from day one and beyond. Thanks to my lawyers, Jason Tuner and Judge Ted Metry.

Thank you to champions always in my corner: Ruta Sepetys, Lynel Harding, and Uncle Mike Shafer.

Thank you to whoever made the annoying meme during the pandemic that said, "Shakespeare did his best work during the plague." At first the meme made me feel lazy, but the world was in lockdown and I was freaked out. Then I thought, "Oh yeah? Watch this. I'll write a book during quarantine"—and I did.

To my many friends in Nashville, Tennessee, and Grosse Pointe, Michigan, thank you for cheering me on ever since the Battle of the Bands. You're in every song I write.

Surrounding myself with people more talented than I am has made all the difference in my life. Every person mentioned on the pages of this book is tattooed on my heart. Thank you all.

If you're thinking about suicide, are worried about a friend or loved one, or would like emotional support, The Lifeline network is available 24/7 at 1-800-273-8255.

About the Author

J.T. Harding is a multi-platinum songwriter who has written hits for Blake Shelton, Keith Urban, Kenny Chesney, Dierks Bentley, Jake Owen, Darius Rucker, Florida Georgia Line, and the four-million-plus-seller "Smile" with Uncle Kracker, among others. J.T. was born and raised in South Detroit. His storytelling lyrics caught the attention of Nashville, where he now resides and continues to churn out the hits in the light of his vintage KISS pinball machine.